The Edinburgh Companion to
Muriel Spark

Edinburgh Companions to Scottish Literature

Series Editors: Ian Brown and Thomas Owen Clancy

Titles in the series include:

The Edinburgh Companion to Robert Burns
Edited by Gerard Carruthers
978 0 7486 3648 8 (hardback)
978 0 7486 3649 5 (paperback)

The Edinburgh Companion to Twentieth-Century Scottish Literature
Edited by Ian Brown and Alan Riach
978 0 7486 3693 8 (hardback)
978 0 7486 3694 5 (paperback)

The Edinburgh Companion to Contemporary Scottish Poetry
Edited by Matt McGuire and Colin Nicholson
978 0 7486 3625 9 (hardback)
978 0 7486 3626 6 (paperback)

The Edinburgh Companion to Muriel Spark
Edited by Michael Gardiner and Willy Maley
978 0 7486 3768 3 (hardback)
978 0 7486 3769 0 (paperback)

The Edinburgh Companion to Robert Louis Stevenson
Edited by Penny Fielding
978 0 7486 3554 2 (hardback)
978 0 7486 3555 9 (paperback)

The Edinburgh Companion to Irvine Welsh
Edited by Berthold Schoene
978 0 7486 3917 5 (hardback)
978 0 7486 3918 2 (paperback)

The Edinburgh Companion to James Kelman
Edited by Scott Hames
978 0 7486 3963 2 (hardback)
978 0 7486 3964 9 (paperback)

Forthcoming volumes:

The Edinburgh Companion to Scottish Romanticism
Edited by Murray Pittock
978 0 7486 3845 1 (hardback)
978 0 7486 3846 8 (paperback)

The Edinburgh Companion to Scottish Drama
Edited by Ian Brown
978 0 7486 4108 6 (hardback)
978 0 7486 4107 9 (paperback)

The Edinburgh Companion to James Hogg
Edited by Ian Duncan and Douglas Mack
978 0 7486 4124 6 (hardback)
978 0 7486 4123 9 (paperback)

The Edinburgh Companion to Muriel Spark

Edited by Michael Gardiner and Willy Maley

Edinburgh University Press

© in this edition Edinburgh University Press, 2010
© in the individual contributions is retained by the authors

Edinburgh University Press Ltd
22 George Square, Edinburgh

www.euppublishing.com

Typeset in 10.5 on 12.5pt Goudy
by Servis Filmsetting Limited, Stockport, Cheshire, and
printed and bound in Great Britain by
CPI Antony Rowe, Chippenham and Eastbourne

A CIP record for this book is available from the British Library

ISBN 978 0 7486 3768 3 (hardback)
ISBN 978 0 7486 3769 0 (paperback)

The right of Michael Gardiner and Willy Maley
to be identified as editors and of the contributors
to be identified as authors of this work
has been asserted in accordance with
the Copyright, Designs and Patents Act 1988.

Contents

Series Editors' Preface

The preface to this series' initial tranche of volumes recognised that some literary canons can conceive of a single 'Great Tradition'. The series editors consider that there is no such simple way of conceiving of Scottish literature's variousness. This arises from a multilingual and multivalent culture. It also arises from a culture that includes authors who move for many different reasons beyond Scotland's physical boundaries, sometimes to return, sometimes not. The late Iain Wright in *The Edinburgh History of Scottish Literature* talked of the Scots as a 'semi-nomadic people'. Robert Louis Stevenson travelled in stages across the world; Muriel Spark settled in Southern Africa, England and then Italy; James Kelman, while remaining close to his roots in Glasgow, has spent important periods in the United States; Irvine Welsh has moved from Leith, in Edinburgh, to a series of domestic bases on both sides of the Atlantic.

All four writers at one time and in one way or another have been underappreciated. Stevenson – most notoriously perhaps – for a time was seen as simply an adventure writer for the young. Yet Stevenson is now recognised not for simplicity, but his wonderful complexity, an international writer whose admirers included Borges and Nabokov. Similarly, the other three have firm international reputations based on innovation, literary experiment and pushing formal boundaries. All have grown out of the rich interrelationship of English and Scots in the literature to which they contribute; they embody its intercultural richness, hybridity and cosmopolitan potential. Some of their subject matter is far-flung: often they are situated not only physically but also in literary terms well furth of Scotland. Yet they are all important contributors to Scottish literature, a fact which problematises in the most positive and creative way any easy notion of what Scottish literature is.

Ian Brown
Thomas Owen Clancy

Brief Biography of Muriel Spark

Muriel Spark was born Muriel Sarah Camberg on 1 February 1918 in Bruntsfield Place, Edinburgh. Her Scottish Jewish father, Bernard Camberg, was a machine-shop engineer. Her English mother, Sarah Elizabeth Maud (née Uezzell) was from Hertfordshire. She had one brother, Philip. Having an English mother made young Muriel acutely aware of language and the distinctive sound of Scots alongside Standard English. Spark attended James Gillespie's High School for Girls from 1923 to 1935, where she fell into the hands of 'that character in search of an author', the inspirational Miss Christina Kay, model for Miss Jean Brodie. Spark wrote poetry from the age of nine, and in 1932 won first prize in a poetry competition to mark the centenary of the death of Sir Walter Scott. After leaving Gillespie's, Spark took a précis-writing course at Heriot-Watt College (later University). In 1937, she became engaged to the schoolteacher Sidney Oswald Spark, sailing from Southampton on 13 August 1937 to Cape Town, then on to Salisbury, Southern Rhodesia (later Zimbabwe), where they were married, and her son Robin was born. She lived there seven eventful years, and Africa inspired her award-winning short story in *The Observer* competition of 1951. By this time single again, London-based and established as poetry editor and biographer, she was persuaded to write novels. After her 1954 conversion to Catholicism and the success of her debut novel, *The Comforters* (1957), she quickly emerged as a writer of sparkling talent, penning twenty-one novels over the next fifty years. Her sixth, *The Prime of Miss Jean Brodie* (1961), cemented her reputation for life. As a novelist, she lived a life of 'exile', moving first to New York, then to Rome, and on to Tuscany, where she lived with her companion, Penelope Jardine; in Italy she continued to forge fantastic fiction, from *The Driver's Seat* (1970) through to *The Finishing School* (2004). She died in Tuscany on 13 April 2006 at the age of 88.

Introduction

Michael Gardiner and Willy Maley

Arguably the most important Scottish novelist since Walter Scott and Robert Louis Stevenson, Muriel Spark is a writer of unsurpassed range and richness. As a biographer, critic, editor, playwright, poet, short story writer and chiefly a novelist, her work is both popular and highly literary, combining experimental narratives with eerily familiar generic forms, including the detective story, gothic, murder mystery, romance and adventure. Technical excellence and a sense of economy which walks on stiletto sentences characterise an *oeuvre* running from journalism for a jeweller's magazine, through a set of much-loved novels, to the peerless late prose published in the *New Yorker*.[1] The same tightness of tone and idea is seen in editorials, drama and various lengths of short story, and even Spark's sorties into children's fiction, as in *The Very Fine Clock* (1968), show a rare integrity of purpose and clarity of expression. She illuminates pivotal areas of literary and cultural history: absorbing influences including Scottish tradition and the *nouveau roman*, she provokes deeply challenging cultural questions. From the ballads to The Book of Job, *Wuthering Heights* to the poetry of T. S. Eliot and Dylan Thomas, her writing is informed by wide and thorough reading and the tackling of topical issues; she becomes a literary transformation of our understanding of familiar material. In *The Abbess of Crewe* (1974) Watergate is reconfigured as a meditation on surveillance and corruption in a convent; in the apparently comic *Aiding and Abetting* (2000), the Lord Lucan case is looked at through the lenses of class, misogyny and the psychological double. And as a poet first and foremost, Spark endows her prose with a poetics and a thematic tension almost unknown in writers of the era. Even as her reputation as a novelist grew, she continued to publish poems and short stories throughout her life, and the essays in this collection take on both Spark's poetry and her poetic prose.

Spark's novels have been translated into many languages and several have been made into films, including the classic version of *The Prime of Miss Jean Brodie* (1969), starring Maggie Smith. Indeed that novel – and that film – have stolen the limelight from her other work and are much

1

more widely known than the cinema adaptations of Spark's favourite novel, *The Driver's Seat* (1974), with Elizabeth Taylor and Andy Warhol, or *The Abbess of Crewe*, filmed as *Nasty Habits* (1977), with Glenda Jackson in the title role. Spark also liked Ingmar Bergman's production of her stage play, *Doctors of Philosophy* (1963). As these collaborations suggest, Spark has long since been accepted on a global scale, known as a popular writer who wears her learning lightly, capturing the major cultural concerns of her time in a deceptively spare style. The combination of sensitivity to cultural processes and literary traditions, and stringent storytelling craft, makes her one of the most significant literary figures to emerge in the twentieth century. Even *The Prime of Miss Jean Brodie*, as Randall Stevenson notes in this collection, is a more complex and politically charged novel than is usually realised. Indeed, a comparison of *Brodie* with *The Driver's Seat* (1970) shows how far Jean and Lise are both marked by the will-to-power, and the questions asked by *Brodie* about education, Enlightenment and progress have often been overlooked in conventional critical accounts. *Brodie*, indeed, is only one incarnation of a thematic tightness characterising her work from the moment she won *The Observer* short story prize in 1951 for 'The Seraph and the Zambesi', emerging as a writer of audacity able to smuggle the most outrageous insights into superficially conservative forms. We should avoid glossing over the malice and menace in short, apparently comic novels like *The Prime of Miss Jean Brodie*, which is as politically provocative and as teasing and testing of time and tense as any of her work.

This volume brings together a 'Brodie set' of critics to trace the history, impact, reception and major themes of Spark's work, from her early poetry to her last novel, *The Finishing School* (2004). It encompasses the range of Spark's output, pursuing contextual lines of approach, including biography, geography, gender, identity, nation and religion, and considering her legacy and continuing influence in the twenty-first century. While she may be a Catholic writer to be set alongside Evelyn Waugh and Graham Greene, both of whom admired her work, she also emerges as a thinker on issues as diverse as the Welfare State, secularisation, decolonisation and anti-psychiatry, and a writer whose work may be placed alongside Marcel Proust, James Joyce, Vladimir Nabokov and Doris Lessing. The essays collected here reflect the fact that, although principally known as a novelist, when she published her first novel, *The Comforters*, in 1957, Spark already had a significant profile through her poetry, biographical criticism and literary journalism, as chair of the Poetry Society and editor of the *Poetry Review*, and was author or co-author of a number of scholarly studies of writers, including William Wordsworth, Mary Shelley, the Brontës, Cardinal Newman and John Masefield.

In the introduction to his long-awaited *Muriel Spark: The Biography*, Martin Stannard says of Spark:

She belonged nowhere, was determined to belong nowhere and to no one. 'It was Edinburgh', she wrote, 'that bred within me the condition of exiledom: and what have I been doing since then but moving from exile into exile?' This was not a lament. Exile for her, as for James Joyce, was the natural condition of the artist. 'It has ceased', she wrote, 'to be a fate, it has become a calling.' Edinburgh was her Dublin, redolent of escaped impositions yet bred in the bone of her art. It was the locus of conflicting memories: of those who had tried to impose guilt for the audacity of claiming independence, of the solid pleasures of a well-regulated, prelapsarian life'.[2]

If Spark's home was indeed her art, this companion concerns itself with the structure and feel of the house of fiction she built up over half a century. The contributors to the present volume understand Spark as a major writer already subject to multi-approach criticism, and historicise not only her own works, but also their reception and their relationship with the work of contemporary – and less contemporary – writers. These are not simply readings from single, enfranchised, critical positions, but also attempts to interweave texts and contexts in a way that speaks to long-term Spark scholars while providing a gateway for relatively new students of her work. In 'Muriel Spark and the Problems of Biography', David Goldie examines Spark's use of character in fictions, including *The Driver's Seat*, *The Public Image* and early stories, exploring conflicts between order and disorder, the registration of complexity and the negotiation of limitations in representing otherness. Goldie considers the relationship between the deception of fiction and the deception of self-representation, and the authorship of speech and the authorship of action, revealing how anxieties of authorship can assume religious significance. In 'Poetic Perception in the Fiction of Muriel Spark', Vassiliki Kolocotroni illustrates the extent to which Spark thought and wrote as a poet in her fiction, and the degree to which her reading of poetry informed and underpinned her prose at every turn. Spark was not only a poet who considered this to be her natural form, she was also an astute editor and reader of poetry whose approach to the novel drew on poetry history. Michael Gardiner relates the themes and form of Spark's fiction of the late 1950s to a waning in the British consensus, placing Spark's early concerns within both a long context of British literary and political preoccupations, and also a shorter one in which Spark picks up on the moment of decolonisation and on Gallo-Scottish intellectual movements which were sceptical of unitary individuals and of detached authorities. Looking at three geographically disparate novels, Marilyn Reizbaum talks about an uncanny effect of the Sparkian voice which seems to emanate from a remote or recessed location, and the transfiguration of the commonplace which renders strange the colloquial statement. In 'Muriel Spark and the Politics of the Contemporary', Adam Piette identifies national allegories in *The Girls of Slender Means* and

The Hothouse By the East River, and reads three levels of narrative significance in *The Mandelbaum Gate* – contemporary-political, religio-historical and socio-sexual – looking at how Spark places readers in narratives, allowing for movement between these different levels. Matthew Wickman discusses Spark's fiction from *Territorial Rights* (1979) in terms of theories of modernity and postmodernity, concluding that it is Spark's preoccupation with the uncanny in later novels such as *Symposium* (1990), rather than the economy of the novellas of the early 1970s, to which we should look for her distinctive contribution to fiction. Gerard Carruthers discusses Spark's description of a god of intangible purposes operating in tandem with free will, including morally unorthodox behaviour, and looks at how the Catholic nature of Spark's work has tended to be an anxiety for many critics. For Paddy Lyons, Spark's approach to fiction is bound up with the dethroning of authorship much pursued in twentieth-century art and commentary, in the stories of Jorge Luis Borges, Vladimir Nabokov or Flann O'Brien, and in the theory of Roland Barthes and Michel Foucault. From the beginning, Lyons argues, Spark was preoccupied with 'voices at play', to borrow the title of an early collection of short dramatic pieces and prose fictions, a preoccupation which, with the attendant undermining of the authority and integrity of the speaking and narrating voice, shows not only a postmodern playfulness, but also a double-edged critique of both realism and romanticism. Randall Stevenson places Spark within a generation suspicious of relations between ethics, intelligence and power, investigating *The Prime of Miss Jean Brodie* in terms of its connecting art and education with control, and seeing scepticism over totalising authorities alongside Spark's proleptic and metafictional techniques relative to recent European writing and also in terms of a Scottish tradition sceptical of overarching powers. Drew Milne's closing chapter, 'Muriel Spark's Crimes of Wit', focuses on Spark as a satirist and wit whose irony and subtlety have confounded critics, so that she has been more praised than appraised. As a sly and suave stylist, Milne argues, Spark is also a writer of substance and stealth who is as preoccupied by the abuse of wit as by its use, and who calls for a criticism attuned to the ruses and rustle of language.

These essays offer a thorough account of the cultural contexts of one of the later twentieth century's most provocative and important writers. They attempt to locate Spark's works in terms of the pressure points of the period, in most of which she intervened, as well as describing how they operate as literary texts. Within a relatively modest space, this *Companion* touches on the whole range of Spark's work and, in introducing the *oeuvre* thematically for those looking to explore this elegant and challenging author further, sets the agenda for future Spark studies.

CHAPTER ONE

Muriel Spark and the Problems of Biography

David Goldie

Spark's short story 'You Should Have Seen the Mess' (1958) features a first-person narrator who appears in the throes of a personality disorder. The irony of this disorder is that it is manifested in neurotic attempts to impose an order where it does not belong. The narrator, Lorna, cannot make sense of what she sees as the chaos in which others choose to live: the disorderliness, the want of cleanliness, the lack of pattern in everyday behaviour. The dark humour of the story comes from her inability to empathise: to understand the very human reasons why her friend Dr Darby might shout in frustration at his young child, for example; or to mistake a 'charming' fourteenth-century cottage for a slum and blithely recommend to the old lady who lives there that she apply to the council to be re-housed. As is rather characteristic in Spark, this thematic humour is reinforced by formal irony: in this story a narrator obsessed with order and cleanliness signally fails to create a clean, coherent narration. Despite her professed facility in English (belied by grammatical errors) and her self-consciousness about her role as expositor, what Lorna offers is a narrative in name only. It remains to the reader to give a shape to what she or he has read.

Such conflicts between order and disorder – along with the difficulties of getting one's life story straight – occur frequently in Spark's writing. Lorna's inability to read the patterns of other lives, to draw lines of significance from what seems a tangled mess of social relationships, is an everyday problem – successful relationships plainly depend on individuals understanding and predicting the thoughts and actions of others. But it is also pre-eminently the writer's problem: how to construct in a sequence of words a plausible simulacrum of the social world and its inhabitants in a way that recognises and respects its complexity while rendering it coherently. A concern with such issues in both their philosophical and technical aspects is fundamental to Spark's writing. One of the principal questions asked of her work – related to the philosophical 'problem of other minds' and her interrogation of the founding premise of liberal humanism that individuals are the authors of their own experience – concerns how much we can ever truly know what is going on in others' inner lives. The other, technical, issue concerns the process of expressing such speculative knowledge in language: in her fiction Spark insists not only on the difficulty involved in knowing others, but also on the ill-advisedness of attempting to put such knowledge into written form. Her characters are never in any simple sense knowable: she frequently raises troubling questions not only of how far they can ever know each other, but of how far we as readers can ever satisfactorily understand them. This is doubly difficult when the issue becomes textual: when characters either try to write about other characters or verbalise their thoughts about them, or the author reminds us that what we are reading is, after all, only a text, not a record of actual lived experience.

The difficulties Spark's characters experience in coming to terms with one another might then be described as the biographer's difficulties – first discerning another's attitudes and experiences and then inducing a plausibly coherent, explicatory life story from them. These difficulties are most explicitly experienced by Spark's artist figures: those who pursue writing or other forms of representation as a career, in Spark's world, are rarely to be trusted. The novelist Charmian Piper, in *Memento Mori* (1959), is one such. Alec Warner is mistrustful of the easy way she can glibly reduce his own experiences to a simple plotted account, believing that 'her novelist's mind by sheer habit still gave to those disjointed happenings a shape which he could not accept, and in a way which he thought dishonest'.[1] Warner's view of Charmian is that she falsifies her account of his life by narrativising it, by insisting on reading pattern and significance into what have in fact been mostly random events and then constructing an account of them that serves her own interests: 'she saw the facts as a dramatic sequence reaching its fingers into all his life's work. This interested him so far as it reflected Charmian, though not at all so far as it affected himself.'[2] When Charmian acknowledges that 'the art of fiction is very like the practice of deception' we are not, then, particularly surprised, just as we are not surprised when another Spark novelist, Fleur Talbot in *Loitering with Intent* (1981), says that 'complete frankness is not a quality that favours art'.[3] Reading such novels, we are frequently reminded, as Bryan Cheyette puts it, that 'fiction, for Spark, is always essentially a distortion, a true lie that arbitrarily fixes meaning'.[4]

Similar difficulties attend other Spark characters who attempt to use their writing as a means to understand others. January Marlow in *Robinson* (1958) writes potted life-histories of Robinson and Jimmie Waterford in her journal, in the hope that if she grasps their life stories she will gain a kind of intellectual purchase on them. But, perhaps typically for Spark, Marlow fails to do this in any satisfactory way, never fully understanding Jimmie's oddness or Robinson's initial opacity and then his final perversity in faking his own death. Not long before Robinson disappears, Marlow is baffled by his irregular habits and irrational cultivation of the island, remarking to herself that 'if you choose the sort of life which has no conventional pattern you have to try to make an art of it, or it is a mess'.[5] The irony is that all this time he has, unknown to her, been artfully preparing to become the author of his own apparent death. The novel's wider irony – and perhaps the reason why it is one of Spark's less loved books – is that despite its gestures towards closure in its final pages, the narrative leaves the reader only partly satisfied by the explanations given for its characters' behaviour. January Marlow's continuing concern for her privacy – refusing to sell her story to the newspapers and remaining opaque to the reader – becomes a sign of the book's wider acknowledgement of others' fundamental unknowability, a rejection of art's order for life's messiness. In the end she perhaps comes to speak for the reader (as well as reminding us of her namesake's similarly unfathomable encounter with Kurtz in Conrad's *Heart of Darkness*) when she says of her fellow survivors: 'their familiar characteristics struck me merely as a number of indications that I knew nothing about them.'[6]

Similar frustrations attend Jane Wright in *The Girls of Slender Means* (1963) as she attempts to write a biographical feature article on Nicholas Farringdon, a poet and Catholic convert lately martyred as a missionary in Haiti. Jane has in the past been an accomplished forger, attempting to put herself into the mind of others by imitating the marks they leave on the surface of events, but for all her arts of impersonation, she is – as we find in the course of the novel – unable to get to the heart of the mysteries of Farringdon's personality. She encounters only other people's deep inscrutability. Although Spark's narrator offers us some additional information about the possible causes of Farringdon's conversion in the form of his unexpressed and unrequited attraction to Joanna Childe, a note in a manuscript by him in which he states that 'a vision of evil may be as effective to conversion as a vision of good', and his witnessing of a murder during the celebrations of VJ day, we finish the novel little more enlightened about the reasons for the change of direction that will eventually lead to his death.[7] He is a figure of contrary impulses, who attempts to impose, in 'a poetic image that teased his mind', his own mistaken construction on the women of the May of Teck club.[8] As such he is most prominent of the many mis-readers in this novel: individuals who interpret their fellows narrowly according to their personal needs and together form a tragicomic world of misrecognition and, ultimately, mutual indifference.

Biography – in its loosest sense of the attempt to make a persuasive life story for an individual out of one's observations of them – seems, then, to be something of an impossible art in Spark's fiction. The problems of truly knowing others disinterestedly, and being able to render such knowledge satisfactorily in language, seem insurmountable. No surprise, then, that her novels contain many characters who might be said to be wilfully resistant to biography. Caroline Rose's efforts to escape the narrative that attempts to write her in *The Comforters* (1957) might be read in this way, as might Sandy Stranger's resistance to the life narrative that Jean Brodie plots for her and other Brodie set members. Elsa in *The Hothouse by the East River* (1973) is another, slightly more unusual instance, who refuses to submit to the limitations of her real life story, instead continuing a posthumous counterfactual existence, Paul saying of her: 'she's a development of an idea, that's all. She's not my original conception any more. She took on a life of her own. She's grotesque.' [9] Lord Lucan similarly seems to enjoy not one but two posthumous lives in *Aiding and Abetting* (2000) in an attempt to evade the limitations and closure of conventional biography. Lise in *The Driver's Seat* (1970) is another figure who tries to overcome the world's defining narratives in unusual fashion, by pre-empting them in authoring the events of her own death.

The reason such characters might want to resist others' attempts to define their identities in terms of their life stories is perhaps highlighted by the rich cast of blackmailers in Spark's novels. Tom Wells in *Robinson*, Joe Ramdez in *The Mandelbaum Gate* (1965), Mabel Pettigrew in *Memento Mori*, Hector Bartlett in *A Far Cry from Kensington* (1988) and Robert Walker in *Aiding and Abetting* all use biographical knowledge for financial leverage. To know the intimate secrets of another life in Spark's fiction is not to own it exactly, but to take out a potentially lucrative lease on it.

This sceptical approach to the possibility of knowing others, and the anxiety over the uses to which that knowledge might be put, is perhaps unsurprising given Spark's religious beliefs. The attempt to exercise authorship over the life of another might be regarded as rather presumptuous to one who acknowledges a higher-level Author in the world. But this hesitation is a little more surprising when one notes how much of Spark's early career involved the activities of literary criticism and biography where such presumptions were, at least at that time, fundamental. In the seven years before the publication of her first novel, *The Comforters*, in 1957, Spark's major published output was as author or editor of eight anthologies and critical biographies which dealt variously with William Wordsworth, Mary Shelley, John Masefield, the Brontës and Cardinal Newman. Spark's major emphasis in approaching this rather diverse group was emphatically biographical: two – *Child of Light: A Reassessment of Mary Wollstonecraft Shelley* (1951) and *John Masefield* (1953) – were relatively straightforward, full-length critical biographies; one – *Emily Brontë: Her Life and Work* (1953), co-written with Derek Stanford, was a critical biography to which Stanford supplied the criticism, while Spark contributed a 100-page biography. The other books, three of them co-edited with Stanford, were *Tribute to Wordsworth: A Miscellany of Opinion for the Centenary of the Poet's Death* (1950), *Selected Poems of Emily*

Brontë (1952), *The Brontë Letters* (1954) and *Letters of John Henry Newman: A Selection* (1957), Spark again contributing introductory biographical essays to each.

Spark's literary criticism in these works is, as might be expected, both insightful and technically informed, for example in her analysis of the language of Shelley's *Frankenstein* or the discussion of the 'tragic error' in Masefield's *Dauber*. But her approach to biography in these books is rarely as cautious or self-reflexive as in her later fiction. Her work on Masefield, for instance, is, she says, an attempt 'to discover the vision in the man and the man in the vision' and involves reading parts of Masefield's poetry as a form of personal revelation.[10] She is concerned primarily with Masefield's achievements as a narrative rather than a lyric poet, and is attentive to the ways in which he transforms personal experience into art, but her reading tends to come back, for validation and authority, to the life experiences and the 'inspiration' from which it came.[11] Much of the book is a detailed, technical reading of Masefield's long narrative poems, with (in an emphasis especially relevant to Spark's own fictional technique) particular attention being paid to the way in which Masefield achieves effects by patient accumulation of closely observed details. For Spark, it is Masefield's rootedness in his own experience and his personal simplicity that give his work its clarity and power, an impression his autobiographical writings, which 'never fail to give the impression that life has always presented itself to him, as it were in the narrative form', reinforce.[12] The insistence throughout is of conventional biography, assuming both its subject's transparency and his life story's teleology. When Spark discusses the books Masefield read in his youth, for example, she describes them as 'unpieced parts of a mosaic, which later was to take shape in his mind'.[13] We get little sense here of a life that might have taken any number of turnings according to chance or circumstance. Instead, we have an assumption that somehow all Masefield's early experiences led ineluctably to his eventual triumph: each a building block in the formation of a mind destined for greatness, not part of an undifferentiated mess from which worldly success somehow emerges.

Similar assumptions underpin her treatments of other writers. If the subjects of her critical biography have anything in common, it is their intriguing personalities existing in tension with the organising forces that surround and threaten to destabilise them. Wordsworth is defined by his relations with the circle of females that orbit him; Emily Brontë by a tight-knit family group dominated by her elder sister, Charlotte; Masefield by the conventions of a conservative literary practice against which his narrative poetry strains; Newman by the machinations of the Roman Catholic Church to which he converts; and Mary Shelley by the overshadowing presence, first of parents and then husband and half-sister. Such tensions are the common stuff of biography, but what arguably unites her subjects is Spark's fascination with the personal, human qualities that each salvages from that experience and transforms into art. Spark asserts, in her introduction to *The Brontë Letters*, that 'where outstanding figures of literature are concerned, surely the greatest benefit to be derived from a study of their lives is that which penetrates the operation of the creative mind, interpreting the spirit which motivated it'.[14] This approach finds expression in the view of Newman as 'a great man' whose 'personality was involved in all his undertakings' and who 'approached practically everything from a personal point of view'.[15] It can be found in her assertion that 'more than is the case with most poets, Wordsworth the man and the poet are interdependent' and in her belief that the best of Brontë's poems are 'a personal projection of the author's spiritual life-force'.[16]

This is never quite as simplistic as it sounds. Spark's interest in biography is focused mainly on those aspects of the life experience that inform the writing directly and that, in her view, become objectivised in the artwork itself. She seems duly mindful in this regard of T. S. Eliot's arguments about literary impersonality as well as the work of contemporary theorists, such as Father Agius, that derive from them.[17] And Spark is always aware that her subjects' personalities are rarely as straightforward and consistent as they might be. Although she tends to downplay this in the case of Masefield (her only living subject), she is alert to her other subjects' difficulties and self-contradictions. She writes apropos Mary Shelley, for example, that 'all people contain within them the elements of conflict. In some, however, the battle wages more vigorously, more unequally and longer than in others, and such people eventually reveal a salient inconsistency to the world.' [18] Newman, likewise, proves by example that 'some temperaments are only true when they are inconsistent'.[19] This idea has its most sustained examination in Spark's long biographical essay in *Emily Brontë: Her Life and Work*. Here she tries to come to terms with the contradictory biographical readings of Brontë: on the one hand, the timid '"problem" girl' who appears in contemporary comments and in Charlotte Brontë's account; on the other, the 'impassioned superwoman' manifested in her novels and emphasised in the 'legend' emerging in later biography.[20] Spark acknowledges the self-contradictions involved and resolves them partly, as she would again in the case of Newman, by talking in terms of the 'development' of a changing personality. But she also offers a more surprising and subtle reading that undermines the assumptions underlying much of her biographical writing. In attempting to come to terms with the disparities in accounts of Brontë's life, Spark ponders whether we should pay more attention to the immediate facts of a life or to the accumulated interpretations placed on those facts by subsequent accounts. 'Which is the more accurate portrayal,' she asks, 'that of the real man whom we chanced to meet, or that of our reconstruction – the legendary figure, in other words?' The surprising answer is that 'the second impression is the more real. The first merely pre-figured the legend.' Spark is careful to add that a mixture of the two is the best of all, that 'we need concrete as well as legendary impressions to bring us somewhere near a true picture of the man', but the welcome acknowledge-ment here is that biographical objectivity is difficult, if not impossible – that life-writing is an inherently unstable practice. Such an admission is as rare in her biographical writing as it is abundant in her fiction.[21]

While Spark's biographical writing is rarely as self-reflexive as her fiction in these terms, her biographies do introduce several preoccupations that are worth noting for the way they recur in her fiction. Perhaps the most salient of these concerns is the creative individual's need for independence. Uniting her biographical subjects is their need to escape the restraints of convention, family and religion to develop their individual voices. Newman's struggle was to assert his personality against the dogmas of the Catholic Church to which he had converted. This created misunderstanding and rejection, but also led to personal growth, 'almost as if the endurance of personal misunderstanding were a condition of his development'.[22] The Brontës are likewise fortunate to have evaded another kind of smothering orthodoxy. As Spark tells it, 'there is every possibility that had their mother lived she would have humanized them to the extent of reducing their creative powers; while their personal sufferings might have been mitigated, their genius might in some measure have been muffled by her love'. This is particularly fortunate as, in Spark's view, *Wuthering Heights* 'could never have been the product of an orthodox mind'.[23] The cases of Mary Shelley and William Wordsworth are less salutary. Shelley can never escape the snares of the world and finds her imaginative powers declining 'as her passion for "status" mounted'.[24] This is also adduced as the reason for Wordsworth's decline, which Spark (writing jointly with Stanford) attributes directly to his marriage. Wordsworth at the height of his powers is 'the rebel, the heretic, the "half-atheist"', but when he marries and finds himself 'adapting to the demands of orthodox opinion' his work is fatally weakened. He is, in this view, an individual who 'seemed to require some profound emotional disturbance before the universe appeared to him in vital and imaginative terms', so that 'a low-voltage domestic feeling for his wife outwardly stabilised the man but inwardly assassinated the poet'.[25]

As these arguments show, it is possible to see in Spark's biographical read-ings an early manifestation of several of her later fiction's preoccupations. The biographical writing's assertion of an inverse relationship between orthodoxy and creativity, for example, can be seen to foreshadow the scepti-cism towards religious institutions many of her fictional protagonists exhibit, usually in their attempts to maintain a semi-detached relationship to religious orthodoxy. A similar case can be made about the common attitudes in her biographies and fiction towards the responsibilities of the individual in their personal and familial relationships. Where she is concerned with family life at all in her fiction, it is usually only to show how stifling and restrictive it is and how ungrateful children are to their parents. And just as she rarely plays happy families in her novels, she is rather short on happy marriages. From her first novel, *The Comforters*, in which the wedding of Caroline and Laurence is endlessly deferred, to the disintegrating marriage of Nina and Rowland in her last, *The Finishing School*, Spark's fiction is overwhelmingly populated by a cast of dissatisfied husbands and wives, and single women in flight from unsatisfactory relationships. In this world marriage is commonly a condition of limitation involving either erosion of self or grounds for powerful mutual resentment, seen most nakedly, perhaps, in Frederick Christopher's vicious jealousy of his wife in *The Public Image*.

It is abundantly clear from her novels that Spark is a highly self-reflexive, sophisticated author who understands, and exploits, the many paradoxes of life writing. Strange, then, that she appears to resist these paradoxes when it comes to dealing with narratives of her own life. As even a casual reader of Spark quickly understands, and as her autobiography readily testifies, there is often a great deal of her own experience at the roots of her fiction. Peter Kemp has noted, for example, how in *Robinson* Spark allows 'barely transmuted bits of personal material [to] break jarringly through the fictive covering'.[26] It is clear there is more than a little of Spark in the character of Fleur Talbot, the first-person narrator of *Loitering with Intent*. Fleur becomes entangled in the machinations of the 'Autobiographical Association' for whose members she invents life stories that are racier and more credible than the real thing. She is at the same time working on her first novel, *Warrender Chase*, and in typical Spark fashion (and perhaps as a reminder of Spark's own first novel) it begins to appear that the people around Fleur are acting in ways predetermined by her fiction. The novel is, in other words, an enter-taining and complex treatment of the themes of identity and the operation of free will often found in Spark's work, as well as being a characteristic Sparkian metafictional experiment. The sense in which the novel is engaged in a series of complex autobiographical games is further enhanced by the ele-ments of direct personal experience that Spark chooses to place in the work. For example, the reader's first encounter with Fleur is in 1950 as she sits writing a poem in a Kensington graveyard. By the time the novel was written it was already public knowledge, thanks to Stanford's critical biography as well as poems such as her 'Elegy in a Kensington Churchyard', that this is the kind of situation Spark might typically have been found in at this time.[27] And this is only the first of several direct parallels to be made between the life experiences and tastes of the writer-heroine and her author. Both are, in 1950, quirky, independent-minded women, existing, as Fleur puts it, 'on the grubby edge of the literary world': both slightly *fast* poets manqué, with an ear for the felicitous eccentric phrase and an abiding passion for the autobiographies of Newman and Benvenuto Cellini. So when Fleur tells us that 'I've come to learn for myself how little one needs in the art of writing, to convey the lot, and how a lot of words, on the other hand, can convey so little', it is difficult not to hear a self-description of Spark's own fastidious approach to prose writing.[28] This closeness in tone is reinforced at the novel's close, with Fleur's account of her early life ending with the phrase that would also close Spark's autobiography: both resolving to 'go on my way rejoicing'.[29]

It would be reductive to suggest that Fleur is simply a thinly veiled portrait of Spark, but it would be equally simplistic to say that she is definitively not Spark. She is, rather, a composite textual being in whom fundamental questions about the stability of fictional and ontological identity contend. Spark's characterisation teases the reader into a game of recognition and misrecognition. She invites us to recognise the seemingly real people behind her characters, and persuades us by her observational sharpness and sensitivity to the niceties of social behaviour that what we are witnessing are rich, thickly cut slices of life. But by constantly foregrounding the constructedness and self-consciousness of her narratives she also reminds us of the opposite case: her scenarios are textual rather than actual; her characters are not autonomous beings preceding the text, but rather individuals having come into being within it. That is, they owe their being to their author and the context in which that author has chosen to place them – an ontological status that has both literary and religious ramifications.

Loitering with Intent, like many of Spark's novels, playfully explores and exploits such issues of autonomy and identity. It does this within both the boundaries of its own world – in the manipulations of personal identity which its characters are subjected to and with which they largely collude – and the wider literary world surrounding it, the world in which the novel is consumed and which is aware of the persona (or, as in Spark's discussion of Emily Brontë, 'the legend') of the author who controls and informs it. One of the several points that emerge from these playful, sophisticated textual games is that the writing of a life story is not so much an act of discovery as an opportunity for creativity and reinvention; less an attempt to fix a simple truth in lines of type than an opportunity to work up some words in ways that might, in all their contingency and partial adequacy, come close to resembling at least a little of individual experience's complexity, inscrutability, and self-contradiction . Fleur Talbot confides in the reader that,

> Since the story of my own life is just as much constituted of the secrets of my craft as it is of other events, I might as well remark here that to make a character ring true it needs must be in some way contradictory, somewhere a paradox.[30]

What is particularly interesting here is not just the opinion – often expressed, as we have seen, in Spark's fiction and in her biographies – of the irreducible complexity of personal identity, but rather the self-reflexiveness of the first clause. In acknowledging that the story of Fleur's life is 'just as much constituted of the secrets of my craft as it is of other events', Spark is stating concisely the fundamental difficulty of arriving at an authoritative biographical narrative and, perhaps, pointing to the ultimate irreconcilability of the two parts of the phrase 'life writing'.

One might expect, then, that her approach to the writing of her own life might show such a reflexive, playful awareness of slippery textuality, the issues of autonomy and authorship, and the pluralities of personhood. But when she becomes in her turn a biographical and autobiographical subject Spark's tone becomes much less ludic and sophisticated. It is on record that she disapproved of Stanford's *Muriel Spark: A Biographical and Critical Study* (1963), perhaps understandably given their once close working relationship had ended some six years previously (with Spark subsequently pillorying him as Hector Bartlett, the mendacious *pisseur de copie* in *A Far Cry from Kensington*, and removing his name as the dedicatee of her biography of Mary Shelley in its second edition). Spark wrote to one early critic of her work, Dorothea Walker, that, in 'the interests of accuracy', Walker should be mindful that 'a number of biographical pieces already written about me are altogether wrong, sometimes pure inventions, which I am sure you would not wish to perpetuate. Especially don't copy Derek Stanford.' [31] This concern with 'accuracy' and setting the record straight is professedly a part of the motivation for the writing of her own autobiography, *Curriculum Vitae* (1992), and arguably what makes it a less interesting and less insightful book than it might otherwise have been. In her introduction Spark talks again of the 'strange and erroneous accounts of parts of my life that have been written since I became well known' and states that the book contains 'nothing that cannot be supported by documentary evidence or by eyewitnesses'.[32] This is admirable for the purposes of consistency and factual scholarship, but it ignores exactly the complex issues that animate her fiction. In mapping meticulously the real events of her life, and in relating them to their transfiguration in her fiction (as well as settling a few old scores along the way), Spark creates a persuasively clear and amusing account of her younger self but denies that self the rich variousness, the openness to self-contradiction and the enabling sense of paradox she customarily allows her fictional characters. She renounces, in other words, the messiness of life as it is lived for the clear certainties of the documentary word, constituting herself author and official keeper of her own life: a position her fiction-writing self – the witty, paradox-loving creator of Caroline Rose, Jean Brodie and the Abbess Alexandra among many others – would surely have mocked for its impossible presumption. And she continues to will this authority over her life's story from the grave. In the 1990s Spark relented in her resistance to becoming a biographical subject and approved the writing of a biography by Martin Stannard. When it became clear, however, that Stannard intended to take an independent line, Spark stalled on its publication, reportedly having 'to spend a lot of time going through it, line by line' in an attempt to 'make it a little bit fairer', and ultimately wishing 'she had not got involved with the project in the first place'.[33] According to press reports, this process of obstruction in the name of clarification continued, with her estate insisting on 'substantial revisions' before the work would be authorised for publication.[34] The result is that the biography did not appear until 2009, long after its completion.

In the letter to Dorothea Walker quoted above, Spark suggested that her long-held reluctance to divulge biographical details was partly natural reticence, partly a concern for the feelings of others who might be implicated, 'but also because I believe my work can be judged on its own'. In the light of her early excursions into biography and in the wake of the indiscretions of *Curriculum Vitae* (not to mention her apparent absence of concern for the feelings of Lady Lucan in bringing her husband back to life in *Aiding and Abetting*) this seems disingenuous. Spark's work can, no doubt, be enjoyed and understood in the absence of knowledge of its author. But hers is an *oeuvre* that is so deeply concerned with issues of identity and authority, and so closely identified with the persona of its author, that to attempt to understand it without taking Spark herself into account is to miss a rich, perhaps the richest, element of its intriguing, playful complexity.

CHAPTER TWO

Poetic Perception in the Fiction of Muriel Spark

Vassiliki Kolocotroni

As a poet, poetry editor, critic, anthologist [1] and a novelist who consistently professed 'a poet's way of looking at the world',[2] Muriel Spark loitered with intent among the pages of the treasuries of verse, always exercising what Fleur Talbot, the protagonist of one of Spark's most autobiographical novels, calls her 'poetic vigilance'.[3]

Poetry punctuates and resounds in Spark's text, channelled through the human voice with an intense, mantra-like delivery. Especially in the earlier novels, poetry speaks *through* characters, who carry and amplify its sound as if possessed. In *The Girls of Slender Means* (1963), Joanna Childe, elocutionist in residence at the May of Teck club, is famous for her 'good voice' and taste in poetry,

> which she loved rather as it might be assumed a cat loves birds; poetry, especially the declamatory sort, excited and possessed her; she would pounce on the stuff, play with it quivering in her mind, and when she had got it by heart, she spoke it forth in devouring relish.[4]

Joanna's raw, passionate, instinctive appetite for poetry points to a relationship with the word that is child-like, as suggested by her last name, and thus unfettered and poignant. Crucially, it is not for relevance to the occasion that her choice of poetic passages for recitation is known: 'It was not usual for Joanna to quote anything for its aptitude';[5] yet her powerful rendition of Gerard Manley Hopkins' *The Wreck of the Deutschland*, unbeknownst to her and her enthralled audience, proleptically speaks of the tragic fate that awaits her and the girls' house of refuge at the end of the novel.[6] There is a collage of voices (or Babel of tongues) in this sonorous text: 'at any hour of the day or night', Dorothy Markham, poor relative of the club's chairwoman, for instance, might be heard 'emit[ting . . .] a waterfall of debutante chatter, which rightly gave the impression that on any occasion between talking, eating and sleeping, she did not think, except in terms of these phrase-ripples of hers: "Filthy lunch", "The most gorgeous wedding" [. . .] "Ghastly film."

"I'm desperately well, thanks, how are you?"' or, more disconcertingly, in an echo of a notorious final scene in Spark's later work, "'He actually raped her, she was amazed"'.[7] Dorothy's 'phrase-ripples' compete with Nancy Riddle's attempts to 'overcome her Midlands accent' through her elocution lessons with Joanna Childe, while Jane Wright, 'tyrannous about her brain-work', is composing her dubious addresses to famous writers, and the beautiful, languid Selina Redwood repeats, 'slowly and solemnly', the 'Two Sentences' prescribed by the 'Chief Instructress of the Poise Course' for recitation twice a day:

> Poise is perfect balance, an equanimity of body and mind, complete composure whatever the social scene. Elegant dress, immaculate grooming, and perfect deportment all contribute to the attainment of self-confidence.[8]

Meanwhile, there are the wireless sets, the 'rippling tinkles' of the girl at the piano and a seemingly endless provision of lyrical verse, recited by Joanna and her pupils. The polyphony of discourses operates at both the aural and visual level (as interruptions on the page), and the effect of simultaneity is conveyed through a collagistic text, riddled with quotation and reported speech.

Delightfully chaotic and riotous as the overall effect might be, as well as reflective of the strong utopian elements associated with the figure of the club – one of Spark's many such spaces occupied by communities of women (though not always as merrily)[9] – the technique here goes beyond the precise observation of plausible characters' peculiar way with words. As glimpsed in the carefully constructed class undertones of all speech-acts in the novel, there is no neutral act of linguistic expression in this girly Babel; some discourses are more equal than others. At the core of this loaded use of language in the novel lies poetry-loving elocutionist Joanna Childe and her trained delivery.

In a sense, Joanna is the voice of the canon, or of the prescribed, valued, anthologised, previously enjoyed and vicariously experienced poetic life. A woman of 'strong obscure emotions',[10] she 'had been brought up to hear, and later to recite, "... Love is not love / Which alters when it alteration finds ..."', as all 'her ideas of honour and love came from the poets'.[11] 'Like the rector's eldest daughter that she was', consumed by the fear of causing offence, Joanna suppresses her love for the newly ordained curate or, to be precise, in the comic but cutting literalism of some of Spark's more determined believers, 'decide[s] to pluck out her right eye, cut off her right hand, this looming offence to the first love, this stumbling-block, the adorable man in the pulpit' and 'enter maimed into the Kingdom of Heaven'.[12] There is humour but also poignancy and pathos in Joanna's hyperbole, as the depth of her conditioning is revealed to the reader. Sublimation takes its course, 'the sensation of poetry replace[s] the sensation of the curate' and Joanna becomes an elocution teacher instead.[13] As it resonates through the novel in recitations of lines from Shakespeare, Marvell, Webster, Wordsworth, Drinkwater, Blake, Coleridge, Arnold, Byron, Poe, Tennyson, Shelley and Hopkins, as well as the Bible and the Book of Common Prayer, Joanna's voice becomes uncannily, eerily mechanical, as if disembodied or agentless, making her, more clearly than other characters in the novel, a perfect representation of what Marxist sociolinguists call the 'verbally constituted consciousness'.[14] For Joanna, rector's daughter and elocutionist, the biblical and poetic word go to form a single, dominant authoritative discourse, which, as Mikhail Bakhtin points out, 'cannot be represented – it is only transmitted':[15]

> The authoritative word demands that we acknowledge it, that we make it our own; it binds us, quite independent of any power it might have to persuade us internally; we encounter it with its authority already fused to it. The authoritative word is located in a distanced zone, organically connected with a past that is felt to be hierarchically higher.[16]

There is a subtle but important distinction between Dorothy's tendency to 'emit' a 'girl-about-town' language in the form of 'phrase-ripples', and Joanna's ability (or compulsion) to 'transmit' poetry and, in Bakhtin's terms, 'the word of the fathers', quite literally in her case, as the daughter of a member of the High Church. There is automatism in both linguistic behaviours and the suggestion that they are both specifically gendered (though sexed in Dorothy's and sexless in Joanna's case), but Joanna's performance carries additional ideological nuances. She is not so much a reader as a speaker of poetry: 'No, she recites from memory,' one of the girls points out. 'But her pupils read, of course. It's elocution.' [17] In his study of the verse recitation movement in late Victorian and Edwardian England, Mark Morrison traces its class dimension in a context particularly revealing for Spark's use of poetic quotation. According to Morrison:

> Victorian elocution and recitation practices, which initially served the clergy, barristers, MPs, and other male members of the privileged classes who envisioned a career involving public speaking, evolved into a much more elaborate and widespread vehicle of cultural reproduction, legitimation, and distinction for the male and female upper and middle classes.[18]

Wider dissemination of the perceived benefits of exposure to the poetic word was considered an important acculturating tool; as 'Mrs S.', a formidable member of the servant class in Spark's *Doctors of Philosophy* (1962) would put it: 'You can't dab a bit of scent on a mind but you can dab poetry on it.

Stands to reason.' [19] More pertinently still for Spark, one of the institutions of this 'culturally legitimating marker of distinction', embodied by the idea of the 'pure voice',[20] was none other than the Poetry Society, originally founded in London in 1909 as the Poetry Recital Society. As Abby Arthur Johnson puts it: 'the Poetry Society talked about reaching the average reader. Such rhetoric attracted many names prefaced by Lady, Lord, or Sir.' [21] Morrison cites in his essay some of the key terms from the mission statement of the Society issued by the then chairwoman, an aristocratic antecedent of Muriel Spark, who was to be the Society's general secretary for a brief but formative period in 1947–9: [22]

> Lady Margaret Sackville's inaugural address epitomized the Poetry Society's goals for recitation [. . .] : 'There should be no striving from outside to produce a definite effect – the soul of the interpreter should be so possessed by the poem that it follows it instinctively in every modulation and inflection as easily as water flows between winding banks'. Significantly, the marker of distinction was always the voice, the one thing that would be almost impossible for a working-class reciter to emulate.[23]

Morrison makes interesting connections between the connotations of the 'pure voice' and the doctrine of impersonality (later to be picked up by T. S. Eliot) and shows that one of the paradoxical results of the verse recitation movement was the provision of a forum for the dissemination of modernist poetry.[24] Following such controversies, as editor of the Society's publication, the *Poetry Review*, Spark herself entered the fray with combative editorials urging an end to the 'railing at the moderns' and ushering in of an 'Age of Reassessment' of poetic value.[25]

Joanna Childe, then, who, we are told, is 'not moved by the poetry of Eliot and Auden',[26] is the medium of the 'pure voice' of a heritage whose hold is both acknowledged and subverted by Spark's ventriloquist tactics. There is more than pure satire, though, in this characterisation; rendered as a virginal and angelic type (in the literal sense of the Greek *angelos*, a messenger), Joanna is also cast by Spark in the role of the ambivalent, ageless figure of the female enigma, as perceived, or rather misconceived, by the novel's main male auditor, Nicholas Farringdon. This misrecognition occurs in the scene where Nicholas, pacifist poet and Catholic convert-to-be, but at the time a follower of anarchism (and of Selina Redwood), loitering as is his wont in the club hall of an evening, hears Joanna recite a verse from John Drinkwater's 'Moonlit Apples': 'if she knew life she would not be proclaiming these words so sexually and matriarchally as if in the ecstatic act of suckling a divine child', he thinks.[27] He had thought along the same lines the first time he heard her voice: 'she is orgiastical in her feeling for poetry. I can hear it in her voice [. . .] . Poetry takes the place of sex for her.' [28] Joanna's voice is soon silenced, however, by the sound of Winston Churchill roaring from the upper floors:

> The wirelesses spoke forth their simultaneous Sinaitic predictions of what fate would befall the freedom-loving electorate should it vote for Labour in the forthcoming elections. [. . .]

> 'We shall have Civil Servants . . .'
>   The wirelesses changed their tones, they roared:
>   'No longer civil . . .'
> Then they were sad and slow:
>   'No longer . . .
>   . . . servants.' [29]

Meanwhile, in Nicholas's mind, Joanna, overcome, silenced by the more formidable declaimer, is curiously de-animated:

> Nicholas imagined Joanna standing by her bed, put out of business as it were, but listening, drawing it into her bloodstream. As in a dream of his own that depicted a dream of hers, he thought of Joanna in this immovable attitude, given up to the cadences of the wireless as if it did not matter what was producing them, the politician or herself. She was a proclaiming statue in his mind.[30]

We are in the realm of ideology here, an echo chamber and hall of mirrors at once, whereby sound alone creates a fantastic identity: to the sexually predatory (though not 'orthosexual',[31] as is succinctly put by Jane Wright) Nicholas, Joanna is an emblem of ambivalent and mysterious femininity, a virginal Madonna (suggested in his account of her recitation as 'the ecstatic act of suckling a divine child'), turned empty vessel, carrier of the master's voice. It is not clear in the text whether Joanna is in fact as enthralled by Churchill's harangue as Nicholas's mediation would have it; what has been activated here is his own desire to imagine her, a woman consumed by the Word, in the manner of a Renaissance sculptor, an animator of stone, or put differently, a de-animator of a living body. Men are often caught by Spark in the act of de-animation, their fantasies, or fears, glimpsed through awkward encounters with overbearing and female fleshly demands – Mervyn Hogarth (formerly Hogg), for instance, who can barely manage to be in the same room as his first wife, the buxom, insufferable Georgina in *The Comforters* (1957): 'He had married her in his thirty-second year instead of carving her image in stone. It was not his first mistake and her presence, half-turned to the window, dabbing each eye with her furious handkerchief, stabbed him with an unwanted knowledge of himself';[32] or Martin Bowles, the grudging confidant of the Chelsea divorcée Isobel Billows in *The Bachelors* (1960):

He saw it would be safer to marry her. Often, when she had said, 'Martin, what should I do without you? I should never be able to manage my affairs without you,' he had recognized her strong-boned beauty and thought how a sculptor might do something about it.[33]

These small epiphanies are more revealing about the inescapable fact of *mis*recognition than about any true insight or union between perceiver and perceived. They also lift the curtain on the theatre of misogyny, as practised by both men and women. *The Bachelors* is particularly rich in such renditions of the sexual insult, with its strong cast of weak characters (or 'ridiculous demons',[34] as the graphologist Ronald Bridges, the novel's main observing consciousness, sees them), as is *The Public Image* (1968), Spark's first of many forays into the world of the fantasy industry, in this case Rome's Cinecittà. Though publicly perceived as a powerful, seductive woman ('the English Lady-Tiger'), Annabel Christopher simply 'transmits' a message, reflecting what is projected on or through her.[35] Like Joanna Childe, who was 'generally assumed to be something emotionally heroic' and thus 'compared to Ingrid Bergman',[36] Annabel is a cipher, more acted upon than acting, caught up and created in the image of many, often contradictory demands and desires, including those of her husband, Frederick, who, in a desperately malicious act of envy and self-absorption, commits suicide in order to script her public fall from grace. His final note, in the form of a letter to Annabel, attempts to expose her in the following terms: '*You are a beautiful shell, like something washed up on the sea-shore, a collector's item, perfectly formed, a pearly shell – but empty, devoid of the life it once held.*'[37] Frederick's hissing insult misfires, however, his scheme falls flat and Annabel escapes relatively unscathed, firmly for a change in the driver's seat. The empty shell, a rather clichéd analogy in his hands, as Peter Kemp notes,[38] is revisited and redeemed at the end of the novel, when Annabel is on her way to Greece, presumably fully to assume her new incarnation as ancient goddess, having relinquished the trappings of her public persona:

> Waiting for the order to board, she felt both free and unfree. The heavy weight of the bags was gone; she felt as if she was still, curiously, pregnant with the baby, but not pregnant in fact. She was pale as a shell. She did not wear her dark glasses. Nobody recognized her as she stood, having moved the baby to rest on her hip, conscious also of the baby in a sense weightlessly and perpetually within her, as an empty shell contains, by its very structure, the echo and harking image of former and former seas.[39]

The image of the empty shell suggests survival, antiquity, purity and fragility, perhaps also recalling the emergence from the sea of Botticelli's Venus. At the same time, Annabel seems unselfconsciously to have struck a Madonna and child pose or, rather, a Madonna *with* child, thus acting out the literal meaning of her second name (*Christopher*, bearer of Christ), but also subtly and economically crystallising the fraught issue at the novel's core, namely the mystification of the feminine image and its persistent misprisions.[40] The suspended duality of this final, redemptive image of singularity is crucial for Spark and it resonates with formulations that recur throughout her work. Spark's argument is with the fallacy of certain forms of Christian dogmatism, which, as she put it in an early piece published in *The Church of England Newspaper* during her brief membership of the Anglican Church, 'takes the form of a dualistic attitude towards matter and spirit. They are seen too much in a moral conflict, where spirit triumphs by virtue of disembodiment. This is really an amoral conception of spirit.' [41] Instead, she argues, 'there is a method of apprehending eternity through our senses, analogous to our sacramental understanding of eternity by faith.' [42] The exemplar she celebrates in that piece is Marcel Proust, the 'agnostic, hedonist, self-centred neurotic',[43] whose 'labyrinthine work' she had 'read deeply',[44] but she revisits this argument frequently in her own work. In *The Bachelors*, for instance, Matthew Finch comments dismissively on the spiritualist Patrick Seton's reluctance to marry his hapless (and pregnant) fiancée:

> 'What do you expect of a spiritualist? His mind's attuned to the ghouls of the air all day long. How can he be expected to consider the moral obligations of the flesh? The man's a dualist. No sacramental sense. [. . .] You've got to affirm the oneness of reality in some form or another'.[45]

More than twenty years later, in *Reality and Dreams* (1996), Spark stages the following exchange between the protagonist, incapacitated film director Tom Richards, and his Greek masseur:

> 'This physical experience is almost a spiritual one,' he observed to Ron.
>   'I hear this before, it's well-known,' said Ron. 'Many persons feel they relax in the spirit from massage.'
>   'What is the difference between body and spirit?' said Tom.
>   'There is a difference but both are very alike, you know,' said Ron.
>   'At least, interdependent I should say,' Tom said.[46]

For Spark, the false duality between spirit and matter is particularly pernicious when it comes to the rendition of female physicality, the fear, or at least lack, of understanding which she dissects often in her novels to hilarious and dark effect. Her bemusement at the persistence of the ancient insult levelled at women in their compromised position as dangerous, impure bodies is palpable in those vignettes where she exposes the blind spots of many an orthodox believer. In *Robinson*, for instance, she has the convert January Marlow confront her brother-in-law, the 'cradle Catholic' Ian Brodie,[47] on the matter of Mariolatry, or what he sees as 'Marian excesses':

> 'Any good Catholic,' said Ian, 'should be horrified to see the Mother of God worshipped as if she were a pagan goddess.'
>
> . . .
>
> Agnes had told me once that her husband was sexually impotent. She had no right to tell me any such thing, but I felt she was not telling me anything that I did not really already know.[48]

Trapped in a near-paradisiacal island, January, a Girl Friday but also Eve of sorts, despite, or perhaps *because* of, her recent widowhood, has to stand her ground against the fixations and prejudices of her male companions, for whom she is decidedly 'a female problem'.[49] She manages this by befriending Bluebell, an 'enchanted' cat,[50] and by staying true to her 'aesthetic sense', or the conviction that 'If you choose the sort of life which has no conventional pattern you have to try to make an art of it, or it is a mess'.[51] A gloss on Spark's own predilection for the unorthodox, contradictory and elusive detail, January's fascination is for the 'misleading element':

> In the course of deciphering a face, its shape, tone, lines and droops as if these were words and sentences of a message from the interior, I fix upon it a character which, though I know it to be distorted, never quite untrue, never entirely true, interests me. I am as near the mark as myth is to history, the apocrypha to the canon. I seek no justification for this habit, it is one of the things I do.[52]

It is this association with the apocryphal and mythical (as a correlative to the canonical and historical) that is suggested by Annabel Christopher's final image. Like the ambivalent figure of the Black Madonna, which features so often in Spark's writing,[53] Annabel's Virgin-with-child pose captures the essence of a very real mystery for Spark – the spiritual potential of female materiality.[54] For Spark, as the wise Sister Gertrude puts it in *The Abbess of Crewe*, "'That isn't a problem [. . .] It's a paradox'",[55] or a conundrum with a colourful past in the history of faith and artistic representation. A keen researcher in the archive of myth and symbol,[56] Spark had a good eye for such paradoxical, transitional moments. In *The Takeover* (1976), for instance, the exploits of the self-styled pagan descendant Hubert Mallindaine include founding a church that 'cultivated the worship of Diana according to its final phases when Christianity began to overcast her image with Mary the Mother of God'.[57] Transfigurations of this type offer opportunities for set pieces of comic staging in her work, such as Pauline Thin's ill-conceived interpretation of her role as one of Diana's vestal virgins, which causes Hubert to scream: "'That woman has no sense of stage management. Tell her to go and remove those objectionable clothes. She's supposed to be the chief of Diana's vestals and she looks like Puss-in-Boots at the pantomime'";[58] but these are also focal points for affirmative, lyrical reflection.

Annabel thus joins the cast of Sparkian characters who seem to attain (or to recover through a 'reversal of circumstances', a favourite Aristotelian term)[59] an archetypal, mythological state. As ever with Spark, this is an ambiguous condition, representing both agency and its lack, an act of will (or even wilfulness) through the pursuit of self-mystification and a relinquishing of it through the compulsion to act as if one were blindly heeding destiny. This is also a condition that often coincides with an act of terrible self-eradication or withdrawal from the world, such as Lise's plotting her own violent death in *The Driver's Seat* (1970), Miss Pettigrew's medieval renunciation of the flesh in 'Come Along, Marjorie' (1958) or, indeed, the fatal 'self-styled superwomanism' of Emily Brontë, which Spark in her biographical essay attributes to a 'torturing self-image', an obsession with 'the ideology of her work' and a penchant for 'mystical intimacies' in the style of the Middle Ages.[60] Such extreme embodiments of self-dramatisation hold a distinct appeal for Spark. One of her most consistent, and consistently hilarious, self-dramatisers, Alexandra, Abbess of Crewe, acts out that part with great self-conscious aplomb: "'Sister Gertrude has charmed all the kingdom with her dangerous exploits, while the Abbess of Crewe continues to perform her part in the drama of *The Abbess of Crewe*. The world is having fun and waiting for the catharsis. Is this my destiny?'" [61] As Spark recalled in the BBC television recording 'At Emily Brontë's Grave, Haworth, April 1961':

> For many years I was intensely occupied by Emily Brontë – almost haunted. What impressed me was the dramatic shape of her life. It's as if she had consciously laid out the plot of her life in a play called *Emily Brontë*. She might have been invented by Ibsen – a parson's daughter with a terrifying soul.[62]

Like Annabel, striking her final pose, Emily seemed to Spark 'as if she had consciously laid out the plot of her life' for the benefit or instruction of a future audience. A subtle ambiguity about the self-consciousness involved in the acting out of a private vision is introduced by the 'as if' formation, suggesting the possibility of the coexistence of fact and legend, actuality and mystification. For Jennifer Lynn Randisi, following Hans Vaihinger's formula in *The Philosophy of 'As If'*, the phrase is a key Sparkian trope, a device that allows for the irruption of the paradoxical and the uncertain within the narrative flow.[63] It is as if the reader's attention is drawn to the artifice of the character or plot in question, while holding on to the plausibility of its reality. Randisi sees this as one of the fundamental features of Spark's 'language of possibility', but it is also an expression of the belief in the fundamental theatricality, or the literally spectacular nature of even the most solitary or singular act. To echo Spark again, it is as if the individual subject is only confirmed through a show, a performance open to the interpretation (or more often than not, misinterpretation) of others, or, as Margaret Murchie puts it in *Symposium* (1990): "'It's a question of *les autres*" [. . .] "One can't live unto oneself'.' [64] That living for '*les autres*' may be a kind of hell, as one of Jean-Paul Sartre's damned characters famously declares in the 1944 play *No Exit* ('Pas besoin de gril: l'enfer, c'est les Autres!'),[65] only serves to underline the tragicomic effect of the attempt, shared by many Sparkian neurotics, to script themselves and control others' interpretations.

Unlike professional purveyors of interpretation, who in a variety of guises are treated with comic scorn in her novels (journalists, policemen and psychoanalysts are the usual suspects), Spark never, however, issues a diagnosis or final account, a full disclosure; characters may meet their fate,[66] but their motive or profile is never caught fully from within. Framed through others' views or memories, they become what they always already are, creatures of the imagination, compounds of fact and legend, figures in a retrospective, there to delight or inspire or baffle a community of readers. This Aristotelian gesture is conveyed quite clearly at the end of 'Come Along, Marjorie': 'But the community was sobered and united for a brief time, contemplating with fear and pity the calling of Miss Pettigrew Marjorie';[67] and it is also invoked in the final sentence of *The Driver's Seat*:

> He sees already the gleaming buttons of the policemen's uniforms, hears the cold and the confiding, the hot and the barking voices, sees already the holsters and epaulets and all those trappings devised to protect them from the indecent exposure of fear and pity, pity and fear.[68]

The zooming in on detail, random and real, detracts momentarily from the weightiness of the occasion, while acting by way of counterpoint to emphasise it. In 'Come Along, Marjorie', The full impact of the event, Miss Pettigrew's removal by ambulance, by 'strange men' carrying 'unnecessary equipment',[69] is both reduced and made more poignant by the observers' bemusement at the fact that she was called by her first name; similarly, the drab details of the 'sad little office where the police clank in and out' convey more a sense of banality than of evil, but in screening the raw, 'indecent' fact of Lise's murder, they also seem to be complicit with it. In much the same way, Nicholas Farringdon's impotent gesture of thrusting a letter down the blouse of the anonymous seaman whom he has just seen stabbing silently and for no apparent reason a woman during the VJ night revels at the end of *The Girls of Slender Means*, conveys in its pathetic irrelevance both the unavoidability of certain casual horrors and the subtle complicity between male aggressor and male bystander, both in attendance at these scenes of random but very 'final [. . .] finality'.[70]

At the same time, a ritualistic, religious aura surrounds such feminine endings, with Lise calling out at the crucial moment of the killing in four languages,[71] Marjorie passing on the message that 'the Lord is risen',[72] and Joanna 'mechanically reciting the evening psalter of Day 27, responses and answers', before the May of Teck club 'sank into its centre, a high heap of rubble, and she went with it'.[73] Spark may be scripting here her female characters' 'ceremony of identity', as Judy Sproxton puts it,[74] but in these final moments something larger, older and more public than the individual subject speaks. What emerges is a fundamental fissure in the performance of individual identity, confirming both the authority and agency of the singular voice (through the speech-act) and its derivative, unoriginal quality in its debt to the legacy of the word (through the act of quotation).

In Spark's world this fissure is neither flaw nor failing; it is not a psycho-logical or moral feature, but a linguistic fact. Keenly aware of the varied, eclectic and collective sources of individual speech, Spark seems more con-cerned with rendering speech than individuality. Aided (and abetted) by her extraordinary auditory imagination, Spark's explorations of 'the literary and conceptual possibilities of the sonic', as Allan Pero puts it,[75] complement her poetic ways with language. Spark's *via poetica* crosses her narrative in subtle and often subversive ways, underlining and undermining the hold of accepted meanings of words, the social resonance of speech patterns, idioms, clichés, mannerisms. As she explained to Stephen Schiff: 'There is also such a thing as poetic vision. It's being aware of the value of words, sometimes in their etymology, in two or three senses, in a very quick flash as one is going along. That I can do quite easily. That is a sort of a poetic method.' [76] As this chapter has argued, the resulting confusions, or misrecognitions, caused partly by chance and compounded by the deep sociolinguistic conditioning of her speakers (and auditors) can have a range of effects, satirical, poignant, uncanny or lyrical, but are always based on acute observation and what might be called a visionary ear (as the narrator of 'Come Along, Marjorie' puts it, 'my ears were windows').[77] Spark can be a literalist in this sense, as the fre-quent use of recording and transmitting devices in her fiction suggests[78] and as her contribution to the provision of 'detailed truth with believable lies' to the enemy during the war demanded.[79] In a way, too, it may be argued, Spark's remained a *counter-intelligence*, that is, counter to the ideal of the 'pure voice' and its attendant assumptions about orthodoxy and deference. In a poet's voice, she once declared: 'Poets are few and they are better / Equipped to love and animate the letter'–[80] and she reserved the right to a poetic rendi-tion of a multi-vocal world.

CHAPTER THREE

Body and State in Spark's Early Fiction

Michael Gardiner

Much of Muriel Spark's work is preoccupied with individuals' negotiation, playful or serious, conscious or unconscious, with the structures of nation, state and empire. Her early fictions often turn a ferociously critical eye on personal reactions to the end of empire and Britain's entry into a postwar technocracy. Her turn to the novel in 1957 was itself a significant gesture in this sense, since although often read against the background of her conversion to Catholicism in 1954, it can also be viewed in terms of the cultural politics of a move towards a Gallophile aesthetic, related more to surrealism and the *nouveau roman* than to British realism. As the Algerian war coincided with scepticism over British consensus around empire and union, a Gallophile turn from the UK state can be read in writers including Alexander Trocchi, R. D. Laing, G. E. Davie and Edwin Morgan. Spark can be read in this company. Indeed, she picks up the aesthetic scent early with her first novel, *The Comforters* (1957), a move towards the *nouveau roman* further confirmed in the period under examination here, from *Robinson* (1958) to *The Ballad of Peckham Rye* (1960).

By 1957 there had been a marked decline in the British consensus secured near the beginning of the Second World War and specifically concretised in the iconic moments of the Blitz (1940–1) and the Beveridge Report (1942). The 1951–5 period under Winston Churchill had been characterised by a sense of a very dim echo of the 'national' consensus of the early to mid-1940s. Growth and high employment encouraged economic policy to settle into the bipartisan Keynesian compromise satirically known as Butskellism (Butler–Gaitskell-ism). Much of Southern Africa, the stage for some of the stories in Spark's *The Go-Away Bird* (1958), was moving inexorably towards independence, and the Suez crisis in 1956 confirmed that Britain was no longer a world policy-shaper. Financially stable and lacking any underlying beliefs or values, in the last years of the 1950s the UK state was settling into a long era of 'decline management', softened by the anaesthetic of commodity consumption.

Against this backdrop, dominant Anglo-British domestic intellectual movements conspired to underwrite consensus in social and constitutional terms – many of them from Cambridge, a place often touched on by Spark. At Cambridge, a Keynesian tradition of social management was joined by Leavisite literary criticism and by logical positivism – a movement which shaded the high-British thought of the philosopher David Hume towards an ideal of standing back from objects in order to make true statements about them without the interference of experience. Logical positivism confirms the impossibility of action, since personal experience is irrelevant to a truth divined only by pre-existing, quasi-metaphysical rules. This context is crucial: the spread of logical positivism corresponds historically to the period of greatest consensus in the British state, and the laying of welfare on top of a constitution held both to be true and to have no anchoring in experience. Correspondingly, one identifiable move in more or less underground or scurrilous literary streams of the 1956–62 period is to recapture the literary in terms of the active, reattaching meaning to the experiential, the tactile and the corporeal, and increasingly identifying the state as a pure, disembodied rationality.

This was especially, but not exclusively, a Scottish phenomenon. Countermovements were also becoming conspicuous in England: there is an obscure but potent scepticism of the fit of state and entrenched interests of capital in the social realism practiced by writers like Alan Sillitoe and John Braine at the time of Spark's first fiction. These writers' critiques of the Establishment are in turn comparable to the historiography of the Scottish commentator Tom Nairn, who would prove an important influence on the New Left emerging at around that time. As well as *The Comforters*, 1957 also saw the publication of the first *Universities and Left Review*, and Richard Hoggart's *The Uses of Literacy*. The way that logical positivism had elevated instrumental reason over experience, tracking a mode of literary address whose knowledge relied on a single organising perspective, would now come under increasing pressure, whether from multiple narrative perspectives or from a critique of the totalising power of the state–capital nexus. The tendency of British novelistic realism to organise sensation into systematic behaviour from the 'rise of the novel' in the eighteenth-century *Bildungsroman* and Romance through the liberal panoramic social conscience of the mid-Victorians had been left largely untouched by the apparently radical modernists of the 1920s and 1930s, even when their aesthetic made a fuss of disrupting word order or event order. It was only when the fundamental intellectual principles of British consensus themselves were threatened in the late 1950s that the positivist realist narrative was significantly thrown into relief.

Correspondingly, in the early Spark the management of the individual is indexed to the management of objects in classical realist narrative. Her first novel, *The Comforters*, turns to the anti-realist *nouveau roman*, particularly Alain Robbe-Grillet's *Les Gommes* (1953, tr. 1966). *The Comforters* picks up on the way the *nouveau roman* had shaken the stable and discrete perspec-tive of classical realism, to leave narration open to viewpoints that change according to the object described – a powerful comment on the universalist certainties which reached their zenith in logical positivism. *Nouveau roman* theorists described a destruction of myths of depth and of cinematic ideolo-gies of perception programmed to arrange objects relative to the observing eye, giving us the sense that the visible world belongs to us as consumers.[1] The *nouveau roman* looked, in other words, for a less mimetic and more didactic method, less dependent on apparently intuitive certainties and so more actively critical.[2] Similarly in *The Comforters*, the writing *of* scenes is linked to the writing done *in* scenes, complicating perspective by turning per-spective itself into narrative. This experiment aroused the suspicion of most British critics – though not, notably, Evelyn Waugh, who was sympathetic.[3] Spark's next novel, *Robinson* (1958), tones down the experiment, while retaining much of its attitude towards perspective.[4] Thematically, though, this second novel explicitly returns to the very foundations of British con-sensus, in tackling one of the earliest models of realist form in the canon of English Literature, *Robinson Crusoe* (1719).

Robinson keeps much of the first novel's thematics of auto-writing: the author herself has a presence, as the book is full of gestures towards autobi-ography, from the naming of Robin-son (Robin is Spark's own son) to the Derek [Stanford] and Muriel mentioned in the small ads (61). Here, as in *the Comforters*, narration arises from the specificity of each viewpoint (it arises autopoetically), as characters' visions of the plane-wrecked island interact with the narrative presented. The novel's refusal of a pre-existing perspec-tive certainly echoes the *nouveau roman* style of *The Comforters*, but also in moving attention away from the knowing and viewing subject to the acting agent, characterises the post-consensus thought of certain elements in mid-1950s Britain. John Macmurray's Gifford Lectures (1953–4) had recently criticised logical positivism's dependence on the stable viewing subject for truth, turning his concentration instead towards the acting agent; and R. D. Laing was working on historicising the myths of the subject in *The Divided Self* (1960). The Laing who adapted Sartre's ideas of revolutionary experi-ence (1964) was also absorbing Frantz Fanon's description of fundamental violence in the visual field on colonial Martinique, which had in turn been influenced by the experiential surrealism of Aimé Césaire. This means that the context into which Spark introduces her island story is one in which what is welded together is not just Scottish and French thought, but also Scottish and Franco-Caribbean, making the revisiting of the island story of *Robinson Crusoe* particularly charged.

Robinson Crusoe is an exemplar of both realism in the English novel and of a certain ideal of British imperial resourcefulness. It is also a constant reference point for postcolonial critique. Spark's *Robinson* is one of the earliest examples of the mini-genre, later common, which reworked the classics of colonial fiction in postcolonial terms. As a gendered rewriting of the Atlantic colony, the book also anticipates Jean Rhys's *Wide Sargasso Sea* (1966) and Maryse Condé's *Windward Heights* (1995, tr. 1998). *Robinson Crusoe* had itself lately been reconfirmed at the centre of the Eng. Lit. canon by a critical consensus running from Virginia Woolf (1935) to Ian Watt (1957). Spark's rewriting immediately followed, and to an extent responded to, this re-canonisation on the one hand – and the desert island wreck story in William Golding's *Lord of the Flies* (1954) – and on the other, the Fanonian moment and the political reading of *The Tempest* by Octave Mannoni in *Prospero and Caliban* (1950). Within the writing-back sub-genre, *Robinson Crusoe* itself would later be influentially reworked after Spark by Michel Tournier (1967) and J. M. Coetzee (1986). Like Spark's, these later rewritings make a point of destabilising agency, offering a critique of empire, introducing the problem of gender and examining ways in which the coloniser's body is seen. For Spark also, however, going back to Defoe also means revisiting the foundations of a narrative regime in which a specific form of mimetic realism is seen to be behind the way that the British state mobilises a certain inscription of the universal properties of the individual in terms of economic vested interests.[5] Her Robinson, an individualist armed with nothing but his work ethic, trying to shape the land in his own image, also proves that no man is an island as he tries to figure political representation around himself. Or as Ruth Whittaker puts it, a certain realist 'contract' is severed by Spark at this key point, reminding us of the social contract which set down universal political rules, yet was never written.[6] In severing a realist contract and writing the conditions of writing, Spark also severs this *de facto* contract with the British state.

By the time he wrote *Robinson Crusoe*, Defoe himself had long since been pamphleteering/petitioning for a statist compromise between a self-reliance associated with Scottish Calvinism on the one hand, and the statecraft of the Hanoverian throne on the other. His *History of the Union* (1709) describes the recent misadventures of England and Scotland before the Union's saving 'master-piece of policy',[7] and sets out the benefits of the new state as primarily *financial*: mercantile activity (especially the East India Company) and government policy are here virtually interchangeable, and the British Union is desirable because it closely maps the movement of capital. So in *Robinson Crusoe*, the fate of the bodies of the shipwrecked characters are tied to the fate of the body of capital as it crosses oceans, the body is rationalised and made instrumental, and life is a series of tasks to be worked on. Similarly, Spark's Robinson, owner of the island, is a manager who divides and rules over his subjects, devolves power, audits ownership of commodities, polices the spiritual lives of his subjects and generally instrumentalises thinking. Into this regime comes January Marlow, her name referencing Defoe's Man Friday and Joseph Conrad's Edinburgh-published *Heart of Darkness* (1899) – as well as introducing a touch of Scottish weather to the tropics. From January's standpoint Robinson, adopting a perspective beyond everyday experience on the island, is also an oddly absent figure – 'I could not think of him as part of the present tense' (131) – like the observer in logical positivism, Robinson aims to exist prior to and stand beyond experience. Here, as in *The Comforters*, the possibility of a detached perspective entails the rejection of the way that action in writing is a form of action itself. A staunch realist, Robinson monitors the veracity of January's journal, telling her to 'stick to facts' (75). Just as Caroline in *The Comforters* is encouraged towards a properly representative 'straight old-fashioned story' (202),[8] January is required to write evenly and mimetically, and has her notebook seized when she strays (18–19, 59). The question of whether writing reflects truths already known or is itself a form of action is crucial to the Spark whose fiction emerges during this period. Later, in *The Only Problem* (1984), she would revisit the Typing Ghost, and the idea that writing is real action, not simply meta-action: 'experience, too; real experience, not vicarious, as is often assumed. To study, to think, is to live and suffer painfully' (153).

It is noticeable how different this post-consensus is from the Bloomsbury modernism that preceded it. Woolf had praised Defoe's classic paradigm for precisely its realist attitude of rooting narrative in objective detail to unify through perspectival control: 'By believing fixedly in the solidity of the pot and its earthiness, he has subdued every other element to his design; he has roped the whole universe into harmony.'[9] Nor, despite her interest in gender, does Woolf say much about the body in Defoe. Spark, in contrast, re-genders Man Friday as January, discussed by Robinson as the 'female problem' (30). The fault-line between Woolf and Spark is even codified by Robinson's bookshelf, where January reconsiders James Frazer's *The Golden Bough*, a comparative study of magic and religion favoured by British modernists, but waiting to be read in terms of Scottish Enlightenment encyclopaedism (124). So *Robinson* is preoccupied with the contexts of knowing and seeing, and with the interplay between the 'facts' worshipped by the island's owner and the 'superstition' apparent in rituals and rosaries.

Correspondingly, the realist stitching Spark sews carefully with one hand is, with the other, carefully unpicked, constantly working at making difficult any naturalisation of the bond between the individual and the disembodied rationality of the state. The difficulty of fixing social expression to individual bodies is exemplified by the way that voices tend to split off echoes generating meaning beyond what any one person has said:

When Jimmie called back to me, 'Is dangerous', the words were repeated again and again on the walls of the cave and its recesses and I listened to the 'dangerous, dangerous' . . . (113)

The embodiment of the echo, of course, suggests another thread arising from the France which was being rocked by Algerian insurrection: supplementarity, in which that archetypal form of cultural echo known as a colony returns to haunt the authority of the centre. In *Robinson*, there are frequent echoes, stutters and mishearings; Miguel's lack of English allows for an echoing kind of repetition, which also signals the prospect of a conversion to Catholicism entailing an attachment to ritual and forms of folk wisdom, related, for example, to the moon (129, 167). It is not that January wants Catholicism to be an alternative structure of truth, but that it represents one escape from the rationalism and realism that equate the will of the individual with the abstracted will of the state; or, as Ruth Whittaker puts it, 'mimesis has a kind of triviality, almost an immorality, since the real concern is with the inimitable'.[10] Moreover, as *Robinson Crusoe* stands behind a realist-Protestant tradition of English Literature (meaning the literature of Britain), so Robinson's linguistic integrity is also a spiritual guarantee – and the echo or stutter links Catholic unreason to the ungodly, as in the Satanic-sounding killing of the goat, Rosie:

Robinson said quickly, 'If you mean the rosary, I do not want the boy to see it.'
Miguel looked interested. 'Show me Rosie.' (89)

If the Miranda-like, in-between character of Miguel has learned language from Robinson, January's influence shows how imperfect Robinson's teaching has been. Here 'Rosie' also recalls the human cipher Caroline Rose of *The Comforters* and anticipates the English roses of *Loitering With Intent*, rose-aries which slide along a string of unfixed meanings rather than staying placed. Robinson and Robinson Crusoe require a control of this environment which is guaranteed by the alignment of the spiritual and the earthly as they are hinged together by Providence and through which God can affirm the will of an industrious person: 'Man proposes and God disposes' (75). Where Robinson Crusoe's will is rewarded by the survival of his body, so Spark's Robinson resists the abstraction of spirit outside of his own body as an affront to his expression of will. A modern Leviathan, he blows up his own body to the size of the known earth – his body *is* the abstraction of the state (10). A Catholic turned rationalist (45), he now struggles to resist idolatry and other enemies of instrumental reason (60). This is a figure, January imagines, whose beliefs would be corroborated by her brother-in-law, Ian Brodie, anticipating the Edinburgh schoolteacher Spark would create three years later, and who would most forcefully link ideas of will, work, authority and Enlightenment reason (91). Universalist assumptions about the individual are therefore contextualised by both Robinson and Jean Brodie as the workings of raw state power. And as a defender of universalist individualism, Robinson resists January's suggestion that '[t]here's no such thing as private morality' (161). For Robinson, Providence, the predeterminedness of judgement, provides an explanation for the eternal rewards which accrue to specific types of individual will, just as the state, with its predetermined constitution, stands beyond experience as a structuring principle.

And yet, there are areas of the Spark island–state–body which remain resistant to this mapping and form networks of secret caves and tunnels. Hidden from enlightenment and producing echoes and short-circuits in the body politic, the island's underground channels are also an underground knowledge (73). The official mapping is dependent on universal light to confirm the spatial arrangement of fixed objects and fixed viewer, but official maps are obliterated when January journeys into the caves, taking with her a pocket torch which only momentarily lights up specific areas, in much the way *nouveau roman* narration settles temporarily on specific objects of attention (153–60). In such a place the echo – the personal excess of the instrumentalised body – can even overtake the body itself: 'My cough echoed around me and, as it seemed, a short distance ahead . . . the echoes from the interior seemed stronger and more frequent than my cough itself' (156). It is in the caves that the presentation of a body as universal, rational and efficient finally breaks down, establishing a link between the unevenness of prose narrative and the breakdown of the visual management of bodies.

At first glance merely comedies of manners, the stories collected in *The Go-Away Bird* (1958) ask similar questions of late empire, the managerial state and the rationalisation of the body. One of the most telling fictions in the early Spark, 'You Should Have Seen the Mess', addresses the instrumental reason reproduced across multiple state agencies to create a single authority in a way which looks something like those contemporary English social realists whose anti-heroes were bounced from school to borstal to Labour Exchange. Here, a girl of an age to embark on adventures of love and work, and going under the pointedly Scottish name Lorna – a name perhaps coined by R. D. Blackmore for his outlaw clan-princess – is beginning to experience various debilitating anxieties about the physical world. She perceives dirt and foreign bodies in every object which has not been worked over and rationalised, from cracks in cups which 'harbour germs' to outmoded painting styles (143, 142; cf. 35). Her aspiration to a state of hygienic grace is less a sickness or anomaly than a literalisation of British state rationality finding its modern form within postwar welfarism. Lorna struggles to differentiate between the apparent cleanliness of schools and the quality of their education, opening with the surprising statement, 'I am glad that I went to the Secondary Modern School' (141). She prefers a chemicals company to a lawyer's office or a publisher's, and a new council flat to a fourteenth-century cottage, and repeatedly turns her allegiance to a state busy reproducing itself across many types of institution. And since her own values have been indexed to values which are managed, technocratic and instrumental, physical bodies represent a particular danger for her. Recoiling from the unhygienic habit of sexual contact, she finds it troubling that, as establishment technocrats and guardians of reason, a doctor and his wife would neglect to sleep in twin beds (144). For Lorna, bodies are separated in space so as to remain knowable, and tactile experience is converted into visual experience – a process increasingly familiar now, in an era of British mass surveillance. Spark's interest in contextualising narrative omniscience, recognised as early as 1971 by David Lodge, would at times become a fully-fledged fascination with surveillance, as most obviously in The Abbess of Crewe (1974), which recasts a convent in terms of authoritarian politics,[11] or Territorial Rights (1979), whose tourists enact a paranoid game of manners, so that the 'place could be filled with spies, how could one tell?' (TR, 25).

In the face of this British modernity, which is ruthlessly rationalising, the old class system dissolves, only to reproduce itself in a new and more efficient form, becoming more and more detached from history. Managerial systems sweep away all the messy values of wealth and art and sex, and any other motive not reducible to instrumental ends. There is some kinship here between Spark and writers like Anthony Burgess and Kingsley Amis in describing how welfare provision can destroy ambition; better comparisons, however, would be with Doris Lessing, a neighbour of Spark's in Africa in the late 1930s and early 1940s, and Alan Sillitoe – especially in Saturday Night and Sunday Morning (1958) and The Loneliness of the Long Distance Runner (1959), filmed in 1960 and 1961 respectively – and those other anti-Establishment writers who recognised that class antagonisms were simply being adapted to an increasingly coherent state–capital nexus (cf. Prime, 32–4; Far Cry, 178).

There is a further wrinkle here in that where in both The Comforters and Robinson the ownership of language has been an element of plot, in 'You Should Have Seen the Mess', although Lorna claims to be 'good at English', the writing ascribed to her voice deviates from prestige forms, containing exclamation marks and rogue expressions – 'etc'. This leaking of spoken language into writing begs questions about the supposed primacy of speech and represents another type of disembodying in which Lorna is given writing mistakes in her voice. This orthographic excess, a disembodied echo of the kind found in Robinson's caves, is a subject close to the heart of the London Scot, since it asks whether language which is meaningful to authority can be produced by the body – and so, in Derridean fashion, what the pitfalls are in seeing writing as simply a rehearsed version of speech. Lorna remains unaware of how many non-standard forms she is inserting into the story – the *writing* is beyond her. Spark's playful concern with the borders of speech and type also signals a long-term anxiety for Scottish writers dealing with a state standard form, giving rise to a writerly experimentalism described by Cairns Craig in terms of a 'typographic muse'.[12] One concentrated form of typographic experiment – concrete poetry – would be taken up only five years later by Scottish writers, including Edwin Morgan, long-term critic of logical positivism, and Ian Hamilton Finlay, who, like Jean Brodie, exposes the apparently intuitive fundamentals of Enlightenment reason to reveal authoritarianism and violence. In this story the disembodied echo, then, can travel from the corporeal body to the body of a text, a dangerous form of metafiction which threatens the institutional power of literature itself.

The echo which troubles the boundaries of the human body can take various other forms, also becoming animal body, as in the case of Bluebell, the ping-pong playing cat in *Robinson* (41–2), or as in the 1958 collection's title story, 'The Go-Away Bird', where the verbal tic becomes the 'speech' of a bird whose message repeats conversation out of context and has a real effect on the story (267). Meanwhile, there is pressure on British ex-pats in Africa to stay rational beyond the animal demands of the body: the frustrated Cambridge graduate Donald Cloete struggles with a country that 'brings out the savage in ourselves' (241). The concern with the limits of the human body can be read across the African stories, and by the time of *Symposium* (1990), the usual candidate for a postmodern reading, this limit is investigated through experiments with artificial intelligence – 'biological prototype(s) for synthetic systems' (21, 108).

Even as early as *Memento Mori* (1959), though, the echo is assuming a machine intelligence, taking the form of an anonymous phone call which promises the disappearance of elderly characters with the same repeated sentence, 'Remember you must die'. This voice is 'telepathic' as well as 'telephonic', an excess of body beyond the experience of the individual.[13] This 'death sentence' kills not the characters but the idea of life as endlessly subject to will and rationalisation. For in the post-Lawrentian world of the Welfare State, 'life' behaves something like 'efficiency', as a general demand to keep performing quantifiably – a Health and Safety-like 'life cult' whose greatest fear is the suicide bomber who feels he has nothing to lose. But in Spark, the promise of death can also be the promise of escape from the individual subject. Soon after the gerontologist Alec Warner warns that he may be 'Jekyll and Hyde' (68), precipitating a typically Sparkian conversation about the possibility of understanding otherness, as well as connoting the Edinburgh Gothic of Robert Louis Stevenson, Jean Taylor assures him, '"This graveyard is a kind of evidence . . . that other people exist"' (72).

This novel also sees Spark using her ability to switch registers to ironise
the gap between the life cult and personal experience, by making a comic
detective story out of a statement of existential truth. The characters that
thrive in Spark are those most suspicious of the life cult promoted by the
rationalist state. Even *will* becomes ironic, where it means not only a desire
for life, but also a last testimony, as in the plotting of the chronics in the
Maud Long Ward – the maudlin ward, long *mort* ward or modern longevity
ward – whose lives have been rationalised down to the disposal of goods. The
writer Charmian, on the other hand, is unafraid of the death threat, since
she connects events novelistically *rather than* realistically, and her writing
exceeds her old life as her novels are reprinted (59, 12, 98). The way bodily
regeneration remains untouchable by the police who investigate the calls
casts a deep irony over the way that the life cult sees death as a crime to be
solved. Here, as in Robbe-Grillet, the figure of the detective is not only a *noir*
gesture, but also a presence moving between the universal and the particular to fracture perspective. It turns out that the detective Mortimer – with
death and time in his name – sees the limitations of his corporeal life where
Robinson could not:

> 'I consider,' said Janet Sidebottome, 'that what Mr. Mortimer was saying just
> now about resigning ourselves to death is most uplifting and consoling. The
> religious point of view is too easily forgotten these days, and I thank you, Mr.
> Mortimer.' (153)

The voice beyond death, here coming by phone, had already been in evidence in *The Go-Away Bird*: 'The Portobello Road' is narrated by someone
who 'departed this life nearly five years ago' (3), and 'The Girl I Left Behind
Me' is a tale told by a murdered woman, prefiguring Lise's determination to die
by her own design in *The Driver's Seat* (1970). 'The Seraph and the Zambesi'
introduces a character whose life seems to exceed her time (77). And the
sudden metaphysical message also appears in 'Come Along, Marjorie', whose
narrator is interrupted by the message, 'The Lord is risen' (153).

These early stories are a staging post for themes of mortality and physicality,
and also an early sign of an interaction between poetry and prose, a tension
which works in a similar way. Poetry is key in the negotiation of realism and
rationalism, since poetry operates 'magically', bunching up realist language
to give it the echo-like effects seen in *Robinson*. In the early Spark, poetic
intentions are often signalled at the outset of a story: 'The Portobello Road'
begins with a dense figure involving a multiple alliteration and an alignment
with the unruly musicality of the New Apocalypse movement associated
with Dylan Thomas and George Barker – 'One day in my young youth at
high summer, lolling with my lovely companions upon a haystack, I found a

needle' (1). As Alan Bold has argued, the ballad mode allowed Spark to fit cultural references onto conversation and observation within modernist form as Eliot had done in *The Waste Land*. Spark's entry into fiction was a recasting of the 'ballad of the Fanfarlo' (Charles Baudelaire's 'La Fanfarlo' (1848)) in a form mixing the realistic and the anti-realistic.[14] As a 'balladic novel', *The Ballad of Peckham Rye* (1960) moves through poetic figures towards the general knowledge of the Peckham chorus – 'they said that . . .'[15] – and motions towards a more direct engagement with a Scottish literary history often directly ranged against the state. Ballads in particular were a shibboleth of national tradition from Walter Scott to Edwin Muir, and a site of negotiation between national art and the state. Ballads are also a charm against the rational. As Spark puts it in *Curriculum Vitae* (1992): 'I was reading the border ballads so repetitively and attentively that I memorized many of them without my noticing it. The steel and bite of the ballads, so remorseless and yet so lyrical, entered my literary bloodstream, never to depart' (98). This is particularly true in *The Ballad of Peckham Rye*, another tale of a London Scot which revisits some of the most cherished and most prosaic assumptions of postwar Britain, and can be read alongside Alasdair Gray's *The Fall of Kelvin Walker: A Fable of the Sixties*, first staged in 1967, then published as a novel in 1985.[16] In *Peckham Rye*, ballad itself is a structuring principle which binds together story, character and echo:

> 'Get away from here, you dirty swine,' she said.
>   'There's a dirty swine in every man,' he said.
>   'Showing your face around here again,' she said.
>   'Now, Mavis, now, Mavis,' he said. (7)

This poetic emphasis makes the echo manifest in the rhyming and parallel figures that haunt the text from the opening, and in the stuttering corrections of speech to the standard that have a hold over the local girl, Dixie, as they had over Lorna. Dixie's highly rational idea of respectability also requires the idea of an authoritative language, and she is constantly correcting grammar with an echoing unconscious tic, although, like Lorna, her social class does not equip her for Standard English. When the Scot Dougal arrives, the Peckham natives are puzzled by his confidence in departing from SE norms – his speech is largely ESSE (Educated Standard Scottish English).

Dougal also sets out to disrupt the instrumentalist work ethic visible in characters like Dixie; he is generally inefficient, encouraging absenteeism, becoming a doubled personality with two jobs and using both to conduct 'human research' consisting of taking in mixed messages from disparate groups (32). He answers instrumental reason with play and gets industrial managers into verbal tangles about the use-value of his work – 'Attractive to us. Useful, I mean useful' (83). Specifically, the contest between the ludic and the instrumental is laid on Edinburgh versus Cambridge education. In a novel published a year before G. E. Davie's *The Democratic Intellect* (1961), an influential account of the distinctiveness of Scottish universities' democratic intellectualism, Dougal comes to London as a presence that is generalist, active and critical, where the Cambridge environment was more associated with the specific, observational and technocratic. There appears the very contemporary nightmare of the provincial graduate working in industry and addressing managerial technocracy, while neglecting the instrumental separation of spheres of knowledge:

> 'I shall have to do research,' Dougal mused, 'into their inner lives. Research into the real Peckham. It will be necessary to discover the spiritual well-spring, the glorious history of the place, before I am able to offer some impetus.'
>   Mr. Druce betrayed a little emotion. 'But no lectures on Art,' he said, pulling himself together. 'We've tried them . . .' (17)

So where the behaviour of the union man Humphrey remains functionary despite his apparent progressiveness, Dougal more subversively suggests that his job title should have 'lyricism', whether or not this 'makes a difference to the Unions' (26). Conversely, for Dixie, Dougal's troubling corporeality is tied to the impossibility of seeing him as a rational figure. Like Lorna, Dixie's sexuality has turned instrumental, and she describes her marriage to Humphrey only in terms of money to be saved. She is suspicious of Dougal's deformity, his hunched back, though he finally comes into his own in a grotesque dance. Dougal's reaction to music is not only cerebral but also corporeal, a mongrelised movement which pastiches consumer culture in a kind of exorcism (102). Dougal is also addressing the messy physicality of the body as against the rationalist ideals of the body seen in *Robinson*, or promoted in the 1940s and 1950s by John Keynes and by Marie Stopes (and vilified elsewhere by Spark), also one of the influences cited in relation to the Edinburgh rationalist Jean Brodie.[17]

Moreover, Dougal Douglas also doubles up to become Douglas Dougal on the other side of the Rye, recalling the Gothic trope of the *Doppelganger*, which reached back through James Hogg and Jekyll and Hyde to the ballad tradition, and codified in G. Gregory Smith's idea of a 'Caledonian Antisyzygy'.[18] Spark's interest in the Gothic double indeed was notable as early as her biography *Mary Shelley: Child of Light* (1951);[19] and Hogg reappears as the Mrs. Hogg of *The Comforters*. As Christopher MacLachlan notes, Spark's recalling Hogg's Gothic is also a 'fundamentally Protestant theological or religious disquietude'.[20] This is inflected throughout in bodily terms: the bumps on Dougal's forehead are like those of a 'diabolical agent' (77, 81) and his moods recall Hogg's Gil-Martin, whose 'countenance changes with . . . studies and sensations'.[21] Dougal is both reason and unreason, Jekyll and Hyde, Prospero and Caliban, a disruptive influence and an independent youth as in *The Prime of Miss Jean Brodie*, 'a solid steady Edinburgh boy' (*PMJB* 42–3; *Ballad* 69). After this, the Gothic doubling seen here would seek fresh forms in Alasdair Gray (*Lanark*, 1981; *Poor Things*, 1992) and later in Irvine Welsh (*Marabou Stork Nightmares*, 1995). It is telling that this doubling returns at the end of the high period of consensus: where logical positivism aims at specialised and absolute knowledge untouched by experience, Dougal's generalised experience-driven thinking is indexed to bodily contingency. And if for logical positivism the ultimate measure of truth is logic as a category independent of the personal, Dougal is as sceptical about impersonal reason as are the other Scottish thinkers of his time, including John Macmurray, R. D. Laing and Alexander Trocchi. Dougal caused trouble by rejecting the Cambridge-inspired findings of a 'time-and-space study' and 'generalises' his research as the results of wide-ranging conversations with workers.

Again in *The Ballad*, instrumental reason stands or falls on the stability of a single perspective, as understood by a discrete and separate subject distinguishing objects visually:

> 'Mr Douglas,' said Mr Weedin, 'I want to ask you a personal question. What do you mean exactly by vision?'
>
> 'Vision?' Dougal said.
>
> 'Yes, vision, that's what I said'.
>
> 'Do you speak literally as concerning optics, or figuratively, as it might be with regard to an enlargement of the total perceptive capacity?' (72)

The ending of *The Ballad* indexes these themes in a way almost identical to that of *Robinson*: Dougal runs away from the Rye – 'to Africa with the intention of selling tape-recorders to all the witch doctors' to counter 'the mounting influence of modern scepticism' (142) – and as in *Robinson* he travels through a tunnel amongst haunted bones, lighting his way with the contingent perspectives afforded by an electric torch (138–40). The 'flashlight' trope is rehearsed as early as 'The Seraph and the Zambesi': 'unreal sounds, as if projected from a distant country, as if they were pocket-torches seen through a London fog' (78). As in all of these stories, management by perspective and disembodying is gradually eroded by fragmentation and embodying. In a state increasingly obsessed with CCTV, visual culture and the other institutionalisations of image capitalism, this attitude to knowledge and realism is a salutary critique.

CHAPTER FOUR

The Stranger Spark

Marilyn Reizbaum

This chapter addresses what some might call Muriel Spark's eccentric narrative style. It is not just that she is unconventional in her techniques and
topics. We may see her in the company of modernists and mystery writers
alike. There is a quality to the writing that is hard to assess – something eerie
that might conform to the mystery genre and also alluringly aversive, as in a
horror story. This chapter asks, why is Spark so strange and yet so fetching?
One is reminded when reading her of Joyce's *Dubliners*, where certain 'sinful
and maleficent' beings fill its inhabitants with fear and yet they long to draw
nearer and look upon the 'deadly work'. 'There was no hope for him this time'
is the opening line of 'The Sisters': a death knell that resounds throughout
Joyce's collection, something very much like the refrain of Spark's *Memento
Mori* – '*Remember you must die*' – which produces early in her career a ringing
note of finality or surrender to some unknown caller. In addressing the question of Spark's strangeness, this chapter contends that her narratives always
reside in one way or another in a remote location, but not that of the perch
on high onto which Joyce's Stephen Vedalus projects his narrative authority,
a condescension she distinctly rejects, as, finally, did Joyce.

There are three uncanny qualities of remoteness examined here; we may
think of 'uncanny' in the Freudian sense of being both familiar and displaced
or mysterious at the same time, and haunting: The first is that distinctive
narrative voice that governs her work and yet is hard to locate or define
– elusive, shifty, insistent and scathing: a formal feeling. Next there is the
physical location, which in the case of the two novels considered here – *The
Prime of Miss Jean Brodie* (1961) and *Memento Mori* (1959) – offers a *kind* of
voice or accent to her narratives, both culturally particular and disembodied, in every case susceptible to misapprehension. Spark said about herself,
somewhat mystifyingly, that she was a 'constitutional exile', which was in
her words a 'calling rather than a condition', bred in her by Edinburgh, the
city of her birth.[1] *The Prime of Miss Jean Brodie*, of course, takes place in that
city and *Memento Mori* in London, whose importance (as with Edinburgh's
in *Brodie*) is arguably novelistic. Spark's characters often seem driven or

inspired, transfigured even, by outside places (even when they are inside); such 'places' are often conveyed as metaphysical, 'a strong religious feeling', though this religious aspect is often over-read in her work.[2] Finally, it is the writerly quality of her fiction that gives the impression of estrangement from the story by the characters – an uneasy feeling. It is not so much writerly, as in the sense of metafiction, where the plot is subordinated to a focus on its novelistic operations: it is, rather, Spark's remarkable capacity to have the plot be coterminous with the embedded commentary on it, and thereby draw in the reader as agents of plot. Spark's critique is often applied, as Allan Pero says of *Memento Mori*, to the 'deductive (and seductive) logic that governs the mystery novel', a genre to which, in some sense, all of her narratives conform.[3] As with most writerly work in the Barthesian sense, Spark's narratives produce enormous stylistic economy and compression which make them seem slippery or impenetrable and thus parody the detective novel, where, as Slavoj Žižek observes, 'the detective is often presented with a "false solution", through which he or she is expected to reveal the true solution'.[4] The narrative performs heuristic display of this generic affect. Spark's novel is a take on the form of a 'whydunnit' (*The Driver's Seat*, 1970) to refer to one of her most mysterious novels and her favourite. The cliché (adjusted from 'whodunnit') removes the actor or author from contention and makes the motive unfathomable. As we shall see, the search for the caller in *Memento Mori* becomes a distraction. In *Brodie*, knowing all along who the betrayer is, we are driven along a different track from Brodie to know why Sandy did it. Through the seeming hint provided by her name, we may deem Sandy the main figure of inscrutability, but finally conclude that Spark's novel itself is the Stranger.

Voice

There is a strange quality to Spark's narrative voices. They always seem anonymous, like the source of the phone calls in *Memento Mori*, even when we think we know whose they are. More than Henry James's unreliable narrators or James Joyce's shifting ones, Spark's narrators are mischievous, sometimes demonic, often maddeningly or charmingly disinterested. Her style of formal economy reminds one of Joyce's 'scrupulously mean' (Joyce's description of his style in *Dubliners*) penchant for settling scores on the page, as with his insinuation of 'characters' from his life into his works, particularly *Ulysses*. Spark's characters seem mistreated, too, abbreviated through epithet or erasure, being killed off. As with the refrain 'Remember you must die', there is a seeming flatness to the style, a matter-of-factness, which in *Memento Mori* mocks its recipients' deafness or tone-deafness, apprehending a threat in the providential statement. Given their age, this is doubly mordant. This perceived threat, to be affronted by the inevitable, is like that Sandy perceived in Jean Brodie, whose 'prime' functions in the same way – standing in for youth, it delimits pastness and inevitable decline. 'One's prime is elusive', she instructs, even threatens. Despite her pretences to linguistic purism, Brodie makes 'prime' a noun to make it stand still.[5] Sandy accuses, 'She thinks she is Providence . . . sees the beginning and the end'.[6] A tonal flatness obtains also in Brodie's pronouncements about the nature of art and politics, where the flamboyance or alarming nature of the sentiments is neutralised by delivery more than motive, which is, anyway, unclear. To the question, who is the greatest Italian painter?, she flatly answers 'Giotto, he is my favourite', displaying her educational philosophy ('*duco*, I lead').[7] The flatness is aided by an aural expectation of a Morningside pinch, 'her best Edinburgh voice'.[8] Certainly, the statement offers an understated critique of aesthetic objectivity and the positivist tradition that precedes Spark. At the same time, the seriousness of such observations is mocked by the absurd quality of such performances.

The mocking voices cut many ways. Just after Brodie's early remark about Giotto, Sandy's voice takes over with lashing effect: 'Some days it seemed to Sandy that Miss Brodie's chest was flat, no bulges at all, but straight as her back.'[9] Having had to bend to Brodie's will, Sandy proceeds to straighten her out. (Later, she and Jenny will straighten Brodie's stomach in a similar effort to desexualise her.) This retributive cut is part of an ongoing wrestling for control, and is highly nuanced since it contains, as throughout, Sandy's fixation and adoration. There is pathos, too, in that what is presented as unwitting discovery of Brodie's falseness, or 'falsies', comes with recognition of the potential to break the back of the 'erect' Miss Brodie, 'head held high'. In the images used to represent their bouts, we see the gendering of such power struggles.

It is difficult to pinpoint Jean Taylor's tone in her commentary on 'the message' in *Memento Mori*, as here in response to Dame Lettie's irate impatience regarding the identity of the caller: '"It's difficult", said Miss Taylor, "for people of advanced years to start remembering they must die. It is best to form the habit while young".'[10] She could be hearing voices or channelling them with such expressions of credo. She may be exuding characteristic wisdom, but the Wildean resonance of satire in her flat response seems to mock Lettie's hysteria, which Lettie attempts to turn back on Jean as dementia, in her mean way ('She's wandering again, thought Lettie'). Here any wish to read Jean's remark as Sparkian moralism regarding the immanence of death in life falls short. Searching for definitive meaning, one may seek to designate her or the former police inspector, Henry Mortimer, as the author's mouthpiece – he even more emphatically concludes that 'to remember one's death is, in short, a way of life'. Charmian's response to Mortimer ('I am sure everyone is fascinated by what Henry is saying') provides the matter-of fact antithesis of the general sentiment.[11] It registers as mockery of such 'facts'. The literal and the metaphorical 'truth' of the statement must coexist. If one is looking for novelistic moralism, it takes no nuance of voice at all to apprehend that Lettie's violent death is shockingly retributive in this seemingly comic novel.

Jacques Derrida, who has written about the telephone, notably in his discussion of Joyce's *Ulysses*, refers to telephonic interiority, or *tekhne*, 'at work within the voice, multiplying the writing of voices without any instruments, as Mallarmé would say, a mental telephony, which, inscribing remoteness, distance, difference and spacing in sound (*phoné*), institutes, forbids, *and at the same time* interferes with the so-called monologue'.[12] In part, Derrida is addressing the expectation of a voice, an authority at the other end. 'In the beginning, there was the telephone,' he pointedly riffs.

> 'I should not answer the telephone, Dame Lettie, if I were you.'
>
> 'My dear Taylor, one can't be cut off perpetually. [. . .] One must be on the phone. But I confess, I am feeling the strain. [. . .] I never know if one is going to hear that distressing sentence. It *is* distressing.'
>
> 'Remember you must die,' said Miss Taylor.
>
> 'Hush,' said Dame Lettie, looking warily over her shoulder.
>
> 'Can you ignore it, Dame Lettie?'
>
> 'No I cannot. I have tried, but it troubles me deeply. It *is* a troublesome remark.'
>
> 'Perhaps you might obey it', said Miss Taylor,
>
> 'What's that you say?'
>
> 'You might, perhaps, try to remember you must die.'
>
> She is wandering again, thought Lettie. 'Taylor,' she said, 'I do not wish to be advised how to think. What I hoped you could suggest is some way of apprehending the criminal, for I see that I must take matters into my own hands. Do you understand telephone wires? Can you follow the system of calls made from private telephone boxes?' [13]

This passage works as a *double entendre*: the 'distressing sentence' that is the locution and the judgement of dying; being a 'back number' to mark Dame Lettie's obsolescence; Lettie's use of Taylor's blunt apprehension of death as an index of her remoteness from life, her 'wandering', used here and elsewhere in the novel like a Brodiean epithet. And there is the narrative voice, overtaking those of Dame Lettie and Taylor with a kind of mockery marking the insistent propriety and eccentricity of these characters in the face of the 'troublesome remark'. Taylor's call for acceptance of death – the call *of* or *as* death – mirrors *Mortimer*'s approach to resolving the mystery with nominal irony: 'Death is the culprit,' he opines.[14] '"Have you considered", said Alec Warner, "the possibility of mass hysteria?" "Making the telephone ring?"

said Mr. Rose, spreading wide his palms.' [15] The phone in this case is the red herring, yet it becomes the communal device or voice of what is in fact their mass hysteria, what Derrida might term the 'coup de téléphone'.[16]

In an essay on Memento Mori, which works as a playful meditation, where the sections are separated or connected by the icon of a telephone, Nicholas Royle makes the case for the telepathic function of the telephone. What he demonstrates figurally as well as discursively is that the telephone performs the function of medium of 'uncanny transmission'.[17] But 'medium' in these terms may take on several meanings – a technological or spiritual enabler, for example. Royle goes on to say that such telepathy or transaction is bound up with the very nature of fictional narration' (a topic we shall come to more explicitly later).[18] The disembodied voice as medium becomes an apt metaphor for Spark's narratives.[19]

In keeping with the idea of uncanny transmissions, one might say that Sandy hears voices that she attributes to various sources, most often Jean Brodie. Brodie's voice is tyranny and therapy. When Sandy thinks of her own mother's voice, it seems like that of a stranger, or at least reminds her of her foreign aspect and yet, though her mother's English term of endearment – 'darling' rather than the Scottish 'dear ' – sometimes embarrasses her, she also exploits this difference, 'making the most of her vowels' in the way that language signals her superior because remote caste, 'her only fame'.[20] This conflict in affinities, in adhering to voice, is often articulated in response to Brodie. When hearing Brodie criticise the scapegoat Mary Macgregor, Sandy, again as though in an act of over-mastery or spite, 'thought of the possibilities of feeling nice from being nice to Mary instead of blaming her', as Brodie would demand. But 'the sound of Miss Brodie's presence, just when it was on the tip of Sandy's tongue to be nice to Mary Macgregor, arrested the urge'.[21] Various acts of ventriloquism evidence her identification with Brodie.

A conflict of affinities may extend to the reader, who, when feeling least sympathetic to Brodie, may be otherwise encouraged by some unidentifiable narrator: 'It is not to be supposed that Miss Brodie was unique at this point of her prime; or that (since such things are relative) she was in any way off her head.' [22] This conflict or uncertainty seems still at work when we see Sandy behind the grille in that haunting image at the novel's end, where what has transfigured or disfigured her is the voice she always hears, and which she has betrayed, in a double sense of revelation: the need to expose her is at once the desire to know her. Spark may be mocking the presumption or hubris of the psychological method that is Sandy's treatise, a revelation it seems of her own devotion to Brodie, whom she mirrors as she acknowledges that 'what went to the makings of Miss Brodie who had elected herself to grace in so particular a way and with more exotic suicidal enchantment than if she had simply taken to drink like other spinsters who couldn't stand it any more'.[23] Sandy writes the book of Brodie's life, which is 'The Transfiguration of the Commonplace', her 'strange book of psychology'.[24] In this Spark seems to take very seriously that other betrayal for which Sandy seems to be doing penance, which is to confuse Brodie's voice with ultimate authority. Like the crazed son in Alfred Hitchcock's *Psycho*, Sandy has sought futilely to silence her beloved Brodie's voice in order perversely to serve or embody it.[25] Sandy's end might register, too, the author's self-mockery for having the hubris to assume the 'calling' of writing, which, as this last image of Sandy conveys, doubles for a kind of banishment, or 'exiledom' as Spark termed it.

Place

Spark uses place in a way that grounds, flavours and mystifies. It ironically creates the condition of displacement that so many of the novels manifest, a kind of wandering, as with Dame Lettie's characterisation of Jean Taylor, perhaps the most grounded of the characters in *Memento Mori*, continually resigning herself to or making peace with her surroundings (Surrey vs. London). The meaning of the location often resides in the question of belonging – national or familial, for instance – but may also recur to the internal world of the novel beyond setting, as reflected in the interiority of the characters. Typically, work is 'placed' outside the confines of the novel, through the author's national and/or political background. Such assignments are compelling but problematic in that they may confer meaning, externally, automatically and prescriptively. Though claiming herself to be 'Scottish by formation', efforts to identify Spark as a Scottish writer have proved difficult, and not only because of her distant relation to her birthplace.[26] The difficulty encapsulates the way place functions in the work. There has been some discussion of her hybrid self as metonymic in these terms.[27] She has been labelled a cosmopolitan writer and by her contemporary, Robin Jenkins, as a 'cosmopolitan misfit', by way of criticising her for a kind of Scottish insufficiency.[28] Whatever Jenkins' intention, such a label as 'cosmopolitan' in the first part of the twentieth century would have been encoded as deracinated. Perhaps Jenkins and others have lamented her refusal to toe a national line. Gerard Carruthers lauds her for avoiding the nets; Bryan Cheyette, for keeping them in play. In 'Edinburgh-born', Spark addresses these matters, if obliquely, at the moment of her father's dying. She is in residence at the North British Hotel in Edinburgh so that she may be 'within call' of the hospital where her father is: 'In those days I experienced an inpouring of love for the place of my birth, which I am aware is psychologically connected with my love for my father and with the exiled sensation of occupying a hotel room which was really meant for strangers.'[29]

One might in these terms also view Spark's conversion to Catholicism as a radical national act as well as a religious realignment – a return to a certain

Scottish history, in keeping with a tolerance for ambiguity or 'scope', as she might call it.[30] She suggests such a reading in 'Edinburgh-born' when she writes that 'it was on the nevertheless principle that I turned Catholic':

> It is my own instinct to associate the word, as the core of a thought pattern, with Edinburgh particularly. I see the lips of tough elderly women in musquash coats taking tea at McVities enunciating this word of final justification . . . I believe myself to be fairly indoctrinated by the habit of thought which calls for this word. In fact, I approve of the ceremonious accumulation of weather forecasts and barometer-readings that pronounce for a fine day, before letting rip on the statement 'nevertheless, it's raining'. I find that much of my literary composition is based on the nevertheless idea. I act upon it.[31]

We see in her remarks here an etching of *Brodie* and Brodie and an address to the notion of loyalties, literary, national, familial and otherwise. In this carefully crafted, brief essay, Spark concludes by marking her father's death in yet another way, through 'the nevertheless idea'. Discussing the distinctive beauty of Edinburgh, she comments on the protrusion of the Castle Rock, 'the primitive black crag rising up in the middle of populated streets of commerce, stately squares and winding closes, like the statement of an unmitigated fact preceded by 'nevertheless'.[32] This site remains constant in the wake of her father's passing, but its solidity does not yield a metaphor of constancy for Spark: 'The influence of place varies according to the individual.' [33] As Carruthers argues, in a way that eschews the essentialist national identification as relevant, 'Spark does not trust that place is easily (or unimaginatively) apprehended.' [34]

Nevertheless, *Brodie* arguably delivers a homage to Edinburgh, while not departing from the idea of place as associative; with all its history, the city is Sandy's personal setting of discovery:

> And many times throughout her life Sandy knew with a shock, when speaking to people whose childhood had been in Edinburgh, that there were other people's Edinburghs quite different from hers, and with which she held only names of districts and streets and monuments in common.[35]

On the occasion of this reflection, rendered out of time as though historical, Sandy is encountering the 'squalor' of the Old Town and is balancing three couples in her sights: the imaginary insinuation of herself into Stevenson's *Kidnapped* as Alan Breck's love interest; the storied Mary Queen of Scots and Rizzio; and the contemporary violent couple. 'It was Sandy's first experience of a foreign country, which intimates itself by its new smells and shapes and its new poor'.[36] Brodie seems to reinforce and gloss over this idea of foreignness with her attribution of cosmopolitanism to Edinburgh: 'We owe a lot to the French. We are Europeans,' she says, in a momentary identification with the former queen.[37] The city with its mnemonic smells and shapes is Proustian.[38] Throughout, Sandy interchanges place with character, as with Spark's association of the dynamic city with her father. The idea of the proxy is a powerful conceptual force in the novel. For Sandy, all the couples are stand-ins for her relationship with Brodie, to which there is an impediment of one kind or another. Each is marked by a betrayal of historic proportions: Alan Breck is wedded to his country whose betrayal is reproduced in the story of David Balfour; David Rizzio, Mary's beloved servant, is murdered by Mary's husband, Lord Darnley, who is in turn murdered by Mary's future husband, the Earl of Bothwell (also, John Knox, as Brodie points out, 'would never be at ease with the gay French queen').

Sandy also imagines, in a Freudian displacement of desire in the 'sex-laden year', that Anne Grey will help her police sex in the city, crucially, 'to find out more about the case of Brodie and whether she is in a certain condition as a consequence of her liaison with Gordon Lowther . . .'.[39] Her interest is more than prurient.

One might account for Sandy's conversion and retreat to the convent through this aspect of her repressed desire. But her motive remains insistently mystified. In her efforts to gain mastery over Brodie and over the loss of her, Sandy apprehends the way in which formal structures may accommodate different 'plot' elements and are compulsively repeated, as exemplified by Brodie's narratives of loves lost: 'Sandy was fascinated by this method of making patterns with facts, and was divided between her admiration for the technique and the pressing need to prove Miss Brodie guilty of misconduct.'[40] In this way, her policing of Brodie and her betrayal of her are the evidence of her love, which she might dare but cannot speak. In this way, too, we see history and the city and the individuals within her purview accommodated to Sandy's grandiose plan, just as they were to her idol's aims. It is a kind of psychology Sandy comes to understand, but which also eludes her.

Sandy might be said to wander through the city, steadily and guiltily gleaning the 'scam' that is the doctrine of the elect that has inflected the city since Knox (or more broadly the vicissitudes of authority), which she metonymises also in relation to her desire for Brodie: 'In this oblique way, she began to sense what went into the makings of Miss Brodie who had elected herself to grace in so particular a way and with more exotic suicidal enchantment than if she had simply taken to drink like other spinsters who couldn't stand it any more.'[41] But the trope of wandering seems more apt for *Memento Mori*, despite the characters mostly being moored within the Maud Long Medical Home, or by virtue of their infirmities. Wandering, by definition, must be linked to the concept of a home base or location; while the wandering mind is a recurring fear and/or accusation among the ageing characters, memory is a place where much of the novel takes place. Such a definitive location is recalled, in Spark's lovely macabre manner, in the conversation between Jean Taylor and Alec Warner about an event in a graveyard almost forty years prior to the time in which the novel is set. When asked *the* existential question by Alec in a rather perverse way – 'how do we know other people exist?' – Jean replies that the graveyard is a kind of evidence. Death's certainty marks life along with the names and dates carved in stone, as Alec goes on to argue rather desultorily. '"Of course", she said, "the gravestones might be hallucinations. But I think not [. . .] The graves are at least reassuring," she said, "for why bother to bury people if they don't exist". "Yes, oh precisely", he said.' [42] Precisely? Again, an inverse logic is employed, one that also points to the reliance on, if not the reliability of, inscription or epithet. The existential cliché gives way to others: death evinces life; life is (imitates) art. Proleptically, the graveyard is the home base to which the novel continually returns (replayed in *Loitering with Intent* (1981), which begins in the graveyard and returns to it in memory at the conclusion).

Reverie or memory becomes a sort of diaspora place, to return to Spark's defining concept of 'exiledom', and to call on a term that has been used by Bryan Cheyette, for example, to discuss Spark as a 'diasporic writer'.[43] As with the unsettled question of authority that persists throughout, the novel acts as a diasporic space, which, through its encounter with readers, is never settled (not to mention the way in which Spark regards her own father as a touchstone in this respect). This passage works at the same time to unsettle the proposition that you can know the existence of others, for in her momentary fear of Alec as they walk in the graveyard, Jean sees that, despite their former intimacy, his style in every sense, through inflections of rhetorical gesture and social class, makes them incompatible, not at home with one another. She does not have the best London speech, which will be noted even among this 'progressive set', who 'would think nothing of her walk with Alec that summer of 1928'. There would be those who would use class in an effort to undermine her or, put another way, to come back to the import of the passage, to deny her existence. (Lettie, for instance, would spitefully *name* Jean Taylor, Charmian's maid.) Alec asks the existential question as he does, because he would seem to have no doubt about his own place in the world; it is a rhetorical refusal of his mortality, which is also marked by his collection of gerontological narratives in the present tense of the novel.

Form

It is striking that *Memento Mori* and *The Prime of Miss Jean Brodie*, two of Spark's most popular novels, are also two of her earliest. Being numbers three and six, they would seem to act as chronological bookends of a sort for those inside the novels: the children of the Gillespie school and the residents of the nursing home. In both novels, though, the chronological order is reversed: the end precedes the beginning. Both also anticipate endings in the way that has come to be known as Spark's trademark use of prolepsis.[44] Judith Roof has brought Peter Brooks' *Reading For the Plot* to her reading of *The Driver's Seat*; indeed his use of the Freudian death drive and pleasure principle, in which the narrative of fiction mimics that of life, may be liberally applied to Spark's works. Freud's premise that 'the aim of all life is death' seems a flat re- or pre-statement of *Memento Mori*'s refrain and a *memento mori* of Spark's novelistic aims.[45] In the same way that Brooks explains the paradox that attends that drive towards the end, Spark seems to ridicule the desire for a 'proper' conclusion, an effect or 'weapon', as she characterises 'ridicule', that Spark gives important value.[46] To paraphrase Pero, death not only exceeds our ability to fashion meaning out of it, in keeping with modernist principles about form, the end is not where the meaning resides. As Brooks argues about the function of repetition in the text, a prominent feature of Spark's style, it paradoxically propels and retards movement, which the reader may pleasurably use both to approach and avoid the end. 'The apparent paradox may be consubstantial with the fact that repetition can take us backward and forward because these terms have become reversible: the end is a time before the beginning',[47] to wit, the advent of *Memento Mori* before – old age before youth – and the 'truth' of *Memento Mori*'s refrain, in which one is reminded that the end is always imminent.

The beginning and end of *The Prime of Miss Jean Brodie* and *Memento Mori*, respectively, display these narrative propositions. '"I am putting old heads on your young shoulders," Miss Brodie had told them at that time,' reminding us on page 5 of the novel that the narration is in part a flashback, though one would not guess it from the opening paragraph:

> *The boys, as they talked to the girls from Marcia Blaine School*, stood on the far side of their bicycles holding the handlebars, which established a protective fence of bicycle between the sexes, and the impression that at any moment the boys were likely to be away.[48]

The image of the boys, seeming very present tense as well as tense, configures the plot as poised to take off and yet signals what is in fact their departure from the novel. The opening gives what is both a false and true impression of what is to come: a pretence to propriety – 'Safety First', which Brodie and Spark reject – and a seeming maintenance of it, in that there will be no boys in the novel even to speak of. However, the rules of neither form nor of desire are observed. The 'old heads' signify both the girls' 'advanced, precocious education' and Spark's narrative method, ageing or eliminating them before their time. By the end of Chapter 1, Mary Macgregor's unhappy fate – death by fire – is interpolated into the narrative like a running legend, a runner. The ends of all the characters are narrated (except most notably for Sandy, who is presented as neither dead nor alive behind bars). The girls' epithets, established from the beginning, act as a sort of abbreviation, but certainly as a rhetorical gesture that remembers, a *memento mori*, in the sense that their naming functions as a literary afterlife or fame. At the same time, such associative naming, or character formation, in accordance with Spark's ideas about writing, is like a killing, a limiting of character that is a literary offence Spark charges other writers with too often committing.[49] The labels mock the affect of such naming as much or more than they mock any character in the novel. (We may be reminded of Charmian's lament about characters' agency and the practice of deception in art.) Mary Macgregor has been discussed as a scapegoat, which functions as a figure of treason within the symbolic domains of pre- and post-Second World War history that the novel bridges and which contextualises it; and also as a figure who reflects the theme of betrayal that pervades the novel. But the recurring image of Mary's bizarre and tragic death is rendered through Spark's method as comic, and therefore acts as a focal point of unease. The reader must question its role, just as, in its wake, the reader, like the characters, must wonder whether loyalty is due to Miss Brodie, herself a stand-in for the novel. We, like her, presume to see the beginning and the end.[50]

In his essay 'Memento Mori', Nicholas Royle describes the last calling out of deaths in *Memento Mori* as a 'check out in the final pages' in a 'bizarre textual supermarket', and suggests that

> The final section of *Memento Mori* operates as a sort of memento, a kind of warning or foreshadowing of – and hinting towards – the eerie structure of *The Prime of Miss Jean Brodie* (1961). In this novel, too, notions of age, in particular youth and prime, are subjected to strange displacements. The final section of *Memento Mori* performs a time-skip and lets us know, in a comically but disquietingly cursory manner, how and when the various remaining characters in the story died. In *the Prime of Miss Jean Brodie* these death-divulging time-skips punctuate the narrative throughout . . . . *The Prime of Miss Jean Brodie* is another *memento mori*, at once about the concept (if it is one) of 'memento mori', and itself a *memento mori*. The earlier novel rings and resonates across it.[51]

Memento Mori realises in narrative terms the phrase 'Remember you must die', remembering what the characters cannot or refuse to recall. It plots out the deaths of all until there is no one except the narrator standing. As Pero suggests, speaking of the anonymous phone calls, 'the problem is that the meaning ascribed to them does not explain why they happen'.[52] In other words, that the would-be admonition may portend death does not, except perhaps by fact of mortality, give it verisimilitude or causality. 'Remembering our death' is the rhetorical equivalent in this sense of the formal non-conclusion of the modernist novel. For while death is conventional, one might say, the end does not have explanatory force. To return to Pero's observation, 'death exceeds our ability to fashion meaning out of it'.[53] The exhortation mocks the disingenuous wish for transparency, since the end is always in one sense revealed. As Spark says, we have to wait to see the picture emerge. We are always waiting.

Spark said about the mixed response to her work: 'Readers of novels were not yet used to the likes of me, and some will never be.' [54] In this, one is again reminded of Joyce, to whom this chapter has consistently returned, and that here ends with a reaffirmation of their connection through Spark's own brand of 're-joycing'.[55] They are conjoined in many ways, certainly by the enigmas that have mystified their works as remote. But like the joy Fleur takes in the process of writing in *Loitering with Intent*, the novel from which the celebrated phrase comes ('from here by the grace of God I go on my way rejoicing'), these writers demonstrate to their readers the pleasures of the text, however dangerous. Spark beckons us to encounter the stranger.

CHAPTER FIVE

Muriel Spark and the Politics of the Contemporary

Adam Piette

Muriel Spark knew her enemy. In *The Mandelbaum Gate* (1965), the Foreign Office official and spy, Freddy, realises, with a life-changing shock, that his mother is a tyrannical liar:

> Ma was a peculiar type of tyrant-liar whose lies could only with difficulty be denounced because of her long-sustained tyranny, and whose tyranny could hardly now be overthrown because of her long-condoned lies.[1]

At the local level of acid social comedy, Freddy's Ma is a minor figure, one of those Waugh-like monsters Spark could so effortlessly fabricate from the comic tradition, a blend of Tartuffe and Ubu Roi. But when Ma is murdered by her religious fanatic carer, Benny (Mrs Bennett), whom she has tormented for years, readers are asked to think twice about what constitutes her wicked influence. For Spark, every institution, every department, every family harbours a tyrant-liar; someone who spreads vicious rumours and who is able to do so because of the longevity of other people's tolerance. Tyrant-liars seduce their victims and accomplices with slanderous texts, too outrageous to be denounced, condoned because there is a conspiracy to pretend they are true. And what they do, the scheming and the bullying, the casual smearing of reputation, is a malignant viciousness that Spark identified as one of the ways evil is done in the world.[2]

The keynote in Spark's satire, what gives it robustness, is not this ability to target the enemy, however. It is the situating of the targeted enemy within a complex textual web that begins to do other kinds of work with the chosen character formation. Freddy's Ma also works with a long view: her tyranny is 'long-sustained', her lies 'long-condoned'. It is this empty stretch of time which establishes her authority over her victims. She has created a tradition of lies which, once tolerated, creates the necessary conditions for its continued infection of the textual environment – textual because Ma works through long, wheedling letters to her brainwashed children – and Freddy must dutifully write weekly letters of flattery to her as she bullies Benny into madness. The conspiracy of letters the four children find themselves in is a lifetime project, in other words; it works because it has always seemed to be what constitutes their lifetimes, structuring time in their lives.

Time is the long frame Spark places her subjects in, but with a novel like *The Mandelbaum Gate* there is a time schema of at least three levels. The characters in the novel inhabit the contemporary space of Israel and Jordan in 1961. Barbara Vaughan's pilgrimage crosses this political temporal zone with the biblical history of the Holy Land, and this chimes with the religio-political uses of history by the different sects and ethnicities in the area. The novel's characters also live within the desiring trajectories of their family complexes, love affairs, community relationships, Freddy with his ex-pat proprieties, his poetry and monstrous mother, Barbara with the story of her parent's 'mixed' marriage, her Catholic commitment and her attraction to Harry Clegg.

These three temporal levels, contemporary-political, religio-historical and socio-sexual/familial, are matched by three narrative levels in *The Mandelbaum Gate*. Every incident in the book can be interpreted in three ways: first, as an event in a love story – we expect Freddy and Barbara to fall in love and then chart their complex sexualised manoeuvres with Abdoul and Suzi. Secondly, each incident is a move in a political allegory – the Freddy–Barbara–Abdoul–Suzi foursome plays out the dance of relations between the still-functioning attitudes of the British Mandate and 'Spinster' British Empire, and the secret movers behind the Arab–Israeli situation. At the same time, every incident is plotted according to the replay of the biblical narratives in the novel's pilgrimage through the Old and New Testament territories. Every place encountered at this level of engagement becomes, in Bakhtinian terms, chronotopic. Bakhtin defined the chronotope as crossing points of geography and history in charged narratives, when 'time, as it were, thickens, takes on flesh, becomes artistically visible; likewise, space becomes charged and responsive to the movements of time, plot, and history'.[3]

Spark effects this by simply allowing the characters to realise the complex weave of time and incident they are involved in, not merely as metafictional guinea-pigs, but as players in the long game of history. In other words, each character is aware of how each place is a thick palimpsest of story, myth and politics across Palestine, as here with Freddy looking at the Potter's Field:

> He stood there, on the stony path on a ridge of the Hill of Evil Counsel which rose behind him to its summit at Haceldama, the Potter's Field, bought, by repute, with the unwanted blood-money of Judas and serving, throughout subsequent generations, both the dead and the living, as a graveyard for itinerant paupers and a hide-out for smugglers. (*The Mandelbaum Gate*, 134)

It is Freddy who does the hermeneutic work for us, reading the landscape of the place where he stands as an ancient Old Testament zone, registering the tradition of betrayal and criminal activity there which brings the dead and living together. The Potter's Field is the chronotopic scene of several cross-ings between Israeli and Arab zones, but since it is always being understood by the agents within the story as a palimpsest, it begins to accumulate thick significance. It becomes a site of 'smuggling' transgression across political-historical, religious and psychological borders, as one of the metaphysical 'gates' of the plot.

If it is Spark's shrewdness which cedes the intellectual work to her charac-ters, it is her wit which thematises the almost impossible burden of unremit-ting chronotopic thinking. The burden is thematised in the amnesia Freddy suffers after the traumatic episodes surrounding the smuggling of Barbara out of Jordan. What makes Freddy blank out is the transgressive nature of his act, but equally, Spark suggests, it is the sheer complexity of temporal events that blows his fuse. Spark suggests this with the fragmented nature of the narrative: it is only years later that Freddy can work out the sequence of the events, and readers are also asked to piece together the broken pieces, like the archaeologists at the Dead Sea piecing together the Scrolls, aware of fakes and forgeries, suspicious of every momentous find.

Freddy's amnesiac reaction to the shards of his own memory after the breakdown is made to parallel the reader's own bewilderment at the confusion of times in the palimpsestic zone of the Mandelbaum Gate:

> The events were to come back to Freddy in the course of time; first, like an electric shock of fatal voltage, but not fatal, and so, after that, like a cloud of unknowing, heavy with the molecules of accumulated impressions and finally when he had come to consider the whole mosaic of evidence, when he had gathered the many-coloured fragments of what had actually happened, and had put the missing parts in place, then he came to discern, too late for action but more and more clearly as the years sifted past, that he had been neither a monster or a fool, but had behaved rather well, at least with style and courage. (141)

The metaphorical phases (shock of electricity, cloud of molecules, mosaic) map out the kinds of staggered recognitions Spark would expect from atten-tive readers. They must make their pilgrimage through the zones of the book, initially unsure, then slowly acquiring a clearer view of the whole matter, generating chronotopes in dialogue with the textual events of the book.

'Cloud of unknowing' alludes to the anonymous English fourteenth-century mystical tract: for the monk who wrote it, the cloud signified the nebulous mass of ignorance that obscures the godhead from the eye of flesh. Men and women must learn to love the unknowing space, sending darts of love from their 'ghostly' eye into the dark cloud. Freddy and Barbara never quite know everything that occurred in the lost days, but that is partly the point. The unknowing must be loved for its own sake to prepare for a more spiritual vision of the disorganised chaos of reality. Spark uses the phrase again at the end of *The Hothouse by the East River*.[4] Elsa's shadow, the uncanny sign that she is a ghost because it does not move with the sun, is described in the last sentence of the book as 'her faithful and lithe little cloud of unknowing'.[5] For the medieval *Cloud* author, there was another rival cloud of unknowing, the cloud 'below', the mass of ignorance generated by the mundane world which attaches us to the earth. Elsa's cloud is a little dog at her feet, faithful to her in her delusive hope that she is still of this world, yet doggedly stuck at a moment of time when she died in the train in wartime London. The invisible 'light shining upon her from the east window' (15) contradicts the sun's light pouring in from the west in the evening. When she gazes out of her high window on the East River, she is rapt, it seems, with the beauty of the sky and with ghost projections on the clouds. But, Spark implies, she may simply be entranced by the mundane reality of the city and its contemporary politics and culture – she stares at the river, at the Pepsi-Cola sign, at Welfare Island, the United Nations building. Her ghostly eyes can only see the vision of the contemporary world laid out like a spaniel at her feet. Her 'sort of friend' (13) is the city itself, not the divine light. The hothouse is a hell of fictions generated by her misguided and worldly views and desires.

What matters to Spark, then, is less the situatedness of the subject in the three chronotopes of political contemporaneity, supra-mundane reality and psychosocial relations. It is the *competing claims* on the subject made by those three chronotopes, and the ethical mistakes and moral luck of her people as they struggle to stay true to specific combinations of those claims, or, like Elsa, persist in their illusions beyond the grave.

Barbara Vaughan, for instance, could be said to trigger the danger of the spy plot of *The Mandelbaum Gate* in her insistence on a Christian interpretation of the spaces she passes through. For her the claim of the long religious view is primordial – the border between Israel and Jordan is a simple inconvenience. Yet by crossing over to Jordan she is also getting closer to her lover, the archaeologist Harry Clegg. And staying on her pilgrimage despite everything also puts off her decision to marry him. These psychological motives are backed up by a political possibility. By crossing from Israel to Jordan she enacts her hyphenated identity as a Catholic Jew: her most passionate experiences take place at the border between the states, with her suspended between Jewish and Gentile identities. In other words, two of the three claims on her may be forced into hiding by her Catholic identity; yet they are still operational below the level of her conscious decision-making. They form the cloud of unknowing that is her own fluid and unstable identity.

What the struggle between the three chronotopes might signify is an object lesson in the forces at work in the contemporary political world. Barbara's dedication to the supra-mundane zone of the holy places makes her contemptuous of any purely social or political animal (as excluding the sexual and spiritual). She anathematises Freddy at the beginning of the book for his mealy-mouthed suspicion of extremism, for his mildly anti-Semitic liberalism. And she cannot understand why she ought to attend the Eichmann trial: 'She had thought of the trial as something apart from her purpose; it was political and contemporary' (175). And yet it is the thrill of the moment, of the adventure in the present time of the actual day, that is foundational to Barbara's journey to a more liberated identity:

> The reality of this hour was her escape from the convent, and there was no room for any sense of a more immediate danger in the face of the familiar and positive dangers of heart and mind that were, in any case, likely to arise anywhere one went, across all borders and through all gates. (164)

The escape from the convent, for Barbara, is a true liberation: 'it was not any escape from any real convent, it was an unidentified confinement of the soul she had escaped from' (165). It is the confinement of a scripted identity (the same which Sandy imposes on herself at the end of *The Prime of Miss Jean Brodie* as an act of penance) that Barbara is escaping. What she cannot identify in the confinement of her soul is the depth of her imprisonment in a range of scripts. The meekness of the traditional unmarried woman, the self-control of British upper-class *sangfroid*, ultra-Catholic prohibition of desire: three levels of confinement tie her to her sour role as a carping, passive, self-censoring woman conventualised into the spinster role.

It is Freddy who saves her from her scripted self by himself acting not according to the stuffed-shirt conventions of a Foreign Office bureaucrat, but with the ease and agility afforded him by a leap into the moment. Barbara intuits this, seeing a relationship between his new 'wild commitment', 'new spontaneity and forthcoming spirits' and 'some temporary quality in Freddy's mood' (167). What she fails to see is how much she ought to attend to the contemporary, how far the dangers and elastic potential of the temporary enable true freedom. The 'familiar and positive dangers of heart and mind' take place at the border between the historical and contemporary. The psychosocial self becomes fluid, a flux, a spontaneity of spirits at the borders and gates between the temporary moment and the host of dead and mythological forces that are summoned by the moment.

The temporary moment is always a political chronotope for Spark. Like the Watergate subtext structuring *The Abbess of Crewe* (1974) and the genteel modernist fascism of 1930s Britain, which is the secret focus of *The Prime of*

Miss Jean Brodie (1961), it is the political world that shapes the temporary dangers of heart and mind she specialises in recording. In *The Hothouse by the East River* (1973), the ghosts are not locked into their wartime moment, the chronotope of 1944 London, but into the contemporary hyperreality of a Hollywood-styled New York. The slow-burning joke here is that the two chronotopes have mutual repercussions: wartime London was obsessed by the Americans in the build-up to D-Day, and Elsa and her ghost entourage dream of escape to the glamour of the US. Equally, the story is about how haunted the postwar is by the Second World War. The Cold War for Britain was launched by Churchill in 1946 as the special relationship between the British Empire and the United States, a concocted, wishful dream of security that would bankroll the Empire, contain the Communist menace and tie the UK to the new superpower. *The Hothouse by the East River* is a satirical projection of the special relationship. New York becomes the dream playground for the ghosts of Britain's Churchillian wartime ambitions. Paul and Elsa's wealth and elegance as high society spectres in 1970s New York are a wry, parodic survival of the glamourised envy of America in wartime Britain, a vision of commodity riches like the presents Paul brought back from his secret trip to the US in 1944, 'all unobtainable in England': 'One by one they were looked at and smiled over and gasped about' (*Hothouse*, 123).

The special relationship also haunts the plot of *The Girls of Slender Means* (1963); as in *Hothouse*, that relationship is analysed as a political and social creature of the Second World War. The bomb that explodes in the garden of the May of Teck club coincides with the Labour Party's election victory in July 1945 – Spark dates it to the very day. Allusions are made in passing to the news of that summer, Churchill's disastrous election speech on radio (he claimed Labour's leader, Clement Attlee, would form a Gestapo), the Trinity test of the atom bomb, VJ-Day. The plot turns discreetly on the relations between a rationed, poverty-stricken UK (signified by the girls of slender means) and the new superpower. The girls are rescued by Nicholas, a writer who works for American Intelligence, saving them from the fire caused by the bomb from the hotel next door, the top floor of which is used by the American secret services. Much is made of the purchasing power of the Americans, which includes the favours of the slender Selina. The little tale, timed as it is to the contemporary events so closely, becomes a subdued national allegory signalling the destruction of the Churchillian Great Britain of pre-war Imperial London and the inauguration of a new American, egalitarian age. The transition is focused through the changes wrought on the lives women led and were to lead. Written in the early 1960s, *The Girls of Slender Means* reflects on the foundations of the new sexual freedoms of the postwar and times them to the escape of girls through wartime trauma into the arms of a new Americanised culture. They squeeze through the skylight and window as if undergoing birth: some of the young women strip naked to get through the narrow opening (Tilly, for instance, 'struggle[s] and kick[s]' and screams, stuck in the 'slit window', her naked body covered with 'a greasy substance' (*Girls*, 137–8)) – what is happening is like a rebirth into new postwar identities.

If British culture is being judged at key moments linking the Cold War special relationship back to the Second World War, in *The Mandelbaum Gate* the political focus shifts to another product of the end of empire and the war, the creation of the State of Israel. 1961 Jerusalem is the contemporary context of *The Mandelbaum Gate* and the novel is thick with detailed, concrete references to the news of the day, from the border disputes between the Arabs and Israelis to the Eichmann trial. What makes this context chronotopic for the characters is the catalyst of Barbara's passage to Jordan as a half-Jew. Everything seen and heard becomes charged with menace and suspense, spy thriller desire. When Freddy gallantly saves her with the help of Suzi, their own identities become chronotope symbols. Barbara re-enacts the movements, tourism and cultural cultivation of the 'the English Spinster under the Mandate' (54). Freddy is a Mandate adventurer, a T. E. Lawrence spy and intrepid colonial. Suzi plays the role of exotic sidekick and trickster, the Arab girl as Mata Hari love interest in the tale of imperial derring-do. But these semi-scripted roles take on more contemporary meanings as the dangers become more pressing: Barbara must hide in the back seat of the car as an Arab servant, Freddy has to abide by the devious schemes cooked up by the Ramdez siblings, Suzi becomes an anarchic sexual and political agent as the story unfolds. Other allegories proliferate – Barbara and Freddy, as figures for the Mandate, must do penance for the past interventions, she by being stifled in the servant's clothes, Freddy by having his memory cauterised as symbolic punishment. Jordan and Israel, after all, with all the suffering involved in the artificial borders, were *both* created by the Mandate. These political allegories have a knock-on effect on the psychosocial story – Barbara hidden in the back seat with Freddy and Suzi in the driving seat is a playful allegory for her split and secretive new identity. Her religious self is concealed as she is driven by her British and Semitic selves into the plot of the new chronotope. The escape from the 'convent' of her subjection means the discovery of these new driving forces – the male adventurer and the sexually free and politically active woman – within the new feminist subjectivity of the 1960s. The allegorical turn triggered by the contemporary has an impact too on the way we respond to the religious tale – Barbara's pilgrimage becomes a post-Vatican II journey towards a new, more progressive Catholic laity, accepting of sexuality, conscious of the ecumenical need to relate to rival faiths, other peoples.

There are darker sides to the three books, however, which Spark's comedy disguises. All three books concentrate on specific contemporary chronotopes

– the V-2 bomb in *Hothouse*, the Labour election landslide in *The Girls of Slender Means* and the Eichmann trial in *The Mandelbaum Gate* – to reveal something about the darker secrets of the political unconscious. All three books have an intelligence plot: Elsa and her companions in the *Hothouse*'s dream of New York were involved in a political propaganda unit during the war, based on Spark's own experiences working for Sefton Delmer's Political Intelligence Compound at Milton Bryan, Bedfordshire. The May of Teck club in *The Girls of Slender Means* is next door to the American secret intelligence office; *The Mandelbaum Gate* features the secret services of three or more countries. The intelligence plots are designed to blow the cover on the political unconscious.

What the subtext generated by the intelligence narratives does is to raise questions about the costs of social change and the new forms evil takes in the political sphere of the twentieth century. All three books feature a bloodletting, a moment of revolutionary change and a reflection on political loss and gain with regard to new identities. The new postwar sexual freedom inaugurated by the mini-Blitz of the bomb blast in *The Girls of Slender Means* necessitates the sacrifice of the Victorian woman. So the devout, self-sacrificing Christian ascetic Joanna dies reciting the Psalms, like the praying nuns in Hopkins' *Wreck of the Deutschland*. The symbolism of this is given weight within the book by the peculiar attention afforded the club by the male observer Nicholas – as a writer and as someone working for Intelligence, he is sensitive to the secret values of things, to their chronotopic significance; he feels sure the May of Teck club holds some covert 'aesthetic and ethical conception' (108). Joanna's death is enough to make him into a Catholic priest and suffer a kind of martyrdom in Haiti; it is one of the moments of evil he writes about ('"He's got a note in his manuscript,"' we're told, '"that a vision of evil may be as effective to conversion as a vision of good"' (140)).

Joanna's death is also enough to turn Selina mad – she had heartlessly gone back into the threatened building to get the Schiaparelli dress. We are not told why Selina reacts as she does, screaming at the sight of Nicholas, and so on. But it must be that there are relations between Joanna's death and her stealing of the dress. Nicholas intuits this by crossing himself when seeing Selina come out with it, and Spark underlines this by correlating the death of Joanna with the stabbing of the girl in the VJ crowd. Empty hunger for commodity is allowed to survive the war, whilst the fervour for religious mysticism which occurred during the war is killed off. The May of Teck bomb is the Blitz in miniature in that it has led to a revival of Christianity in London, but also to the poverty-stricken virtues of making do and making the best appearances of things. Only the latter survives 1945 – Christian Britain ended with the Labour Party victory and its secular vision of universal welfare, and with the bombing of Hiroshima the same month, destroying the pre-war world. The effects on Selina and Nicholas play out a national guilt at the cheapening of the Blitz spirit to mere capitalist commodity worship (the fetishising of the dress) and a traumatised recall of all the innocent victims of the war (Joanna as martyr). And, obscurely, there is this lingering guilt of the liberated feminists of the 1960s that someone had to die to allow them this new space: secular feminism had to forgo and deny the Joannas of this world (and the next). Elsa senses, at one level, the new culture being generated, as shown by her gleeful disruption of her son's production of *Peter Pan* which casts the older generation as the Lost Boys.

In *The Hothouse by the East River* the intelligence story also features bomb victims, a revolutionary moment and an exploration of loss and gain. Elsa and her entourage play out a 1940s novelette of adultery and spies as though locked into a parody. The Helmut–Elsa–Paul triangle is repeated as if in traumatic dream recall, an acting out which bears the traces of always having happened before, with some eerie suspicion of treacherous (and postmodern) faked performance. The revolutionary moment that occurs is the dropping of the V-2 rockets on London and the transformation of the world into the Cold War of missiles, long-range death and a radical scientism created by wartime technology. The end of the war was a watershed, but it left the postwar survivors and new generations with an obscure triple relation to the victims of the war: partly the traumatic need to remember them, just as Elsa and Paul learn to wind their New York stories back to the events of 1944; partly an envy of the radical life lived by men and women during the war ('In the summer of 1944, [Paul] is telling his son, life was more vivid than it is now' (29)); and partly a difficult acknowledgement of how the postwar world is haunted, still, by the measures taken during the war.

For what Elsa, Paul and Helmut are engaged in at the Compound is 'black propaganda and psychological warfare', which involved a mimicking of fascist beliefs to the point of infection: 'the propagation of the Allied point of view under the guise of the German point of view [entailing] a tangled mixture of damaging lies, flattering and plausible truths' (52). This is the state of mind Elsa and Paul are stuck in after the war, in a dead afterlife of damaging lies and flattering, plausible truths, based on points of view tangled up with the enemy's. Their deaths in 1944 have not put paid to the habits learned by Anglo-American culture during the war. The lies and half-truths of the war survive, Spark's ethical allegory implies, in the damaging pop psychology of psychoanalysis, in the advertising dreams of commodity culture, in the vulgar, self-seeking and godless hatreds between members of the nuclear family. The covert anti-Americanism of the book senses relations between the empty postmodernism of the postwar metropolis and the propaganda invented by fascism to subdue and seduce a dream-rapt populace.

Spark's own trade of fiction writer is under judgement too, of course. It is a measure of her ethical drive that the roots of her fictionalising skills should also be shown to be the black propaganda of the Second World War. Cold War postmodernism is in many ways an exploration of the relations between the networks of simulacra late modernity's commodity culture creates and the systems of persuasion fabricated in the wartime information wars. The black hole at the heart of postwar culture is a shadow cast by those intelligence operations.

Which brings us full circle to Freddy's Ma, the tyrant-liar we began with. Freddy is a creature of her lies, and given his job as an agent in Her Majesty's secret service, it becomes tempting to read her as a monstrous caricature of the British Empire. It was the Empire, as we have seen, which created Israel and Jordan and conjured the Arab–Israeli conflict into being. It was the secret services and their propaganda which justified operations in the name of ethical empire whilst indulging in power-broking *Realpolitik*. Ma's tormenting of Benny could stand as a figure for the relation of the lying Empire to the countries of faith under its dominion: she fosters violence and extremism by false accusation of those believers, then enjoys the fruits of flattery from those faithless civil servants of her political honour. Yet she is also prey to deeper, Freudianised enmities against her dominion, as when Freddy contemplates matricide: 'She would goad anyone to strangle her or slit her throat' (133).

The darkest secret of *The Mandelbaum Gate* lies in the relations between the 'Ma' murder plot and the story of the Eichmann trial. Just as Goebbels' lies seduce Elsa into dangerous fantasy through mimicry, so too do the resemblances between the Empire's *Realpolitik* and Eichmann's bureaucracy raise awful questions. Barbara refuses to see the value of the 'political and contemporary'; yet her love affair, her faith, her Catholic-Jewish identity have been scarred and shaped by the active effects of the lying machines of Empire and of German fascism. As Saul reminds her, '"This trial is part of the history of Jews"' (*The Mandelbaum Gate*, 175), and as such has chronotopic power to ramify beyond the present moment back into time. Spark had covered the trial for *The Observer*, but what she had seen in the dock was not fodder for the newspapers, but a lesson in twentieth-century history and its dreadful impact on the history of the Jews. The gigantic lie propagated by the Nazi tyranny was the self-sufficiency of its own bureaucracy as god of this world, a god founded on the nihilistic and blank vices of an absolutist contemporaneity. This fascist religion, worshipping the system of lies and death channelled through the bureaus which organised the Holocaust, founded its faith on empty timetables, pure dead and killing time. This sensation of dreamlike abandonment in empty time Spark identified with the French anti-*roman* and Beckett's *Waiting for Godot*: 'repetition, boredom, despair, going nowhere for nothing, all of which conditions are enclosed in a tight, unbreakable statement of the times at hand' (177). Beckett is explicitly quoted when the presiding judge asks: 'What are we waiting for?': '– We're waiting for Godot,' Barbara answers (180).

The dreamlike abandonment to the times at hand turns round a black hole at the heart of atheist, postwar culture: 'She was thinking of the Eichmann trial, and was aware that there were other events too, which had rolled away the stone that revealed an empty hole in the earth, that led to a bottomless pit' (283). To sense that pit is also to register the political sin committed by the British in their imperial calculations. Like Freddy's mother, the Empire generated lies to subjugate the peoples of alien faiths under its jurisdiction, bullying the regions into fake political spaces, imposing unreal borders and secretly relishing the violence that ensued. The murder of Ma by Benny is a curious anti-colonial act of emancipation, for Freddy at least, signalling the end of Empire. His liberation begins when he tears up his correspondence with his mother and embarks on a dream of post-imperial adventure.

All three books analyse the relations of postwar British international relations in terms of traumatic residues of the war: *The Hothouse by the East River* sensing the effects of black propaganda on the Cold War special relationship; *The Girls of Slender Means* tracking the American-influenced emancipations of the postwar back to guilt over the war dead and wartime ecstatic faith; *The Mandelbaum Gate* timing the end of Mandate-style operations in the Near East to the purgative effects of the Eichmann trial. All three books use intelligence activity as a trope for the revelation of the political secrets of postwar British culture. And all three books meditate on the kinds of activism necessary to liberate the mind from the bonds of wartime (wartime being time without chronotopic relations): *Hothouse* with Elsa's fitful knowledge that she is caught in false time, her tomato-throwing zest; Nicholas's atonement in Haiti for Joanna's death; Barbara's pilgrimage. Only in the chronotopic present, as a fully experienced political event, can this liberating activism occur, a present that negotiates with the complex pasts of the region, resists the unreal contemporaneity of the public bureaucracies and propaganda agencies (like the anti-Semitic communist double agent, Ruth Gardnor), and can establish a living relationship between the social, political and religious vectors of selfhood.[6]

CHAPTER SIX

Spark, Modernism and Postmodernism

Matthew Wickman

In *Symposium* (1990), Muriel Spark's character 'Annabel, who is a television producer,' opines that "'Some people . . . are eighteenth century, some fifteenth, some third century, some twentieth . . . Most patients are blocked . . . in their historical era and cannot cope with the claims and habits of our century.'" This goes for Annabel, who later professes herself 'eighteenth century too'.[1] Spark wrote the same thing of her grandparents, whose 'parlance often retained some flavour of the eighteenth century' and also of her one-time consort, Derek Stanford, who, in the time Spark knew him, began 'to display ever more eighteenth-century affectations'.[2] One is tempted to say the same thing of Spark: her penchant for 'ridicule' as a deadlier shaft of satire certainly conjures Swift.[3] But even if we restrict our purview to the twentieth century, Spark often seems out of step with her own historical moment. For Liam McIlvanney, the meticulous design and authorial control of Spark's fiction fail to imbibe the democratic (e.g. plotless, polyglottal) spirit of novels by Alasdair Gray, James Kelman and other writers of the Scottish cultural resurgence of the 1980s and 1990s.[4] Martin McQuillan puts a happier face on Spark's anachronistic *oeuvre*, proclaiming it 'untimely' in being at once before its time and also politically disquieting.[5]

The question of Spark's place in literary history grows more vexed when we consider the reputedly 'postmodern' era in which she wrote. Our difficulty arises not only from asking whether Spark's work corresponds with features of postmodern fiction, but also from uncertainties about what postmodernism is. Definitions of the term abound, but one of the most useful heuristics for an engagement of Spark is Ihab Hassan's famous chart dividing modernism and postmodernism. As Hassan has it, modernist literature privileges design whereas postmodern texts highlight the play of chance; modernism strives for depth whereas postmodernism celebrates surfaces; modernism exhibits features of paranoia whereas postmodernism bears the hallmarks of schizophrenia. In all, his list entails some forty categories.[6] Without denying the schematic value of Hassan's exercise, critics have, unsurprisingly, concluded that the polarities of modernism and postmodernism often inhabit the same text, many not twentieth- or twenty-first-century texts at all.[7] The same holds true of Spark, whose 'hybrid background – part English, part Scottish, part Protestant, part Jewish – [makes] her a diasporic writer with a fluid sense of self'.[8] This bespeaks postmodernism. And yet, her influences – T. S. Eliot and Marcel Proust, to say nothing of Cardinal Newman, gothic fiction, the Celtic Twilight or the Scottish border ballads – are hardly postmodern in any conventional sense. So Allan Massie, for instance, situates Spark within a post-realist tradition whose work evokes 'the fragmented manner in which we perceive reality' – a modernist *and* postmodernist convention, as evident in William Faulkner or as in Donald Barthelme.[9] Hence, whether we look to the architects of postmodern theory, Spark's national and religious identity or critics, we find little direction.[10]

This chapter suggests there is something evocatively Sparkian about the plight of a displaced, anxious, delusional and perhaps nonexistent postmodernism; it recalls the paranoid atmosphere of a novel like *The Abbess of Crewe* (1974), or the ludic image of the Marxist nuns in *Symposium*, whose sense of dialectical history corresponds to Sister Lorne's conviction that 'four-letter words were the lifeblood of the market place, the People's parlance and aphrodisiac, the dynamic and inalienable prerogative of the proletariat' (104–5). But then again, as Magnus says of Sister Lorne's position, 'some of [this] may [just] be the fruit of a fertile Scottish imagination' (106). And that is the heuristic value of reading Spark: she implicitly re-channels our energies from efforts to situate her within cultural history to attempts at reading culture by way of her. Spark's fiction does not function as yet another exhibit of postmodernism as much as act allegorically as a kind of metanarrative helping to explain the conundrums of a literary history which culminates in postmodernism as an unsatisfying narrative climax. This chapter sketches its lineaments by discussing the Sparkian devices of repetition and prolepsis – figures which implicitly direct our attention towards the past and future while defamiliarising our relationship with the present.

Territorial Rights (1979) is no bad place to begin. The novel comes at the end of a group of narratives which marked a departure from minutely crafted 'crystals' like *The Driver's Seat*.[11] Beginning with *The Hothouse by the East River* (1973), Spark seemed increasingly to 'relish the worldly confusions which she had hitherto transfigured in her fiction'.[12] As Ruth Whittaker puts it:

> the plot involves spies, adultery, murder, blackmail, betrayal, kidnapping and terrorism, plus, it is insinuated, any other sins you can think of which are not specifically mentioned. The complexity of the plot takes us a long way from the uncluttered story-line of . . . Spark's elegant novellas.[13]

Certainly, prolepsis, metafiction and paranoia inform *Territorial Rights* as surely as any other Spark offering. However, they more closely resemble 'gratuitous puzzles' here than integral organs.[14] They ask us to entertain the machinations of a male prostitute, and would-be art historian, as he learns of and then threatens to write a novel about the covert Nazi double-dealing of his former lover, a wealthy, middle-aged man of pleasure. Along the way, we encounter an anti-Semitic Bulgarian defector, her Communist lover, the male prostitute's father, the father's paramour, the protagonist's trash novel-reading mother, the mother's indignant and shrewish friend, the man of pleasure's co-conspirator, the agent for an international private investigation agency, a butcher looking to exploit his bombshell of a secret – and also his bombshell of a niece – and two elderly sisters who protect the butcher's secret and bury their own complicity in a murder. Eventually, among other things, the defector returns to Bulgaria with her lover after unknowingly dancing on her murdered father's grave; the male prostitute's mother finds the tenor of the novels she reads creeping into her less than thrilling everyday life; and the prostitute himself runs off with the butcher's niece and becomes a famous international terrorist. Or something like that.[15]

While this thumbnail sketch hardly captures all the nuances of the characters or their relationship with each other, it does indicate the multiple threads of Spark's narrative. *Territorial Rights* is actually most interesting *before* it begins tying together these various threads – that is, before the narrator begins exerting an all-too-heavy hand. At its outset, the narrative creates an air of mystery through subtle effects of repetition. We find ourselves in Venice, where the protagonist, Robert, has come after falling out with his lover, Curran. Curran's redundant dismissal – 'Goodbye, goodbye, goodbye, good*bye*' – still rings in Robert's ears and stings his ego.[16] It is clear that there has been a lovers' quarrel, though its substance or cause remains unknown. '"Goodbye, goodbye, goodbye, good*bye*." It was as if the older man had said, "You bore me. You can't even leave in good style. You haven't any slightest savvy about partings. You've always bored me. *Goodbye very much.* Good*bye*"' (6). Curran's dismissive words enter the text as memory; repeated several times in the first couple of pages; they are thus an echo at their origin, carrying with them a past, which they obscure as much as divulge.

The novel amplifies this dynamic through other phrases, many linking and reconfiguring sections of text. The Bulgarian refugee Lina, for instance, asks Robert when he plans to see Curran, who seems to have had second thoughts and has come to Venice in search of him. '"Tomorrow, in the evening,"' Robert replies (20). The section concludes there, with the next one beginning: 'Tomorrow, in the evening, Robert walked through the lanes and across the bridges, under the clear stars and over their reflection in the waters, to Harry's Bar, took a place downstairs and waited' (20). This sentence both reiterates and displaces Robert's terse reply to Lina; its lyricism alters the mood of the narrative even as it modifies the clipped prose which we often associate with Spark and which dominates much of the rest of the narrative. A few pages and one morning later, after their initial conversation, Curran greets Robert by telling him he 'look[s] good'. 'Go to hell,' Robert replies (26). The narrator then informs us that 'Robert had found Curran in the front hall of the Pensione Sofia', the hotel in whose garden Lina's father is buried, 'seated at a table with Katerina and Eufemia', the hotel proprietors and older women mentioned above:

> It was mid-morning. Robert had come in the front door with the English newspaper in his hand, and there was Curran chatting away as if he had known the women all his life.
>   The women dispersed discreetly as Curran got up to greet Robert. And 'Go to hell,' Robert had said when Curran came out with, 'You look good.' (26–7)

As with Curran's dismissal of Robert, the exchange with which the section opens is an echo in its first incarnation; the fuller explanation and 'original' utterance subsequently provided by the narrator is thus an echo of the echo. Here, shadow is substance; the narrative moment emerges textually as its own repetition.

Perhaps this is what the astute Ian Rankin means when he observes that Spark plays with our notions of reality and literary realism: what we see, what is 'there' in the text, is not necessarily what is most essential to its plot.[17] We might add that there is a deeply existential-phenomenological dimension to the sort of 'originary repetition' that resounds in the early pages of Spark's novel. It echoes such formulations as Kierkegaard's when he opposes repetition to memory, Nietzsche's when he writes of the eternal return or Derrida's on *différance* and the erasure of primordial traces.[18] These are the types of dynamics which inspire scholars like McQuillan to assert a strong and even self-conscious rapport between Spark and literary theory. But Spark's writing is less about its conformity to elegant paradigms than the havoc it wreaks on them, and consequently on our cultural and historical bearings. In *Territorial Rights*, for instance, the narrative echo chambers at the novel's outset leave the impression that crucial events and meaning are elsewhere, and that episodes of which we read only partly capture what is most pertinent. For instance, we eventually witness Lina dancing on her father's grave, but we get only an inkling of the machinations which killed him; we behold Robert turning against Curran, Lina, his father and the other characters, but never get a clear sense of the factors – intrinsic or environmental – that drove him to become an expert saboteur. At most we get a character's explanation that 'The really professional evil-doers love it' (235), the equivalent of a *Just So* story. This effect of myopic belatedness creates an atmosphere of paranoia – of powerful agents exerting a causal force from distant but hidden locations. Such effects, we recall from Hassan, evoke a 'modern' more than a 'postmodern' aesthetic.

But this is not to deny Spark's novel its postmodern schizophrenia – its division into multiple personalities, or at least persons. The text's internal echoes partly achieve this effect by revealing themselves as fragments of unassembled diegetic wholes, that is, of the larger worlds (for instance, the past relationship between Robert and Curran, the history of Lina's father, and so on) suggested by the story. But these echoes also acquire a baiting quality at the rhetorical and, by extension, narrative level, as when Robert's mother, hoping to locate her son, speaks with the representative from Global Equipment Security Services, GESS, an international private detection agency. His words to her are as soft as slow-drip water torture:

> 'Well, [Robert] isn't in Venice with us, Anthea, any more. He's walked out on everyone including his kind friend Curran, Anthea. He's left his belongings in his hotel room and gone off into the blue, Anthea. Curran paid up his hotel bill, Anthea.'
> 'Why do you "Anthea" me like that?' said Anthea. (161)

Anthea's question invites the humorous fillip at the conclusion of the sentence, serving not only to underscore Anthea's haplessness, but also rhetorically to conflate the narrator with the agent for the surveillance network. Like Mr. B., as this agent is called (evoking the ambiguously [a]moral convert in Samuel Richardson's eighteenth-century novel *Pamela*), the narrator seems at once attentive to and contemptuous of the characters she engages. And the narrator resembles Mr. B. in other ways, as well. The pun inscribed in the acronym GESS bears itself out in the perpetual half-smile worn by Mr. B. – a physiological defect similar to Jack Nicholson's Joker character in the 1989 film *Batman* – acting as an apt figure for the uncertain air of irony which pervades the narrative:

> It was not quite a smile that [Mr. B.] gave but a shape of mouth and lips that he had been born with, a wide, fat-lipped mouth . . . Who would have known but that his mouth-smile . . . might have got him into trouble in a court of law . . . should he have been giving evidence in a desperately serious case. (54)

This 'trouble' would have ensued, presumably, from Mr. B.'s inability to present a suitably grave image, much like Spark's fiction, irrespective of its 'serious' subject matter, whose topics in *Territorial Rights* include fascism, murder and terrorism. Mr. B. is thus, by narrative position, rhetoric and illegible physiognomy, an extension – a double and perhaps a disfiguration – of the narrator.[19] His half-smile hypostatises Spark's narrative tone.

However, the text's schizophrenia extends beyond the narrative's reflection in its characters. Indeed, not only are characters like Anthea uncertain about the status of events, and not only are Spark's readers forced to withstand the narrative's climate of paranoia, but the novel itself seems fundamentally unsure about its own narrative stance. Its effects are structurally beside themselves. For instance, what one critic calls the novel's air of 'mysterious diffuseness'[20] depends on the narrative's subtly repetitive (re)turns of phrase, but these delicate touches are occasionally overrun by ham-fisted prolepses. One example occurs early in the novel, when Robert meets Curran at a hotel restaurant:

> Around them was the buzz and the small-clatter of multifarious activities, such as the shuffling of chairs and feet, the conversations at the bar and at the other tables, the sound of the door swinging open with the entrance of new arrivals and the constant clink of bottles and glasses at the bar. It made for a good environment for their meeting. Robert was relieved that Curran had not asked him to come somewhere quiet, and it did not occur to him now, as they waited for their whiskies, that in fact he need not have come at all. (21)

Why exactly Robert 'need not have come' never seems entirely clear and never feels truly integral to his subsequent descent into blackmail and terrorism. We are a long way from the startling disclosure in *The Driver's Seat* when the narrator informs us that the protagonist, Lise, 'is neither good-looking nor bad-looking. Her nose is short and wider than it will look in the likeness constructed partly by the method of identikit, partly by actual photography, soon to be published in the newspapers of four languages'.[21] There, the revelation of Lise's impending death prompts the incorrect but logical conclusion that this will happen without her consent; Spark's famous 'flash forward' technique thus generates suspense, which only accentuates the surprise ending. In *Territorial Rights*, though, we get little more than a cinematic summary of the characters' futures: 'Robert and Anna were sent to the Middle East to train in a terrorist camp. Lina returned to Bulgaria . . . Curran . . . went to India to see his guru' (238–9), and so on. The narrative, however, draws inordinate significance from these vignettes, punctuating them with this self-reflexive commentary which concludes the novel: 'the canals lapped on the sides of the banks, the palaces of Venice rode in great state and the mosaics stood with the same patience that had gone into their formation, piece by small piece' (240), imputing a similar, mosaic-like quality to the novel. The narrative pieces are certainly there, but Spark's success in fitting them together is questionable and they do not provide ample pay-off for their earlier, proleptic announcement.

Nevertheless, Spark's 'flash forward' device is compelling in *Territorial Rights* if only because it underscores the impression created by the narrative's rhetorical echoes – the conviction that meaning is elsewhere. When the narrator informs us that Robert 'need not have come at all' to his rendezvous with Curran, this seemingly prophetic utterance implies that what we are about to witness is somehow beside the point, much in the way the textual echoes suggest diegetic origins in extra-textual realities. In each case, our readerly experience is one of fragments; returning to the trial imagery through which the narrator describes Mr. B.'s smile, the 'evidence' the text presents to us is inconclusive. Hence, and appealing to Hassan's categories, we might say that *Territorial Rights* mimics an aesthetic of schizophrenia – of narrative consciousness split between extrinsic voice and hypostatised embodiment (for instance, in Mr. B.'s smile) – while instilling impressions of a more broadly encompassing paranoia (through its insinuations of recoverable truth 'elsewhere').

In doing so, *Territorial Rights* uncannily anticipates Fredric Jameson's influential diagnosis of postmodernism. Here, it may be useful to step back from Spark's narrative to consider its relation to the larger, literary-historical problem outlined above. Commenting on the waning modernist ethos, Jameson remarks that there has been a 'shift in the dynamics of cultural pathology' since the 1960s, a shift which 'can be characterized as one in which the alienation of the subject is displaced by the latter's fragmentation'.[22] Schizophrenic in our habitudes, we are no longer able to unify past, present and future, and are consequently relegated to 'an experience of pure material signifiers' (27). And yet these fragments do not derive principally from evolving cultural sensibilities; contrary to a Bloomian model of influence, postmodern playfulness does not amount to a creative digression from modernist anguish; a poet like Tom Leonard does not simply push the limits of vernacular poetry further than an oppressive literary 'father' like Hugh MacDiarmid.[23] Instead, postmodern art finds its material basis in the forces of late capitalism: 'postmodernism is not the cultural dominant of a wholly new social order . . . but only the reflex and the concomitant of . . . [a] systemic modification of capitalism itself' (xii). Hence, Jameson argues, the architectural designs of Robert Venturi, the silkscreen prints of Andy Warhol or in the context of Scotland (which Spark continued to claim as her national identity) the installation pieces of Douglas Gordon are monuments of aesthetic innovation which merely reflect commodifying market norms.[24]

What this implies is that Jameson, in concert with Spark in *Territorial Rights*, circumscribes schizophrenic effects within a broader hermeneutic of paranoia. Jameson's vision is thus oddly reassuring, if only because it holds out the possibility of a fully conceptualised, coherent and hence non-fragmentary experience. For this reason, Jameson seems almost nostalgic for the era of (mere) alienation, of (mere) paranoia. Indeed, Jameson has been criticised for the un-postmodern flavour of his postmodern analysis.[25] His 'aesthetic of cognitive mapping', whereby we superimpose boundaries on the atemporal, Vegas-like landscape of the contemporary Now and thus provide ourselves with a basic sense of critical orientation, essentially resembles

Sparkian prolepses, which intrude into the plot in order to direct us to some end that is illegible within the narrative framework at that moment. Hence, by this reading, Spark does not assume her place in Jameson's late-capitalist universe as much as Jameson compulsively repeats the narrative logic of Spark's fiction.

And so, we might say, Spark's fiction inverts the presumed norms of literary history, lending structure to the categories which purport to explain the fiction. And yet, prolepsis in *Territorial Rights* – a novel that seemingly reveals the 'paranoid' (or 'modern') underpinnings of a 'schizophrenic' (that is, 'postmodern') heuristic – only lends grist to criticisms like McIlvanney's regarding the putatively 'undemocratic' nature of Spark's work. But is such a criticism fair? What if we were to change the governing model of contemporary fiction from postmodernism to something else? What role would Spark assume then? Bruno Latour presents a particularly interesting argument here because, without addressing Jameson's cognitive mapping *per se*, he characterises it as a quintessentially 'modern' formation. Modernity, he argues, is born of 'two sets of entirely different practices . . . The first set,' which he calls *translation*, 'creates mixtures between . . . new types of beings, hybrids of nature and culture.' [26] These hybrids are not literal products of genetic engineering, but represent fusions of human subjects with the objects they engage, as when electronic gigabytes redefine how we think about 'memory'. Machines become 'human', and vice versa. This conjures the postmodern wasteland of effaced boundaries which Jameson decries, and also evokes the character William Damien in *Symposium*, who works in artificial intelligence, and more specifically in 'the study of animal intelligence-systems as patterns for mechanical devices, a mixed' – that is, hybrid – 'science involving electronics and biology' (31). But the second criterion of modernity, Latour argues, which he calls *purification*, divides humans from nonhumans and thus reinstitutes distinctions which our transformative technologies had eradicated. Here, we rediscover Jameson's impulse towards cognitive mapping and the initiation of differences.

As it turns out, this is where the relationship in Spark's work between repetition and prolepsis becomes most provocative. Spark was in many ways a conscientiously 'modern' writer, in terms of both topicality (e.g. the Watergate scandal as an underlying motif in *The Abbess of Crewe*) and style (e.g. her well-documented imitation of the methods of the *nouveau roman*). And yet she drew on traditionally 'premodern' influences as well, especially the Scottish border ballads, which may be where she learned how to repeat phrases with haunting effect.[27] Indeed, it is repetition which makes these phrases feel haunted, dense with the aura of 'elsewhere'. For instance, her 1994 poem 'Standing in the Field' describes a scarecrow as essentially a hybrid creation with 'turnip face / [. . .] battered hat [. . .] open arms / flapping in someone else's shirt, his rigid, orthopedic sticks / astride in someone else's jeans [. . .]'. But the tenth and final line of the poem, which Spark punctuates as a single sentence (the only other sentence in the poem taking up the first nine lines), creates an altogether different impression: 'He stands alone, he stands alone.' [28] Using Latour's terminology, we might say that with this final line Spark derives 'purification' – the scarecrow's singularity – from 'translation' – his embodiment of others' leftovers. At one level, Latour argues, this is the logic of modernity: it proliferates hybrids then disavows them. But Latour imagines this process as one of rationalisation, whereas here, in Spark's poem, the final line is less the 'rational' consequence of the preceding nine than their uncanny repetition. By emphasising the scarecrow's derivative status *and* his solitude, the poem retroactively makes 'someone else's shirt' and 'someone else's jeans' appear odd, *unheimlich*.[29] This may not be the 'democracy' McIlvanney lauds in other writers, but nor is it the authoritarian poetics he ascribes to Spark either. In this poem Spark implicitly emulates Latour's 'modernity', but she turns it to different effect. That is, she 'repeats' modernity and makes it appear, if not exactly postmodern, then para-modern, outside the modern/postmodern binary altogether.[30]

If 'Standing in the Field' casts Sparkian repetition in a different light, then *Symposium* does the same for Sparkian prolepsis. Like *Territorial Rights*, this novel is something of an ensemble piece, centring on five London couples at a dinner party, weaving in and out of their neurotic existences. Gradually, we hone in on the Scottish *arriviste* Margaret Murchie, the new wife of a young businessman and wealthy heir, whose art-collecting mother is found murdered. Margaret, we learn, has long been linked with shocking deaths, whether coincidentally or through the interventions of a crazy uncle. At this point in her life, having grown tired of being a mere token of evil, Margaret arranges her mother-in-law Hilda's murder. Alas, the best-laid schemes of mice and men gang aft agley, and Hilda is capped by a band of professional thieves in a heist gone bad. Margaret misses her moment.

Spark's patented 'flash forward' technique is on full display here. However, it operates in dual registers, with the effect of rendering it, and its narrative, uncanny. We have, on the one hand, standard Sparkian prolepsis when the characters discuss Hilda's imminent appearance at the dinner party only to have the narrator break in with this disclosure: 'But Hilda Damien will not come in after dinner. She is dying, now, as they speak' (45). And, on the other hand, we also have the repetition of names and phrases which function proleptically. For instance, the characters – and, by extension, the narrative – begin calling attention to Margaret's unsettling presence through the resonant effects of her family name: '"the name Murchie," [Chris, the hostess,] said. "I'm sure I've heard it before in connection with some affair, some case in the papers; something"' (38–9). '"Murchie, the name Murchie . . ."' said

Chris [later], "it rings a bell"' (48). "'Murchie?" said [another character,] Roland. "Well, it's an old Scottish name,"' Annabel replies (60). "'There was something about the Murchies last year,"' Roland remarks shortly thereafter (63). Finally, the narrator pulls back the veil – partway – on the Murchie mystery. The crazy uncle, Magnus, 'had . . . been [the family's] guru for six years. He it was who had suggested a course of action which was to cause the Murchie scandal' by arranging to have the 'Murchies' aged mother' strangled in her Edinburgh nursing home (67). The perpetrator of the deed was an escaped inmate at the mental hospital where Magnus was a patient. Thenceforward, the work of death, often vaguely affiliated with Magnus, begins trailing Margaret. Her determination to murder Hilda thus represents her desire to evolve from 'the passive carrier of disaster' into an active agent of destruction (143).

Of course, an accident waylays her scheme, reversing the seeming course of narrative destiny or at least of readerly expectation – another characteristically Sparkian trait. But this climax unifies repetition and prolepsis even as it renders them uncanny, turning these conventions to unfamiliar ends. In Latour's terms, we might say that the repetition of the name Murchie acts as a device of 'translation', conjoining Annabel, Roland, Chris and their motley array of conversations, plots and diegetic situations. Prolepsis, meanwhile, functions as an instrument of 'purification' in that it winnows out significant details from a mass of observations, asides, quips and other strands of meaning. In Latour's narrative of how modernity and postmodernity came to be, 'purification' emerges in order to make sense of 'translation'; indeed, narrative itself, Latour's included, already is an act of purification inasmuch as it takes the welter of experience and imbues it with a legible beginning, middle and end. This is what happens in *Symposium*: repetition ('Murchie' as an instance of 'translation') shapes details from the past into a suspenseful present leading us, proleptically (in the mode of 'purification'), toward a destined outcome –Margaret's arrangement of Hilda's murder. And then, suddenly, things go awry. Contingency triumphs over destiny. In *Symposium*, as in *Territorial Rights*, the 'modernity' whose logic Latour criticises simply ceases to be, at least in his terms.

Does this make these novels 'postmodern'? No more or less so than Spark's poem 'Standing in the Field'. *Symposium* in particular shares with that poem sensitivity to the ballad tradition: Magnus often repeats them, and the novel is filled, Bryan Cheyette remarks, with 'emotionally charged supernatural resonances' evocative of balladry.[31] There are several references to ballads in *Symposium*, as when Magnus recites a fragment with a haunting refrain: 'As I went down the water side / None but my foe to be my guide / None but my foe to be my guide' (81). But Spark is not producing traditional ballads any more than an artist like Ian Hamilton Finlay is creating classical art.[32] Still, we might ask, what critical value lies in asserting or reasserting the resistance of Spark's work to classifications like 'tradition', 'modernism' or 'postmodernism'? Haven't we long grown tired of such labels? Indeed, this is what Latour's landmark book implied in the mid-1990s: 'We Have Never Been Modern' because the 'purifications' by which modernity differentiates itself from the past are ultimately little more than intellectual parlour tricks. Latour foreshadowed the fascination with 'hybrids' which would soon permeate cultural theory (to say nothing of the automobile industry). Posthumanism, cybernetics, biotechnology, informatics, quantitative methods for literary analysis – these are but a few of the 'translational' media which today have conspired to make postmodernism appear almost quaint.

But this only makes Spark more relevant than ever. In the odd effects generated via the fusion of techniques like repetition and prolepsis, Spark's work would seem to conform nicely to Latour's revisionist history, and hence to the post-postmodern hegemony of hybrids. The only problem is that it does not. By mimicking and occasionally overturning the relationship between 'translation' and 'purification', novels like *Territorial Rights* and *Symposium* out-Latour Latour. We have never been modern, Latour says; but neither have we been that thing Latour says we have been, Spark's novels imply. When we think of Spark's work relative to literary and cultural history, we are thus placed in the strange position of desiring one of her famous narrative intrusions, if only to tell us where she, and we, are going. *Territorial Rights* and *Symposium* render such prolepses (real or imagined) problematic, of course, which may be why we should consider them, and not 'crystals' like *The Driver's Seat*, among Spark's most important works. In the absence of any firm basis of orientation – stylistic, historical or (in Spark's case) religious – our identities will most likely develop from the echoes we convert into prolepses, and also from prolepses which disintegrate into uncanny repetitions. Alas, we are like Spark's scarecrow: we stand alone, we stand alone. And so it is that Spark's work puts a finger on the peculiar state of our para-modern condition, one that is neither 'democratic' nor totalitarian as much as thoroughly, remorselessly uncanny.

CHAPTER SEVEN

Muriel Spark as Catholic Novelist

Gerard Carruthers

In the early 1960s Muriel Spark was regarded as yet another prominent British writer of fiction working from within a Roman Catholic sensibility. She was seen as bringing a moral intensity to her novels and short stories, somewhat akin to that of Graham Greene, and purveying a satirical *contemptus mundi* that had some commonality with the mode of Evelyn Waugh. If the 'Catholic' identity of Greene and Waugh has remained more or less secure (though modern theoretical perspectives have also made some attempts to undermine the supposed Catholic 'centre' of these two writers), Spark has seen several, sometimes challenging, claims against what was previously taken to be her core writerly concerns and identity. Rightly, Spark's previously undervalued Scottish, Jewish and gendered identities have been retrieved and emphasised by commentators, most especially since the 1980s.[1] The broad materialist presuppositions of modern critical theory, however, represent a particularly stark reappraisal of Spark in relation to her avowed religious predilections. We see this most clearly in the volume edited by Martin McQuillan, *Theorizing Muriel Spark: Gender, Race, Deconstruction* (2001), where none of the contributors has any regard for Spark's religion as representing something tangibly special with which to work.[2] Implicitly, Spark's religious values are not really to be respected amidst such clear sociological priorities as 'gender' and 'race' and the critical practice of deconstruction, which will not accede to any privileged or unitary idea of the author's perspective. Arguably, McQuillan, in attempting to open up the definition of Spark's Catholicism, is rather reductive as he suggests that Spark's fictions 'are "Catholic" in the sense that they treat the theological-political issues of the West over the course of the last five decades, which in so far as they are concerns for the West intrude upon the rest of the world and become "universal" or "catholic"'.[3] With that movement from 'Catholic' to 'catholic' we see precisely the evacuation of Spark's religious centre and an insistence on common, secular (especially 'Western'), human experience. With McQuillan's volume and other work on Spark an appreciable critical trend has been an emphasis on sexuality in her work with 'Queer' readings especially now very much to the fore.[4] Such shifts in critical perspective might represent an interesting tension with one of the master-narratives of Spark's *oeuvre* read straight, that the world is too preoccupied with secular, materialist, even sociological concerns. A question can be posed: is Spark's confessed spirituality now to be disregarded by critics as either irrelevant in her work or, at best, seen as a quaint delusion which brings some thematic structure to her work even though the 'real' or 'most important' themes of race, sexuality, and so on, lie elsewhere in her fiction?

Spark's most pronounced statement on her faith is found in 'My Conversion' (1961) for the magazine, *Twentieth Century*. Candidly she reveals that:

> [. . .] I decided at last to become a Catholic, by which time I really became very ill. I was going about, but I was ready for a breakdown. I think it was the religious upheaval and the fact I had been trying to write and couldn't manage it. I was living in very poor circumstances and I was a bit undernourished as well. I suppose it all combined to give me my breakdown. I had a feeling while I was undergoing this real emotional suffering that it was all part of the conversion. But I don't know. It may have been an erroneous feeling.[5]

Even in her description of 'conversion' we find a characteristic Sparkian element of dubiety. Her personal experiences are open to contrasting interpretations, which she will neither fully accept nor deny. Her 'undernourished' state (at a time when she was taking the slimming drug Dexedrine) may be responsible for her altered state of consciousness or it may be down to genuine religious experience. Spark had become a Catholic in 1954 and around this time underwent Jungian therapy at the hands of a priest, Frank O'Malley. Her experience can be read as cementing a keystone of her sensibility already informing her fiction. Before her conversion Spark had scored her first success as a fiction writer with 'The Seraph and the Zambesi', which won *The Observer*'s Christmas short story competition in 1951. In this text, the appearance of a real, ostentatiously six-winged angel in a Nativity play being staged by expatriate Europeans beside an African river represents a typical Sparkian collision of the (spiritual) sublime and the (everyday) mundane. Comically, the Europeans are outraged at the unscripted intrusion and drive the celestial being away. Spark's point here, as elsewhere in her *oeuvre*, is that there has been a disastrously discriminating separation in the human outlook between the sacred and the profane, the supernatural and the natural, the rational and the irrational even. Her Jungian therapy typically sought to create harmony between the inner individual and the outer world. In the context of Catholicism (as well as in orthodox Jungian analysis), this meant not being too ready to dismiss the irrational so as to achieve a too neat or tidy, 'normal', rational apprehension. In Spark's first novel, *The Comforters* (1957), its central character is hearing voices either because of her extreme dieting or due to genuinely numinous events. Echoing Spark's own experiences at the hands of Father O'Malley, Caroline Rose is casually told by Father Jerome who is ministering to her, 'these things can happen'.[6] The point is certainly that the supernatural can intrude into the human world, but equally that we should not be too quick to identify this. Spark's breakdown may have been part of her process of conversion or it may have been due to Dexedrine consumption. As she admits with a deceptive casualness, in 'My Conversion', she simply does not know. More important for Spark, in fact, is the religious instinct rather than any religious certainty. In *The Mandelbaum Gate* (1965) Barbara Vaughan listens to a priest preach at the Holy Sepulchre who says that 'where doubts of historic authenticity exist, they are as thrilling in their potentialities for quest and discovery as a certainty would be'.[7] In Spark's short story 'The Gentile Jewesses' the narrator, like Vaughan, Rose, and Spark herself, is again a Catholic convert who addresses her family background:

> My father, when questioned as to what he believes, will say, 'I believe in the Blessed Almighty who made heaven and earth,' and will say no more, returning to his racing papers which contain problems proper to innocent men. To [him] it was no great shock when I turned Catholic, since with Roman Catholics too, it all boils down to the Almighty in the end.[8]

We note again the throwaway, clichéd, mundane secular language ('it all boils down to the Almighty in the end') with which Spark's narrator addresses the mystery of mysteries, or the holy of holies, God's being. Two things are going on here: Spark is bridging the modern chasm that she is so often concerned to identify between the supernatural and the natural as she has the godhead talked about in the most banal way. At the same time what is also recognised is the unknowable, the unnameable reality of the Almighty. Spark's Jewish background, of course, also provided her with a strong sense of this latter religious logic. As she herself said, 'the Roman Catholic faith corresponded to what I had always felt and known and believed: there was no blinding revelation in my case.'[9] Spark's Catholicism sometimes leaves critics sceptical of its validity as an expressed artistic context. Bryan Cheyette, for instance, claims, '[t]he problem with placing Spark in a tradition of Catholic writing – or any other monolithic tradition for that matter – is that she self-consciously resists such classifications'.[10] However, for Spark her Catholic faith is no mere set of easily followed dogma or any 'monolithic tradition'. It is an outlook that sees the world, whether physical or in terms of human action, as not entirely knowable or definable and it is informed by a belief related to this apprehension that God's grace (or purpose) is often ineffable. Cheyette is, though, entirely right that Spark resists 'classification' or essentialism in identity as we see in her short story title 'The Gentile Jewesses', which simultaneously asserts and undermines its narrator's Jewish identity. In this text, the central, narrating character claims her Jewishness through the orthodox mechanism of matrilineal transmission, while at the same time acknowledging that in pure terms neither she nor her mother can be Jewish since this female line, in being not 'wholly' Jewish, is transmitting a 'Gentile' identity. Identity in Spark's fiction is often hybrid, contradictory even, so that it can be difficult to define with any certainty and this reflects her Catholic outlook that life itself is rather wonderfully mysterious and humans should not presume to define it in very limiting ways.

Spark's most famous book, *The Prime of Miss Jean Brodie* (1961), about a Presbyterian central protagonist, is not simply a Catholic novel in its apparent critique of Calvinist teleology, especially the belief in predestination. Certainly in the first instance though, the novel continuously explodes what it takes to be Brodie's limited Calvinist-tinctured mind. Her pupil, Sandy Stranger, opines at one point, 'She [Brodie] thinks she is Providence [. . .] she thinks she is the God of Calvin, she sees the beginning and the end.' [11] Among other acts of believing herself to be in control of Providence, Brodie feels sure of executing a plan whereby her pupil Rose will be placed in the bed of her former lover, Teddy Lloyd, as a kind of substitute for her. Amidst such shocking circumstances, however,

> Sandy felt warmly towards Miss Brodie at those times when she saw how she was misled in her idea of Rose. It was then that Miss Brodie looked beautiful and fragile, just as dark heavy Edinburgh itself could suddenly be changed into a floating city when the light was a special pearly white and fell upon the gracefully fashioned streets. In the same way Miss Brodie's masterful features became clear and sweet to Sandy when viewed in the curious light of the woman's folly, and she never felt more affection for her in her later years than when she thought upon Miss Brodie as silly.[12]

What is registered here is the puniness of Brodie, her 'silliness' when compared, implicitly, to the potency of God and his control, and this also leads to a tender sympathy from Sandy for this 'fragile' human creature. Brodie's nefarious designs, defeated in the novel as Sandy subverts these by herself becoming Teddy's lover, are not to be used in definitive judgement, and not only because these are ultimately thwarted. This is a 'gracefully fashioned' world so that 'dark heavy Edinburgh' can 'suddenly be changed into a floating city'. The world is a place full of alternative possibilities and, in one sense, human evil is not to be taken too seriously or portentously in its singular moment. The supposed Calvinist view that time is already immutably written, that things cannot be changed and humans are set on courses from which they cannot deviate, is undermined. God's 'story' and ultimate judgement of humanity is that which counts and is that to which we do not have anything like full access. For believers, God's infinite mercy or forgiveness should not allow us to dwell too much in a horrified way upon sin. Free will brings the possibility of change, and anyway only God has access to the full inner sanctum of the conscience, or human motivation.

Sandy, as the most explicated point of judgement in *The Prime of Miss Jean Brodie*, is not entirely to be trusted in her condemnation of Miss Brodie. For a start, her methods of opposing her teacher are dubious, to say the least, as she seduces Lloyd not only to interfere with her mentor's plans but also, in a sense, to put herself in Brodie's preferred place. We are invited to consider Sandy's motivations as competitive, probably jealous, certainly in her behaviour with Lloyd, immoral. Indeed, we are allowed to read Sandy's sinister outsider signifying surname – Stranger – and her sibilant, serpentine moniker generally as somewhat demonic. In the Gospels of Luke and Mark, Christ's driving out of one or more demons into the Gadarene swine confirms a long-standing cultural association between pigs and the Devil. On a number of occasions we are told of Sandy's pig-like eyes, and her porcine activity is presented in her affair with Lloyd, where 'By the end of the year it happened that she quite lost interest in the man himself, but was deeply absorbed in his mind, from which she extracted among other things, his religion as a pith from a husk.' [13]

It is as though the duplicity of Brodie, who constantly creates untruthful new stories, who is herself clearly contradictory in her Scottishness as a character part-Mary Queen of Scots, part-John Knox, has transferred to Sandy in her set of deceitful relationships. Duplicity is quite precisely also here part of the biblical subtext of the passages on the Gadarene swine, in which Christ interrogates the identity of the demon possessing a man, to which it replies, 'My name is Legion for we are many.' If Brodie might be read in her dubiety as rather demonic for much of the novel (at the beginning of Chapter 3 we are told 'there were *legions* of her kind'),[14] it is as though the demon jumps into Sandy. However, following on from her scooping from his brain Lloyd's Catholic 'religion as a pith from a husk' we have a sudden change of metaphor where the perspective shoots from husks lying on the ground to the heavens. Her mind was full of his religion as a night sky is full of things visible and invisible. She left the man and took his religion and became a nun in the course of time.[15] Throughout Spark's *oeuvre* we find the characteristic Catholic gesture that good can come from evil, since God never allows the Devil definitively to win a soul before the hour of death. Here Sandy's adulterous relationship brings the unexpected bounty of a belief system to which, like her author, Spark, she converts. Paradoxically, it is her newly dawning Catholic religion that allows Sandy to read Brodie in less melodramatic fashion as rather 'silly' and to begin to extend towards her compassion as a 'fragile' human soul.

Also, we should be aware that in the same moment that Sandy is fixing on her teacher's perfidious Calvinist outlook, she is full of other, very different attempts to identify Brodie's faulty morality:

> And Sandy thought, too, the woman is an unconscious Lesbian. And many theories from the books of psychology categorized Miss Brodie, but failed to obliterate her image from the canvases of one-armed Teddy Lloyd.[16]

Clearly, Sandy at this point is flailing around, attempting to pin down a definition (Calvinism, lesbianism and 'many [other] theories') for her teacher's behaviour, though none of these will ultimately do. Brodie is not to be explained away, or out of Teddy Lloyd's recurrent realising of her form in his paintings ostensibly of other people. Sandy is both jealous of, and intrigued by, the love of Lloyd for Brodie. Brodie may at times be foolish, transparently lying, unpleasant, but she is loved (as much, perhaps, by Sandy as by the art master), and love is deeply mysterious as it transcends the individual.

Like love, human life generally (which Spark reads in orthodox Catholic fashion) is not to be gainsaid or simply defined by science or anthropology. We find a sly pointer to this again at the beginning of Chapter 3, where we are told that the woman of whom Miss Brodie was to some extent a type during the interwar years, among other things, 'preached the inventions of Marie Stopes'.[17] We ought to be aware of Spark's intense dislike for Stopes (1880–1958), pioneer of birth control, sexual libertarian and possibly an anti-Semite. Probably for all of these reasons, as well as a personal one, Spark despised Stopes. During the 1940s as editor of the *Poetry Review* Spark felt herself undermined by a number of old-fashioned individuals, including Stopes, for her promotion of new currents in verse. In *Curriculum Vitae* (1992) Spark comments acidly:

> One enraged reader who joined in the campaign of harassment against me was Dr Marie Stopes, the famous birth control expert – on that account much to be admired. She was absolutely opposed to my idea of poetry. Up to his death three years earlier she had been living with Lord Alfred Douglas, the fatal lover of Oscar Wilde, an arrangement which I imagine would satisfy any woman's craving for birth control. I met her at one of our meetings and knew she disliked me intensely on sight. I was young and pretty and she had totally succumbed to the law of gravity without attempting to do a thing about it.[18]

Spark's utterance here helps us make sense of the women 'preaching the inventions of Marie Stopes' as in the same scene in *Brodie* the disembodied voice of one such woman is heard pontificating to a grocer, "'I tell you this, Mr Geddes, birth control is the only answer to the problem of the working class. A free issue to every household . . .".'[19] Here, rather casually embedded in her narrative, we glimpse Spark's religious 'pro-life' sensibility. This is not simply to do with an orthodox Catholic opposition to birth control, though that is part of the story, but speaks of a larger fear. We should remember the novel is set in the context of the 1930s and that Brodie has a certain admiration for fascism and is loath after the war even to condemn Adolf Hitler. Programmatic, clinical direction of life (or of preventing it) is what Spark's unnamed woman, a disciple of Stopes, clearly is advocating and most especially for her social inferiors, 'the working class'. Arrogance, both political but especially spiritual (since God alone in Spark's religious outlook ought to channel life), is what Spark is attacking. The author has a famous and comically exploded litany of 'problems' from the perspective of the denizens of New York in *The Hothouse by the East River* (1973) who register over-anxiety to rationalise human dilemmas and their world into machine-like functionality. Problems from the human point of view, Sandy's disturbed contemplation of 'lesbianism' or the woman's smug identification of 'the problem of the working class', are rather like these New York misidentifications. 'The only problem', in the title of another of Spark's novels from 1984, at least in the eyes of the central character, Harvey Gotham, writing a monograph on the Book of Job, is the problem of suffering, or how to make sense of evil and discord in a world created by a supposedly benign creator. For Spark, one suspects, even 'the problem' of suffering is not much to be brooded over in the sense of wondering why it persists. Not a Manichean (heretics who saw good and evil as co-equal in mutual definition), Spark, operating from within the most orthodox Catholic epistemological traditions, nonetheless suggests that good and evil are constantly in collision and that humans never have an entirely absolute sense of these things. All that is certain is that both conditions pertain.

The case of the anarchist writer Nicholas Farringdon in *The Girls of Slender Means* (1963) casts some light on Spark's fictional resistance to any one-dimensional hagiography of good or, indeed, of evil. Two other characters discuss Farringdon:

> 'What has he written?'
> 'A book called *The Sabbath Notebooks*.'
> 'Is it religious?'
> 'Well, he calls it political philosophy. It's just a lot of notes and thoughts.'
> 'It smells religious. He will finish up as a reactionary Catholic, to obey the Pope.' [20]

Nicholas does indeed become a Catholic and is even martyred in Haiti as a member of a religious order. Is he, then, following and refining the religious instinct identified within him, albeit witheringly by the cynical character, or, in the implication of this same speaker, does he die merely trying out his latest idealistic fad? Farringdon's is one of two serious conversions to the Catholic life in Spark's fiction, the other being Sandy Stranger's. Her treatise for which she becomes famous is 'The Transfiguration of the Commonplace' with the clear implication that this has been inspired by the colourful, larger-than-life Jean Brodie over-brimming with stories and poetry. However, at the other extreme we view Sandy in the very final scene of the novel seeing the world not as a wonderful, potentially transfigured place, but as somewhere from which she is desperately trying to retreat within the confines of her convent cell: '"The Transfiguration of the Commonplace" [. . .] had brought so many visitors that Sandy clutched the bars of her grille more desperately than ever.'[21] Some readers are perhaps tempted to read Sandy 'clutching the bars' as merely symbolic imprisonment for her crime against Miss Brodie, but what is actually described here is the difficult process of 'unselfing' in the religious life, of divesting oneself of worldly concerns. The novel ends, then, with the options in the foreground: should humans engage imaginatively with the world, as Miss Brodie in a sense does, seeing it as a place in which to operate a creative imagination, or should they retreat from the world as undoubtedly a place of delusional human perspective? Either way, no complete satisfaction is to be found in this world.

Let us turn to a Spark short story, 'The Black Madonna' (1958), which helps us obtain some purchase on her apprehension of the Catholic experience of the world. It is a darkly comical text about grace which opens thus:

> When the Black Madonna was installed in the Church of the Sacred Heart the Bishop himself came to consecrate it. His long purple train was upheld by the two curliest of the choir. The day was favoured suddenly with thin October sunlight as he crossed the courtyard from the presbytery to the Church, as the procession followed him chanting the Litany of the Saints: five priests in vestments of white heavy silk interwoven with glinting threads, four lay officials with straight red robes, then the confraternities and the tangled columns of the Mothers' Union.[22]

Here all is ordered, though there are hints perhaps at something else less straight lying beneath the surface (we have things that are 'curliest', 'interwoven' and 'tangled'). The official Church is here in much of its pomp, but even its priestly protocols are not utterly definitive of the quality of religious experience to which it ministers. We understand this as childless, devout Roman Catholics Raymond and Lou Parker pray to the icon of the Black Madonna for a baby and, in a typically Sparkian manoeuvre of sinister humour, are rewarded with Lou giving birth to a black baby. Understandably, this leaves the couple open to gossip, not least because in their sense of Christian hospitality they have previously provided lodgings to Jamaicans working in the motor-car factory near where the Parkers live. Tests are done and the baby is found to be entirely legitimate, a 'throwback' to African blood in Lou's family. Unable to stand the social stigma, however, the Parkers have their baby adopted. Towards the end of the story an acquaintance, the uneducated and hideously incorrect Tina Farrell, comments, "'If that child was mine [. . .] I'd never part with her. I wish we could afford to adopt another. She's the loveliest little darkie in the world".' [23] One might well feel a modicum of sympathy for the Parkers as their prayers and their genuinely well-motivated social activism seem to have combined to play a horrible trick on them. The point, of course, is that God is testing the couple even as he bestows on them a gift which is perfect, except in the eyes of a mean-minded society. The Parkers fail their test, as many might, and reject God's grace. They conform to the standards of the world rather than to those of God, just as, conversely, Tina's political incorrectness might be frowned upon by the world, though she has wished the Parkers to do the moral thing of keeping the baby and clearly would follow this course herself if she were in their place, with all her disregard for social niceties. The story represents a version of one of Spark's frequently resorted to pieces of scripture, The Book of Job. The Parkers are genuinely trying to be good people and they do not deserve to be 'punished'. Like Job, however, they are visited by strife of a kind, though one that is not simple misfortune. However, the point is not that they have brought this upon themselves, but lies in how they respond to their 'misfortune', that is whether or not they can rise above a racist society. As with *The Prime of Miss Jean Brodie*, the paths of the world are crooked and moral certainty is difficult. This is because the world is a fallen place, but not as in the most puritanical forms of Christianity and other religions, belonging, therefore, to Satan. Rather, the imperfection in the human world is available so that humans might exercise their free will and choose good, however uncomfortable this might sometimes be. Even the imperfect state, then, is part of the Divine Economy where God allows full moral dignity, even if, as in the case of 'The Black Madonna' full worldly dignity would seemingly be denied to the Parkers if they chose this path. Such 'dignity', of course, is bought dearly at the cost of giving up a child in the face of society's false gossip.

Spark's manipulation of the novel form to make the anagogic point looms large throughout her *oeuvre*. In novels such as *The Prime of Miss Jean Brodie* and *The Girls of Slender Means* this involves flash forwards, or giving away later action, to take the reader outside chronological time and give a sense of a larger controlling hand. Here the narrator, perhaps even the author, is to be seen as a metaphor for God, with her panoptic view of past, present and future. Spark's most experimental period, however, is to be found in two formally claustrophobic novels, *The Driver's Seat* (1970) and *Not to Disturb* (1971). In the second of these the complete moral bankruptcy of a cast of characters predestines them to a tragic dénouement, and their unavoidable fate is dressed up in a relentlessly clichéd, but witty, gothic apparatus of character description and plot mechanics. Here we have an unnaturalistic scenario, humanity entirely denuded of the dignity of free will as a version, perhaps, of Hell. *The Driver's Seat*, though, is a much more telling novel, arguably the high point of Spark's career and the novel she herself regarded as her supreme achievement. Its central character, Lise, is a variation of Jean Brodie in that she similarly seeks to control, indeed fabricate, the story of her life and the parts in it of others around her. Lise, though, is a hyper-version of Brodie, stripped of Brodie's joy in life and attempting to set up the story of her own death as a murder so as to attain a dramatic and noticeable status which has previously been denied to her life. In orthodox Catholic terms, Lise is guilty of the sin of despair, having given up on life. She exercises a meticulous control of the empty props of her final days, going on holiday supposedly to meet a mysterious lover, leaving presents behind for nonexistent people and mounting various disturbed scenes, actually meaningless but contrived simply so that she will be remembered afterwards as the police attempt to reconstruct the events leading to her death. Having somehow identified a homicidal sexual pervert, Lise has him kill her with a weapon that she has provided. Only one detail remains outwith her control: 'I don't want any sex,' she shouts. 'You can have it afterwards. Tie my feet and kill, that's all. [. . .] All the same, he plunges into her, with the knife poised high.[24]

A thoroughly disturbing novel, *The Driver's Seat* presents a story that is almost entirely predetermined (by Lise) and so devoid of life, devoid of possibility. The one piece of contingency which she fails to control, her killer penetrating her sexually contrary to her instructions, represents a particularly bleak puncturing of the omnipotence of the individual human. This is the darkest moment in all of Spark's fiction. Is it the author, Spark even, as simulacrum of God reasserting control over the life of the lost soul, Lise? If it is, this would seem to be very far from a loving, compassionate God. One way to read this moment, theologically, is that God is attempting, in the final instance, to shake Lise out of her complacency, to rouse her perhaps to fight for her life rather than, as she originally intends, surrendering it.

Muriel Spark's practice as a Catholic novelist is to warn us against too readily judging the moral status of others. Her characters are sometimes presumptuous in their belief that they can read the moral nature of others, or that their constructed narratives of their own and other people's lives are properly definitive. A paradox pertains as Spark warns against consummate storytelling, but often provides this herself as a kind of warning against others doing the same. Ultimately, her Catholic practice is to acknowledge an omnipotent God, sometimes mimicked in the fabric of her novels by the narratorial or authorial character, whose implied perspective is supposed to overarch all human perspective. Suffering and evil are seen in her fiction, but these are also not to be simply acceded to, or seen as absolutely circum-scribing anyone. Spark's fiction allows a definitive version of this, arguably, in only one novel, the fictive exemplar of *Not to Disturb*. Even here and throughout her *oeuvre*, however, her message is Catholic in being relentlessly 'pro-life', where the message for the reader is never to believe that in the real world understanding of others or ourselves is ever fully ours, or that the larger presence of God can be dismissed. Complete and final meaning lies always beyond the ken of human beings and the life that He has engendered is to be loved, as unselfishly as we can.

CHAPTER EIGHT

Muriel Spark's Break with Romanticism

Paddy Lyons

I said I would have a look at the manuscript. I said that, after all, the advice of St Thomas Aquinas had been to rest one's judgement on what is said, not by whom it is said. 'So never mind the author. I'll look at the actual book.' [1]

Nancy Hawkins, the publisher's editor at the heart of *A Far Cry From Kensington* (1988), mobilises the support of a saint when she is faced with a book authored by Hector Bartlett, the odious *pisseur de copie* and the bane of her life. The medieval principle she calls on runs counter to mainline twentieth-century culture, but dethroning authorship was much called on by the century's novelists. 'Never trust the artist. Trust the tale,' D. H. Lawrence had proclaimed,[2] and resistance to the canonisation of authorship is recurrent in the fiction of Jorges Borges, Vladimir Nabokov, Samuel Beckett and Flann O'Brien. Doris Lessing produced two novels under the pseudonym Jane Somers: the secret of their authorship was carefully guarded, eventually giving her grounds to mock commentators who had shown themselves unable to read a book without a prior view of its author; and she remarked on the liberation gained through this abnegation of authorship: 'as Jane Somers I wrote in ways that Doris Lessing cannot'.[3] Throughout her novelistic career Muriel Spark too was lucidly opposed to the elevation of authorship as the linchpin of writing. By way of introduction to her autobiography, *Curriculum Vitae* (1992), she set out one single protocol: 'I determined to write nothing that cannot be supported by documentary evidence or by eyewitnesses.' [4] This is a defiance of popular opinion which would suppose autobiography to be a flowering of authorship, and a cornerstone in her consistent response to what Alain Badiou has usefully identified as a core dilemma for twentieth-century art: 'finding the means for a decisive break with romanticism'.[5]

In the early 1950s, while still hesitant about novel-writing, Spark made close studies of the lives and works of celebrated women writers of the romantic era: Mary Shelley, Dorothy Wordsworth and the Brontë sisters. The conclusion to her 1953 appraisal of Emily Brontë's biography argued that it was

Emily's distinctive embrace of authorship which brought about her inflexible refusal of help or medical care during her grim and painful death. By the time of her final illness, Spark observed, 'Emily had begun to dramatise, in her own person, the aspirations expressed in her work [and] saw herself, in the end as the hero and cult of her own writings.' [6] To understand this further, she proposed that Emily differed from her sisters in her capacity for love, tending towards a love not inclined to sexual union but to 'passionate and in many ways mystical unions'.[7] This mode of love involves, she explained, desire for an Absolute:

> Desire, either to possess or be possessed by, another of such nature, is not the motive of this type of union. Desire for the Absolute, which Emily possessed in passionate quantity, is seen as the motive.[8]

Before the publication of *Wuthering Heights*, this love was exercised through Emily's 'passionate friendship' with her sister Anne; but after the novel was published and won reviews, there arose for Emily

> a shift of apprehension of the Absolute; she shifted it from an objective to a sub-jective position. She became her own Absolute; so that she would be forced to expend passion, adoration, worship, contemplation, on herself – a destructive process, since sources of replenishment are not self-generated. Emily's inspira-tion would dry up; her whole being would be thrown into disorder.[9]

Propelling this argument is opposition to the Romantic embrace of author-ship; and, notably, it is for secular reasons that Spark identifies it as a pitfall to be avoided: what she diagnoses in Emily Brontë is a mode of grave self-harm, ruinous to an artist: 'inspiration would dry up'. Badiou's more generalised formulation of the difficult legacy left by Romanticism coincides with her response and introduces a further issue:

> [the Romantic] artist lifts subjectivity to the heights of the sublime by testifying that it possesses the power to mediate between reality and the Ideal. Just as the work is sacred, so too is the artist sublime.[10]

When a twentieth-century artist shuns the Romantic posture of sublimity, the stance of high priest, does it follow that the artwork follows suit, and settles for ordinariness and the everyday?

In her discussion of Mary Shelley's *Frankenstein*, Spark looked briefly towards another option, considering the form of the book as neither reduc-tive and everyday, nor elevated through Romantic gesturing towards the sacred. She proposes that underlying the novel is a pattern of movement based on pursuit which takes a seemingly impossible shape:

If we can visualise this pattern of pursuit as a sort of figure-of-eight macaberesque – executed by two partners moving with the virtuosity of skilled ice-skaters – we may see how the pattern takes shape in a movement of advance and retreat. Both partners are moving in opposite directions, yet one follows the other. At the crossing of the figure eight they all but collide . . . Once these crises are over, however, we find Frankenstein and the Monster moving apparently away from each other, but still prosecuting the course of their pattern . . . No collision occurs, and the pattern is completed only [when they] merge . . .[11]

Whereas Romanticism's usual allusions were towards an infinite located in some Beyond, this reading of *Frankenstein* proposes an infinity embodied in the book itself. The 'figure-of-eight macaberesque' replicates a traditional mathematical symbol, the figure eight on its side, which designates Infinity. The couple in movement approach each other as they separate from each other, and yet, however closely they come to intersecting, the pattern persists, 'no collision occurs'. Departure from Romanticism was complicated for twentieth-century artists, Badiou suggests, 'because the infinite is at stake', posing the dilemma 'How can art assume the compulsory finitude of its means while incorporating the infinity of Being?' [12] Imagining a book as somehow folded on itself provided a particularly literary answer and outlined for Spark one method for lifting art out of ordinariness, while steering clear of Romanticism's liking for endowing art with the aura of the sacred and the tones of religiosity. Such complicated literary structures were later to gain zest through her penchant for peopling them with performance artists, theatricalised so as to throw Romantic aspirations into satiric disarray.

Folds: the Book-within-the-Book

The Comforters (1957), Spark's first novel, addressed novelistic form by way of fiction and is unremittingly irreverent whenever the infinite is invoked. Deconsecration extends to the figure of the artist in the novel, Caroline Rose, who is troubled by a voice from beyond transmitting to her the narrative of her life, sometimes just after the event, sometimes predicting it; a voice that is quite certainly not numinous, being accompanied by a very finite clicking and tapping of typewriter keys. Evelyn Waugh, in his appreciative review of the novel, described it as follows, encapsulating it in psychological terms:

The area of Caroline's mind which is composing the novel becomes separated from the area which is participating in it, so that, hallucinated, she believes she is observant of, observed by, and in some degree under the control of, an unknown second person. In fact she is in the relation to herself of a fictitious character to a story-teller.[13]

Nonetheless, though the typewriter's clacking marks a clear break with any romanticised concept of the artist as channelling an infinite force for a finite universe, the overall construction makes this novel a strange and less straightforward experiment with form, which leaves even Waugh's brilliant formulation looking too neat and tidy.

The Comforters can most readily be described as akin to a Möbius strip, that odd and impossible geometric object which is formed from two surfaces that become one surface in such a way that neither inside nor outside remains distinct. Such are the paradoxical dimensions outlined in the course of gossip:

> Caroline is embroiled in a psychic allegory . . . I told you of her experience with the voices and the typewriter. Now she has developed the idea that these voices represent the thoughts of a disembodied novelist, if you follow, who is writing a book on his typewrite-r [sic]. Caroline is apparently a character in this book and so, my dears, am I.[14]

Narrated in the third person and almost entirely in the past tense, the first five chapters (which constitute Part One) slip and slide between the viewpoint of Laurence Manders, Caroline's boyfriend, and Caroline's. On each occasion when Caroline is troubled by the disembodied typewriter-accompanied voice, what she hears are sentences which have appeared as part of the narration of The Comforters. Towards the end of Chapter 5, she tells Laurence angrily:

> 'I won't be involved in this fictional plot if I can help it. In fact, I'd like to spoil it . . . I intend to stand aside and see if the novel has any real form apart from this artificial plot. I happen to be a Christian.' [15]

The car in which this conversation is taking place then crashes, both Laurence and Caroline are injured and hospitalised, and Caroline disappears. Part Two continues in the third person, dipping into more of the viewpoints of more of the cast, until midway through Chapter 7, when Caroline reappears, hearing from her hospital bed the typewriter ghost narrating parts of the plot that concern other people, in other places. As the novel's narrator gleefully underlines this strange turn, it is suddenly no longer possible to decide how far the narration is taking its viewpoint from Caroline:

> It is not easy to dispense with Caroline Rose. At this point in the tale she is confined in a hospital bed, and no experience of hers ought to be allowed to intrude. Unfortunately, she slept restlessly . . . Caroline among the sleepers turned her mind to the art of the novel, wondering and cogitating, those long hours, and exerting an undue, unreckoned, influence on the narrative from which she is supposed to be absent for a time.
>
> *Tap-tick-click. Caroline among the sleepers turned her mind to the art of the novel, wondering and cogitating, those long hours* . . .[16]

This is an extraordinary reversal, outside becoming inside as the commentary on Caroline is relayed and replayed as if it is what Caroline can hear, as if by some means a containing envelope can be enclosed within the letter it holds. The question this begs, though, is whether the trickiness marks more than a twentieth-century escape from the Romantic enshrinement of the artwork as a sacred object. Does its paradoxical shape give it reach towards an infinity or towards closure?

As a formal experiment, *The Comforters* can be read as building, albeit more tersely, on Marcel Proust's *À la recherche du temps perdu*, itself a novel much admired by Spark. Proust's novel presents itself as a book-within-the-book: by the end, it appears to be itself the triumphal and redeeming achievement of the would-be novelist whose life it has been chronicling. A similar device shapes Doris Lessing's *The Golden Notebook*, published in 1962, five years after *The Comforters*, also a novel centred on a blocked and troubled novelist, and also deploying a book-within-the-book schema, though differently: the outcome of the unusual structure of *The Golden Notebook* is release, *à la* Proust, in that the book itself ultimately emerges as a manifestation of the creative powers its protagonist has struggled to recover. By such means, Proust and Lessing dismantle and dismiss the Romantic glorification of the artist as bringing the reader in touch with an outside higher force, the understanding that belongs to an Infinite Absolute or Ideal. Instead, it turns out that the novelist has been caught in the act, that the reader has all along been privy to the movements of a creative process. Viewed though this lens, the structure of *The Comforters* can also be read as itself the manifestation of its protagonist's breakthrough, and thus achieving an outreach beyond its own finitude. In this sense, in Badiou's phrase, 'finite form can be equivalent to an infinite opening'.[17]

There are, however, grounds for an opposite reading, depending on the weight that is given to the final sentences of *The Comforters*, which point towards enclosure. The viewpoint at the ending is no longer Caroline's but that of Laurence, who writes her a letter and, instead of sending it, tears it into small pieces and casts it to the wind. The novel finishes:

> He saw the bits of paper come to rest, some on the scrubby ground, some among the deep marsh weeds, and one piece on a thorn-bush; and he did not then foresee his later wonder, with a curious rejoicing, how the letter had got into the book.[18]

For all its considerable elegance, it is fair to ask is this release or is it, rather, a celebration of closure and containment? Perhaps the question is one of relative tone, for although Spark was to return to the device of the book-within-the-book, she would later direct it more definitely towards enlargement and openness.

Performance Artists

Restless formal experimentation is the hallmark of the novels that followed, engineering fresh interrogations of authorship and of the book:

> With a novel you know the dialogue. It belongs to each character. But the narrative part – first or third person – belongs to a character as well. I have to decide what the author of the narrative is like. It's not me, it's a character.[19]

In fact, only her second novel, *Robinson* (1958), featured a narrator with a name. *Robinson* takes the form of a memoir, told by January Marlow of her time on a remote island, in such a fashion as to have her seem a not altogether reliable witness. From then on, until the 1980s, Spark's narrators were anonymous, but with traits tending to make them not exactly neutral, partial rather than all-knowing. For *The Ballad of Peckham Rye* (1960) she had drawn on an extreme device special to Ivy Compton-Burnett, employing a narrating voice that sees and reports while never attempting interpretation or understanding. But, more usually, her narrating voices were characterised by distinctive blind spots, by placed absence of explanatory information. Spectacular in this regard is *The Prime of Miss Jean Brodie* (1961): at no point does the narration ever render the thoughts or feelings of its magnetic central figure, Jean Brodie, whose vivid utterances are given, as if in a Compton-Burnett dialogue, without a commentary attributing to her any subjective elements. Jean Brodie is purely dramatic, a performance artist, with the immediacy and the fragility which that entails, presenting herself as she invents herself, her girls becoming the *crème de la crème* because and while she is their author and says that it is so. She is constructed on an entirely theatrical basis, and from this has followed her rich appeal for actresses, on stage and on screen. Nonetheless, to other figures in the novel an inner world of contemplation, speculation, division and uncertainty is attributed, and by this means the authorship and authority Miss Brodie takes for granted come under scrutiny:

> Sandy puzzled . . . and took counsel with Jenny, and it came to them both that Miss Brodie was making her new love story fit the old. Thereafter the two girls listened with double ears, and the rest of the class with single.
> Sandy was fascinated by this method of making patterns with facts, and was divided between her admiration for the technique and the pressing need to prove Miss Brodie guilty of misconduct . . .
> Sandy and Jenny completed the love correspondence between Miss Brodie and the singing-master at half-term . . . That intimacy had taken place was to be established. But not on an ordinary bed . . . They placed Miss Brodie on the lofty lion's back of Arthur's Seat, with only the sky for roof and bracken for a

bed . . . It was here that Gordon Lowther, shy and smiling, small, with a long body and short legs, his red-gold hair and moustache, found her.

'Took her,' Jenny had said when they had first talked it over.

'Took her – well, no. She gave herself to him.'

'She gave herself to him,' said Jenny, 'although she would fain have given herself to another.' [20]

Free indirect style here weaves into the narration the efforts and reflections of the little girls until they have hammered out their composition. Jay Presson Allen, the dramatist who made a Broadway hit from the novel, placed Sandy as the implicit narrator of her play, framing it in flashbacks from the nunnery where Sandy has become Sister Helena. However, in the novel the narration is designed quite otherwise, and from time to time deliberately views Sandy from the outside, unflatteringly, dwelling repeatedly on the size of Sandy's eyes – her small eyes, tiny eyes, short-sighted eyes, piggy eyes, narrow eyes in need of spectacles – as if to impute an ongoing poverty to Sandy's vision, a limitation of which Sandy herself could have no awareness. Like *The Comforters*, this novel ends on an image of enclosure, with Sandy clutching the grille in her convent which keeps the world at bay; but unless the novel is read as the product of Sandy's authorship, enclosure is not endorsed; rather, Sandy's attempts at containment – like those of the mean-minded headmistress, Miss Mackay – are mocked by their juxtaposition with Jean Brodie's reach towards expansiveness and possibility, at least while in her prime.

Through the 1960s this mixed method of narration served Spark well; alongside free indirect style she stitched in passages of blankness and rendered her anonymous narrating voices not omniscient, and thereby well cut off from any direct link to an Infinite. The narrator of *The Public Image* (1968) may know the plot, but is blank as to whether the resourcefulness that comes to Annabel is instinctual or consciously intelligent, as Annabel resists being framed as the cause of her scriptwriter husband Frederick's suicide. The novel ends by re-invoking an image that was part of Frederick's stage-management, his attempt to diminish Annabel. Know-all Frederick had summarised her reductively as no more than 'a beautiful shell, like something washed up on the sea-shore . . . empty, devoid of the life it once held'.[21] The ending transforms this image 'with a new vitality', as Peter Kemp remarks.[22] Annabel has escaped from the situation, feeling 'both free and unfree':

> She was pale as a shell. She did not wear her dark glasses. Nobody recognised her as she stood, having moved the baby to rest on her hip, conscious also of the baby in a sense weightlessly and perpetually within her, as an empty shell contains, by its very structure, the echo and harking image of former and former seas.[23]

Here the shell has become – like the form of this novel – paradoxical, at once containing 'by its very structure', while at the same time generating echoes that stretch out allusively towards multiple secularised infinities, 'former and former seas'.

In the 1970s, Spark departed from this combination style with which she had juggled the finite and the infinite through a mix of Compton-Burnett blankness and the free indirect mode. Taking her cue from the French *nouveau roman*, she adopted the present tense for a run of novels Peter Kemp has aptly grouped under the heading 'Tense Present'.[24] The first of these was *The Driver's Seat* (1970), its story interrogating its title, asking who is driving, querying from the outset the authoring of events. Between the narrating voice and the events it recounts an unbridgeable gap is maintained: everything is observed while nothing is comprehended, and the word 'seems' is recurrent. Narration in *The Driver's Seat* is proleptic, flash-forward passages telling how events will turn out before the route to their outcome has been described: Chapter 2 finishes with the main protagonist, Lise, on her way 'to the flight now boarding at Gate 14';[25] the next chapter begins in future perfect mode, with a complex sentence eventually whorling back to the present and the now:

> She will be found tomorrow morning dead from multiple stab-wounds, her wrists bound with a silk scarf and her ankles bound with a man's necktie, in the grounds of an empty villa, in a park of the foreign city to which she is travelling on the flight now boarding at Gate 14.[26]

Lise's gestures and behaviour are given in meticulous close-up; but the narration disowns comprehension so forcibly it becomes feasible to assume Lise is quite deliberately authoring her course towards this grisly ending:

> Lise is lifting the corners of her carefully packed things, as if in absent-minded accompaniment to some thought, who knows what? . . . She puts a little cross beside one of the small pictures which is described on the map as 'The Pavilion'. She then folds up the map and replaces it in the pamphlet which she then edges in her hand-bag . . . She puts the bunch of keys in her hand-bag, picks up the paperback book and goes out, locking the door behind her. Who knows her thoughts? Who can tell?[27]

Roland Barthes once remarked that the past tense (the preterite, the tense of completed action) is fundamental to narration because 'it presupposes a world which is constructed, elaborated, self-sufficient, reduced to significant lines, and not one which has been sent sprawling before us, for us to take or leave'.[28] The present-tense narration of *The Driver's Seat* proceeds as if in defiance of any such past-tense containment, refusing the finitude it would confer. Instead, the unknowing present tense produces Lise as like Miss Brodie, another performance artist, caught only in action, not defined by any thoughts or intentions, which are left for a reader to surmise.

There is no containment, no enclosure, not even in the ending. A brief exchange with his police captors has Lise's killer employing the past tense, the tense of causality and closure, to attribute authorship of her death to Lise: 'this one took me. She made me go. She was driving. I didn't want to go. It was only by chance that I met her.'[29] But thereupon the narration switches to the future tense and draws on shell imagery to render the future it speaks of imperfect, ongoing and unrelentingly repetitive: 'Round and round again will go the interrogators, moving slowly forward, always bearing the same questions like the whorling shell of a snail.'[30] Following this prediction, the narration returns to the present tense, and a blow-by-blow account of Lise's last moments of life ensues as she instructs her killer in the moves that bring about her death. This reads like a dark sex game gone awry, a syntax so twisted that 'no' could mean 'yes':

> 'I don't want any sex,' she shouts. 'You can have it afterwards. Tie my feet and kill, that's all. They will come and sweep it up in the morning.'
> All the same, he plunges into her, with the knife poised high.
> 'Kill me,' she says, and repeats it in four languages.
> As the knife descends to her throat she screams, evidently perceiving how final is finality. She screams and then her throat gurgles . . .[31]

The last paragraph of the book focuses again on the killer and his perceptions after the deed is done, adopting a free indirect style centred on a typewriter, in 'the sad little office where the police clank in and out and the typewriter ticks out his unnerving statement'.[32] The very last sentence is proleptic, as if the police typist is gesturing forwards:

> He sees already the gleaming buttons of the policemen's uniforms, hears the cold and the confiding, the hot and the barking voices, sees already the holsters and epaulets and all those trappings devised to protect them from the indecent exposure of fear and pity, pity and fear.[33]

Two different and discontinuous orders of finitude are juxtaposed: the killer's summary to the police; and Lise's final scream, the gurgle in her throat 'perceiving how final is finality'. To the last full stop there remains a gap between recording and the event recorded.

Commentary seeks to explain, to domesticate and to tame, and it cannot help but be caught off guard by such unfamiliar moves. Writing shortly after the novel's publication, Malcolm Bradbury sought to rationalise *The Driver's Seat*, labelling it as at once 'black humour' and macabre 'casuistry', both

religious and aesthetic, where 'a character who, at the start, seems the subordinated victim of writerly manipulation in a pre-ordained world suddenly
becomes, by virtue of the maximation of the greatest risks she can take, a
consort of the writer herself and hence an ironically free agent'.[34] Twenty
years later, this line still held some appeal for Lorna Sage: 'Spark's concerns
are with literary theology, and the way contemporary life looks from the
improbable perspective of Almighty irony.' [35] Yet corralling *The Driver's Seat*
within a theological twist was a facile way to blunt its dangerousness, tidying
it away into a drawer marked 'oddities'; and Sage then launched towards
another mode of reading, placing *The Driver's Seat* as a genre piece with
fiction of its decade, alongside victimology novels of the early 1970s such
as Judith Rossner's *Looking for Mr Goodbar* and Joyce Carol Oates' *Do With
Me What You Will*, in which the victim-heroine is revealed as the perpetrator of her own destruction. This can readily extend to marking *The Driver's
Seat* as a version of those well-known anticipatory mechanisms of defence
whereby the worst is envisaged in detail so that when it occurs it has already
happened, a move that allows the victim of assault at least the mental solace
of not being ambushed and overwhelmed by surprise; and further, exploring
how indulging such moves risks becoming predictive, how taking possession
of destruction may even bring about in all its awfulness the very event it seeks
to contain. But it is feasible too, and maybe more feelingful, to consider the
narration as coming from that police typewriter, and thereby dramatising
whatever crude voices have pronounced smugly that women who suffer rape
are somehow 'asking for it'. In this reading the novel becomes a Brechtian
outcry, angry protest drawing its resonance from Lise's final scream.

Just as *The Driver's Seat* can take its cue from the police typewriter that
appears in the last pages, so too can *The Abbess of Crewe* (1974) be read as
an emanation of the recording devices that feature inside it so ubiquitously.
Again, narration is in the present tense, with even the flashback chapters
recounted in the present, as if all is on a current and immediate level. Like a
shell, it loops and whorls upon itself. At first, the high-octane opening sentence is memorable for its sharply modulated phrasing:

> 'What is wrong, Sister Winifrede', says the Abbess, clear and loud to the
> receptive air, 'with the traditional keyhole method?'[36] But later, much later,
> when it is patent that the air is receptive because the convent is bugged
> and the Abbess has been summoned to Rome to answer for this, the first
> sentence returns, looping back as the Abbess proclaims loftily to her cronies
> Mildred and Walburga how the very tapes she has commissioned absolve her
> of blame:

> 'There is one particular tape in which I prove my innocence of the bugging
> itself. I am walking with Winifrede under the poplars discussing the disguising

and ensconcing as early as last summer. It is the tape that begins with the question, "What is wrong, Sister Winifrede, with the traditional keyhole method . . .?" I replayed and rearranged it the other day, making believe the moon is green cheese with Winifrede's stupid reply which I rightly forget. It is very suitable evidence to present to Rome, if necessary. Sister Winifrede is in it up to the neck.' [37]

This declaration of her powers of authorship to command meaning puts the Abbess on a par with previous would-be authors, with Jean Brodie at her most outrageous and Lise at her most determinedly perverse. It introduces too a desacralisation of the very text the reader is reading, insinuating that the book is inside itself, that the damningly hilarious exposé of Alexandra's nefarious activities is at one and the same time *her* revised edition of reality on terms she deems favourable to herself, that her narcissism is so advanced it renders her most appalling intrigues radiant and glorious to her. Her instructions in the novel's second last paragraph – 'for the selection and orchestration of the transcripts of her tape-recordings' – both query and confirm that this may be so. The novel bulges with poetry, whereas her orders are to 'Remove the verses that I have uttered';[38] but the novel's cover carries the same title she calls for: 'entitle the whole compilation *The Abbess of Crewe*'.[39] The issue stays open as to whether the present tense here is ultimately that of the tape turning, playing and looping as if every old word is once more new and of the now.

Alexandra's primary dedication is to authorship, to realising what she takes is her own destiny, and this is presented with none of the doubt that arises from the fissure between the narration and its object dominant in *The Driver's Seat*. When facts present her with difficulties, she turns unhesitatingly to imagination and invention:

'Think up your best scenarios, Sisters.'
'What are scenarios?' says Winifrede.
'They are an art-form', says the Abbess of Crewe.[40]

Like Lise and Jean Brodie, the Abbess is known to readers only through her gestures, actions and words; there is no delving into inner speculation or hesitant uncertainty: in private moments she recites well-known verses from the English poets, their cadences blanking out any subjective stirrings. This is a stratagem from spy school, a mechanism whereby not to twitch when wired up to a machine that can detect fluctuations between truth and untruth. Alexandra remains a performer, mesmeric on a grand scale, and with this the narration is wholly in comfortable accord. It applauds her. John Updike observed that it 'dotes' on her. The narration not only echoes and amplifies the Abbess's opinions, it does so in tones of uncritical adoration that mimic her fondness for multiplying a phrase, spiralling just as she does, as for instance in its mockery of Sister Winifrede:

> her whine of bewilderment, that voice of the very stupid, the mind where no dawn breaks . . . Winifrede, land of the midnight sun . . . Winifrede in dark naivety . . . Winifrede the absolute clot.[41]

This coincidence between the idioms of the Abbess and the alarmingly excessive adulation of the narrating voice puts authorship under interrogation at every level. Yet, whether the narrator is picturing the Abbess's attire so as to elevate her to an iconic level or the Abbess herself is admiring the Machiavellian cunning of her verbal intrigues, the present tense suggests all this is on a par, ongoing and familiar, accepted as how things are. The effect is to propose the Abbess as a metonym for power and government today, mistress of spin, with the Infant of Prague safe in the bank, bejewelled with the dowries of all of the sisters, a nest egg just in case luck should leave her. The immediacy of the present tense is an assault on the finitude of contemporary comfort zones, opening up instead an infinity of implications: what if power manipulations like those of the Abbess already rule our world today?

In Spark's later fiction the postulates of Romanticism continue to be reversed, and the nineteenth century's comfortable notions as to what a book is are turned inside out even further. Fleur Talbot, the novelist-narrator of *Loitering with Intent* (1981), recurrently imagines her first novel, *Warrender Chase*, as somehow magical, somehow predicting events that will befall those who come in contact with it. But the joke is on Fleur: to recover her manuscript and bring *Warrender Chase* into publication, she relies on theft and blackmail, which expose to her how her book-within-the-book had been taken as a bag of tricks and was being put to use by the psychological bully who had stolen it. Like Jane Eyre, the arch-romantic heroine and narrator of her own life story, the tale told by Nancy Hawkins, the narrator of *A Far Cry from Kensington* (1988), is that of her entry into lasting love. Nancy, like Jane Eyre, in the end is announcing: 'Reader, I married him.' But, unlike Jane Eyre, Nancy is no missionary: she interrupts herself with practical advice, nothing numinous, just handy hints on dieting and on bananas as a cure for rheumatism. Narrating is not triumphal but rather is a way to unravel the finitudes and closures of a bustling secular world that block vision, and to reproach herself: 'we were all too busy with the foreground of our lives to notice what was happening to Wanda.' [42] Nancy's excavations of the past are as likely to awaken grief as comedy – and not redemption:

> I regretted I had ever thought ill of Mabel, or treated her like the nuisance she had been. Oh Mabel, come back; come back, Mabel, and persecute me again.[43]

Particularly moving is Nancy's remembrance of moments of secular tenderness in the early days of her romance with William, in which she retells anonymous stories:

> He could analyse Shostakovich and Bartók. He quoted Schopenhauer. But he didn't know Humpty Dumpty, Little Miss Muffet, the Three Bears, Red Riding Hood. He knew the story of Cinderella only through Rossini's opera. And all that sweet lyricism of our Anglo-Saxon childhood, a whole culture with rings on its fingers and bells on its toes, had been lost to him in that infancy of slums and smelly drains, rats and pawnshops, street prostitutes, curses, rags and hacking coughs, freezing bare feet and no Prince Charmings, which had still been the lot of the really poor in the years between the first and second world wars. I had never before realized how the very poor people of the cities had inevitably been deprived of their own simple folklore of childhood. At night, I used to sing nursery rhymes to William. I told him fairy stories. Occasionally one of them would vaguely recall to his mind something he had heard before, somewhere along the line. But most of them were quite new to him. They were part of our love affair.[44]

Romanticism had drawn on elaborate and learned culture for the enlargement of its world – Keats looking into Chapman's Homer, for instance. Nancy has read the Brontës and Proust, but with William in her arms she identifies another finitude ('the very poor people of the cities . . . deprived') and mobilises simple, authorless folklore to make unbookish, unsacred love, seductively dissolving those boundaries. And in this she is Spark in miniature, addressing the twentieth century, and doing so not burdened by the lumber of Romanticism that too often bedevilled other writers of her times.

CHAPTER NINE

The Postwar Contexts of Spark's Writing

Randall Stevenson

'God', the old joke suggests, 'seems to be a novelist, and on the whole a realist.' Joking apart, twentieth-century fiction contains several comparisons of authors' relations to their creations with those of the deity to his universe – often as a way of questioning tactics of realism or omniscient narration, or the nature of free will. Muriel Spark's patron and fellow Catholic Graham Greene, for example, speculates in *The End of the Affair* (1951) about ways human beings must be 'pushed around . . . we are inextricably bound to the plot, and wearily God forces us, here and there, according to his intention, characters without poetry, without free will'. Greene's narrator, Bendrix, is pushed around particularly disturbingly by God's 'improbabilities' and by the radically different version of events he discovers in his lover Sarah's religiously-oriented diaries. A novelist himself, Bendrix is forced in the end to consider whether his 'realism has been at fault all these years'.[1] The life he envisages and the realities his work represents may be controlled not, as he has supposed, by his own will and perception, but by transcendent, supernatural agency – almost literally, by a more powerful author.

Concerns of this kind are returned to regularly in Spark's writing, and discussion of them can shed light on both her own imagination and the mid-twentieth-century context in which it developed. They may even have played a part in her move into the novel genre in the first place, which occurred fairly late in her writing career, soon after her conversion to Catholicism in 1954. The protagonist of her first novel, *The Comforters* (1957), Caroline Rose, is also a recent convert, finding 'the demands of the Christian religion . . . exorbitant, they are outrageous'.[2] This outrage extends into – or genuinely derives from – the sound of voices and typing, which Caroline construes as 'a writer on another plane of existence [. . .] writing a story about us [. . .] an attempt being made to organise our lives into a convenient slick plot' (63, 104). Caroline's own literary-critical intelligence and her 'work on the structure of the modern novel' (167) ideally might have equipped her to resist or escape the imposition of this story on her life. Yet despite determined initiatives to 'hold up the action of the novel' and to continue 'asserting free will', her attempts to escape the 'slick plot' prove fruitless (97, 105). Readers likewise can hardly escape the conclusion that Caroline's intuitions are correct. She obviously is a character in a novel, less than fully equipped with personal will. This position is confirmed by comments Spark makes, apparently in her own voice as author, speaking from 'another plane of existence' about her fiction and the mechanics of its creation. Teasingly explicit relations of this kind between author, character and plot may have provided a convenient analogue for Spark's own encounter with the will of God following her conversion, and the consequent experience, like Caroline's, of her 'mind [. . .] working under the pressure of someone else's necessity' (103). Moving away from her earlier work in poetry and the short story, Spark may have found in the longer form of the novel a more appropriate vehicle for exploring forces controlling an individual's destiny and the unfolding of personal life in time.

Alongside its metaphysical concerns, *The Comforters* is on one level simply a novel – like one Caroline herself contemplates writing – about 'characters in a novel', and about the novel itself (202). Spark's début shares in this way in the manner of the *nouveau roman* popular in France at the time, or the postmodern, self-questioning idiom more firmly in evidence in Britain a decade or so later in the work of John Fowles, B. S. Johnson or Spark's friend Christine Brooke-Rose. This idiom did not reappear fully in her own work until *The Driver's Seat* (1970). As the title suggests, free will and control are once again central issues in this novel, which shows another character seeking autonomy and a destiny independent of authorial intentions. In the later 1950s and 1960s, though, and to an extent beyond, Spark's fiction con-tinued to explore comparable tropes and interests, rarely far from those of *The Comforters* and *The Driver's Seat*. Though concerned less explicitly with gods, authors and their relations with characters' free will, much of Spark's writing continues to show the supernatural entering into the quotidian or hints at other 'planes of existence' that may sinisterly influence the immediate one. Mysterious phone calls in *Memento Mori* (1959) may emanate from Death himself. The shady psychic in *The Bachelors* (1960) seems to some characters to be genuinely in contact with the beyond. The protagonist of *The Ballad of Peckham Rye* (1960) may be a devil who has renounced his horns, while retaining a wish to 'wander through the world for the ruin of souls'.[3]

Rather than worrying, like Bendrix, about how improbabilities encounter the everyday, Spark's writing in these novels remains realistic but conven-iently porous, communicating in convincing detail the dreary atmosphere of postwar London, but also opening up brief hints or glimpses of other worlds beyond it. Means of departing from everyday life and its constraints, through narrow apertures or mysterious passages, even figure explicitly as a repeated theme in her early fiction. This appears in the skylight escape hatch in *The Girls of Slender Means* (1963), 'the narrow Mandelbaum Gate' in the novel of that name,[4] the subterranean secret passages in *Robinson* (1958) and the tunnel that strangely assists the central character's hasty retreat in *The Ballad of Peckham Rye*. At times involving hellish fires, whiffs of sulphur or dismembered bones, these episodes suggest descent into or escape from various kinds of underworld. Other novels practise changes of level and suggest escape or transcendence in another way: by means of textual metalepsis, the transgression of established 'narrative levels' or 'planes of existence' defined by Brian McHale, employing Gérard Genette's narrative theory, in his influential critical study *Postmodernist Fiction* (1987).[5] Throughout much of *Robinson*, for example, the remote location of the characters' adventures seems real enough to them. Yet it turns out perhaps to have been no more than 'an apocryphal island', an 'island as a place of the mind' or an extension of the 'dead woman's dream' the narrator fears she may be experiencing following the plane crash that begins the novel.[6] *The Hothouse by the East River* (1973) likewise offers a reorientation of most of its action, similarly recast in its closing pages as something close to a dream. And in *Loitering with Intent* (1981), the narrator and other characters find the supposedly real world they inhabit conforming more and more to versions of it they reproduce in their writing, until reality scarcely seems to exist independently of fictional or biographical versions of it. Spark, in other words, is a writer for whom religious or metaphysical interests regularly interrelate with, and are reinforced by, metafictional or metaleptic tactics. Such tactics ensure that, even when not explicitly the novel's subject, issues of authority, authorship and the control of worlds, fictional or real, inescapably figure among the interests of her writing.

Spark's most celebrated negotiation of these issues appears in her most enduringly popular novel, *The Prime of Miss Jean Brodie* (1961), also one of her least unconventional. The only unorthodox tactic much employed is frequent prolepsis, replacing the metalepsis and metafiction of other novels. Its use adds substance to the judgement that Jean Brodie 'thinks she is the God of Calvin, she sees the beginning and the end'.[7] Almost divine powers and influences are confirmed by regular glimpses of the future and of the various 'ends' of her pupils – in particular, the death in a hotel fire of a character whose fatal bewilderment may well result from her teacher's convincing her of her clumsiness and stupidity. Yet Brodie's powers are examined not so much as those of a god, or even a teacher, but as ones particularly appropriate to an artist or writer. Whereas *The Comforters* may have used artistic control as a figuration of irresistible divine will, *The Prime of Miss Jean Brodie* is more interested in artistic creation itself, and in its imposition of order and pattern on a recalcitrant reality. Brodie's tactics are essentially novelistic, dependent on 'making patterns with facts', then ensuring that the personalities of her 'Brodie set' are forced as far as possible to conform to her designs on them (72).

Vision and manipulations of this kind are also practised extensively by other characters, including the art master Teddy Lloyd, whose portraits of members of the Brodie set invariably, startlingly, resemble Brodie herself. The other principal visionary is Sandy Stranger, as adept as her teacher at weaving narratives around herself and moved towards 'betraying' her when she begins to realise that they are engaged in direct competition. This is partly sexual, as each has an interest in Lloyd, and partly religious – Brodie's talents for fabrication eventually running counter to Sandy's penchant for 'moral perception' (35). But it is also partly narratological: a struggle to see who can shape reality most adroitly around her visions and versions of it. Any victory of Sandy's seems Pyrrhic at best. Though she acquires some disciples of her own, for her work on 'The Transfiguration of the Commonplace', Sandy addresses them only while desperately clutching the grille on the door of her nun's cell.

That concluding image, and repeated references to Sandy's 'abnormally small eyes', suggest her attempts to resist Brodie are as presumptuous or procrustean as the teacher's visions themselves – ones that Sandy herself later realises do have some 'beneficent and enlarging effects' (124, 86). *The Prime of Miss Jean Brodie* offers in this way very equivocal suggestions about the ethics and 'moral perception' involved in art and imagination. These may once again reflect the thinking of a recently converted writer: at any rate, they have clear implications about the nature of literary art in general and about Spark's own writing in particular. As Valerie Shaw suggests, 'all of Spark's fiction certainly displays a fascination with authority of diverse kinds and forms'. Such fascination is especially appropriate to a novelist who is unusually aloof, satirical and superior throughout her fiction: 'high-handed [. . .] both with her readers and her characters', as Malcolm Bradbury suggests.[8] Of all later twentieth-century British novelists, it is probably the high-handed Spark who brings omniscient narrative into closest alignment with old faiths in an omniscient God.

Critics, of course, have long recognised what Dominic Head describes as 'Spark's preoccupation with the authority wielded by the author of a fiction, presuming to play God'.[9] The above discussion scarcely leads to new conclusions, unless through the issue of conversion and the analogy of Spark's work with Graham Greene's. This suggests that the religious convert might be faced with many challenges, but at the same time is equipped with specific narrative opportunities. As Brian Cheyette reflects, in recognising Spark's 'abiding doubleness', conversion may contribute to 'an interpretative act which perceives one world through the eyes of another [. . .] a form of heterodoxy which endlessly multiplies official discourse'.[10] Converts may be uniquely placed to envisage, simultaneously, the commonplace, immediate texture of life, alongside transfigured versions of it. This may facilitate the regular metalepses and encounters with the supernatural, discussed above in Spark's work, or the juxtaposition of radically different versions of the world which Greene achieves in *The End of the Affair* through the inclusion of Sarah's diaries.

Spark's 'preoccupation with authority' does take on further and more far-reaching implications, though, when considered not only in religious or literary-critical terms, but also alongside the work of her contemporaries, and in its historical and political context. Sandy's – and the reader's – scepticism of Brodie is after all not solely for religious, ethical or aesthetic reasons. It is principally on the straightforward political grounds that Brodie is 'a born Fascist' (125). Sandy's betrayal of her teacher is eventually made inevitable when she realises that Brodie is responsible for encouraging another pupil, with fatal consequences, to fight for Franco's fascist forces in Spain. Brodie tours Hitler's Germany and Austria as late as the summer of 1938, after earlier visiting fascist Italy in the same admiring spirit. Such allegiances contribute to a moulding of her pupils into a 'set' naturally enough described as 'Miss Brodie's fascisti' (31). Spark's central character, in other words, employs extreme forms of authority, and rigorously imposes patterns of behaviour on others, in ways strongly identified not only with artistic practice, but with the dictatorial, regimenting tactics of fascism.

That such concerns should figure so centrally in a novel published in 1961 (though set in the years on either side of the war) might seem surprising. Might not the threat of fascism have faded from imagination by then? Yet the timing of Spark's novel is both consistent with wider movements in contemporary historical awareness and indicative of her particular relations with them. Revulsion at fascism and the monstrosities it had wrought could scarcely be exhausted in 1945 or the years immediately afterwards. Rather, it extended strongly through British writing for at least a quarter of a century, sometimes appearing more powerfully later than it did at the end of the 1940s. The exhaustion generated by the war tended if anything to postpone imaginative assimilation of what Ted Hughes describes as its 'colossal negative revelation'. As he suggests, there prevailed in the years immediately following a 'post-war mood of having had enough [. . .] enough of the dark gods'.[11] Spark's narrator in *A Far Cry from Kensington* (1988) confirms that this mood extended into the 1950s, when the novel is set, when she describes as 'uncontemplatable' events which 'had blackened the previous decade'.[12] Some of the darkest experience of the war remained 'uncontemplatsble', or suppressed in the collective psyche, until the early 1960s, released again at that time by the Israelis' capture, trial and execution of the senior SS Holocaust administrator Adolf Eichmann in 1960–2. This ensured that fascism and its consequences once again entered general discussion and awareness, probably more fully even than they had during the Nuremberg trials at the end of the war. As Elaine

Feinstein suggests in her novel *The Survivors* (1982), people 'had read the newspapers after the war [. . .] knew the facts . . . had seen the photographs'. Yet in reporting the Eichmann trial in 1961, 'every day, the newsprint in *The Times* brought the truth into . . . consciousness in a new way', communicating 'as if for the first time what had been done to the Jews of Europe'.[13]

Spark herself attended the Eichmann trial, and its vivid, troubling entry into her consciousness is manifest in *The Mandelbaum Gate* (1965). Characters find the paraphernalia of Nazi nomenclature – '*Sturmbannführer, Obersturmbannführer, Superobersturmbannführer*' (18) – sinisterly recalled at the time, and the novel's central figure, Barbara Vaughan, visiting Jerusalem, is brought close to the trial through the work of her cousin, a lawyer earlier involved at Nuremberg. Her experience of it occurs after 'the impassioned evidence from survivors of the death-camps was over', but in time to endure something almost worse. This is the 'dull phase [. . .] in reality the desperate heart of the trial' in which Eichmann delivers his numbed, automatic, almost meaningless responses to cross-examination:

> Minute by minute throughout the hours the prisoner discoursed on the massacre without mentioning the word, covering all aspects of every question addressed to him with the meticulous undiscriminating reflex of a computing machine. Barbara turned the switch of her earphones to other simultaneous translations – French, Italian, then back to English. What was he talking about? The effect was the same in any language, and the terrible paradox remained, and the actual discourse was a dead mechanical tick, while its subject, the massacre, was living. (177)

Such experiences of the trial Barbara finds 'had rolled away the stone that revealed an empty hole in the earth, that led to a bottomless pit' (283).

Spark is one of a few British novelists to describe the Eichmann trial directly, but there were many others during the 1960s who took up its implications, or those of fascism and the Holocaust more generally. Iris Murdoch is one of these and also, like Spark, is regularly concerned in her work with matters of artistic vision and the god-like roles assumed by authors and artists. 'We have not recovered from two wars and the experience of Hitler,' Murdoch remarked in 1961, adding, 'it is curious that modern literature [. . .] contains so few convincing pictures of evil . . . in spite of Hitler.'[14] Murdoch provides one such picture herself in *A Fairly Honourable Defeat* (1970), focused on a survivor of the concentration camps who consider himself an artist and whose malign powers seem magical or god-like to other characters. Could it then be said, as Spark and Murdoch suggest, that postwar British writers found a whiff of remembered fascism tainting not only authority, but also authorship, or art generally – committed, after all, in their own way, to decisive imposition of pattern and order on the world?

Only to an extent. Interests in power and artistic control shape much of Murdoch's writing, but are seldom connected explicitly to memories of fascism. Spark remained interested in the war and its deathly aftermath as late as *The Hothouse by the East River*, but after *The Prime of Miss Jean Brodie* and *The Mandelbaum Gate* generally moved away from explicit mention of fascism or the Holocaust. Explanations for suspicion of artist-figures, and for the authorial self-scrutiny which extends from it, therefore need to look further than straightforward analogies between artistic ordering and the dictatorial authority of fascism, yet probably not much further. An inevitably disturbing reflection for writers and artists in the later twentieth century was that, even if artistic powers might be innocent of complicity or analogy with fascism, they had proved singularly unable to resist the ravages the latter had wrought on recent history. Resulting crises of confidence influenced the period generally, with an uneasy attitude to artist-figures symptomatic of wider views of art and writing after the Second World War radically different from those prevailing in the decade or so after the First World War.

At that time, modernist fiction generally affirmed the ameliorative, transcendent powers of art and vision, emphasised, for example, by the ending of Virginia Woolf's *To the Lighthouse* (1927). This does little to console characters for the grief and loss of the Great War or to resolve the novel's plot or action. Mr Ramsay reaches the lighthouse, but it has 'become almost invisible, had melted away into a blue haze'. Woolf's last paragraph concentrates instead on the artist Lily Briscoe's final brushstroke: a 'line there, in the centre' completing her painting and making her 'vision', as she calls it, congruent as well as coterminous with the tripartite novel in which she appears. Both Lily's conviction that a painter's brush is 'the one dependable thing in a world of strife, ruin, chaos' and the novel's self-reflexive ending are of a kind which figures much more widely in modernist writing.[15] The chaos or nightmare T. S. Eliot and others feared in contemporary history during the 1920s still seemed containable within the kind of transcendent orders produced by Lily, or by Elstir, Vinteuil and Bergotte – painter, composer, novelist – in Marcel Proust's *À la recherche du temps perdu* (1913–27).

Some of this possibility continued to seem open even during the war, though it scarcely survived its end. In Joyce Cary's wartime trilogy *Herself Surprised, To be a Pilgrim* and *The Horse's Mouth* (1941–4), the central figure is as much rogue as artist. Yet his shortcomings if anything emphasise modernist faiths that art can transcend both the world it surveys and even the intelligence that produces it. Such confidence is reversed in two outstanding novels of the immediately postwar years, one from each of the principal combatant nations – Thomas Mann's *Doctor Faustus* and Malcolm Lowry's *Under the Volcano*, both published in 1947. The protagonist of the former is a composer very different from Proust's Vinteuil, one who, at least in his own unstable estimation, and perhaps literally, has sold his soul to the Devil in return for genius required for musical achievements. Spanning the first decades of the twentieth century, Mann's narrative shows the character and spirit of the German nation comparably led towards insanity and destruction by a Faustian pact of its own, with the dark powers of fascism. Though the principal abuse of 'spirits' in Lowry's novel is through alcoholism, its central figure, Firmin, appears equally Faustian. This is emphasised by frequent references to versions of the Faust legend and by Firmin's possible responsibility for the hellish, Holocaust-like incineration of German officers during the First World War. But it is confirmed above all by his implacable descent towards darkness and destruction while in full knowledge of what might be supposed sources of light. Throughout, Firmin's hectic consciousness is shown to be saturated not only with alcohol, but with unusually comprehensive knowledge of centuries of European art and writing. None of it avails to restrain his self-annihilation – itself an image, Lowry suggests, for the wider self-destruction of the world in the war. Art's ineffectiveness is further highlighted by a range of creative figures almost as wide as Proust's. One of Firmin's friends has 'made great films [. . .] so far as he knew they had not changed the world in the slightest'. His half-brother Hugh considers equally futile his own attempts, as a journalist, at 'persuading the world not to cut its throat for half a decade or more'.[16]

Stephen Spender suggested in the 1940s that the war and fascism showed that 'the angels and the demons of an earlier time, have simply been suppressed in our consciousness'.[17] Lowry's work, and Mann's, incidentally confirm Spender's conclusion, indicating angels and demons, along with an attendant range of moral issues, once again returning regularly to writers' attention. They strongly retained this attention in writing in succeeding years – in Spark's novels a decade or more later and in the work of contemporaries also emerging in the 1950s, notably William Golding, as well as Murdoch. The suggestion of art's impotence to resist darker forces – or, worse, its possible complicity with demonic energy – marks an equally decisive shift in contemporary imagination. Such a change from the views of the 1920s suggests that the term 'anti-modernist' might appropriately be applied to the art and writing concerned, at any rate if 'postmodernist' had not generally, over recent decades, been widely adopted instead. Since it has achieved such widespread currency – though rarely a very confident definition – it may as well be employed here. It has the advantage of allowing, in most understandings of the term, a wide range of later twentieth-century thought and imagination to be considered extending scepticisms so far identified mainly in relation to art. 'Postmodernist', moreover, is a self-definition Spark was tentatively prepared to accept for her work, though – typically perhaps – somehow taking the term to refer to 'another dimension [. . .] supernatural'.[18] There is scope for views of the postmodern context of her writing that are more productive than those suggested by Spark herself, or indeed by many of her critics.

For most analysts, the late twentieth-century's postmodern phase was marked by radical scepticism about *all* the achievements and devices of intellect and reason; about all the bases on which progress and modernity had advanced since the eighteenth-century Enlightenment. Directed towards far more than the ways the artistic imagination embraces the world, such scepticism followed Nietzschean philosophy in questioning whether intellect could in any way validly encounter a reality external to itself. Significantly for literature and writing, it also questioned how far, if at all, language could reliably mediate any such encounter. Spark's work is particularly indicative in relation to this issue. The scene, quoted earlier, in which Barbara overhears Eichmann's interminable, vacuous testimony highlights the historical origins of the postmodern outlook in the 'colossal negative revelation' of the war. Whatever other philosophic or epistemic issues may have contributed to postmodern scepticism, the scene emphasises how far the monstrosity of twentieth-century history was itself responsible for overwhelming any language that might have been relied on to represent it, or any reasonable intelligence that could be directed on it. As a consequence of two wars, the experience of Hitler and the deadly bureaucracy they helped generate, words thin and pale into emptiness: the 'dead mechanical click' of the computing machine, annihilating differences between languages and ultimately the representative power of language itself. Among contemporary British novelists, probably only John Fowles is as direct in registering this failing of language in the face of twentieth-century history, when in *The Magus* (1966) his hero – another victim of quasi-artistic 'god-games' – considers the ways

> Words had lost their power, either for good or for evil; still hung, like a mist, over the reality of action, distorting, misleading, castrating; but at least since Hitler and Hiroshima they were seen to be a mist, a flimsy superstructure.
> (190)

In *The Mandelbaum Gate* Barbara's encounter with this evacuated language has a further, literary-historical resonance when she concludes that 'it all feels like a familiar dream' and goes on to describe this feeling as 'one that the anti-novelists induce [. . .] the new French writers' (177). Though the term 'anti-modernist' never gained much currency, 'anti-novelist' did, and was widely used in the later 1950s to describe another form of radical scepticism about art's ordering powers, expressed in the *nouveau roman* of Alain Robbe-Grillet, Nathalie Sarraute, Michel Butor and other French contemporaries. For these new writers, the limitations of art – or even mind generally, in interpreting the world it envisaged – were a matter less of explicit commentary or subtle analogy than of direct enactment in puzzling, fractured fictions. Impossible chronologies are characteristic of the novels concerned, also marked by obsessive but apparently pointless description, by fractured, indecipherable characters and subjectivities, by language flaunting its distorting detachment from any 'reality of action' and by self-reflexive interest in the artificiality of the novel's own procedures. The influence of this writing was acknowledged by Fowles in *The French Lieutenant's Woman* (1969). It has often been seen shaping Spark's work too, though in his article 'Parodying Postmodernism' Aidan Day sounds a note of caution by quoting equivocal views she expressed in 1971. Questioned about modern novelists she admired, Spark cited 'Robbe-Grillet certainly, though I don't in the least accept the theory of the anti-novel'. Such views confirm the kind of 'partial complicity' Day identifies[19] – a kind of sibling relationship of resemblance and affinity, but alongside some critical distance and wish for separateness and individuality. The idea of a sibling relationship also implies common parentage – appropriately, as Spark herself suggested when she remarked of French intellectuals in the 1950s and 1960s: 'I was thinking the same thoughts they were thinking, people like Robbe-Grillet. We were influenced by the same, breathing the same informed air. So I naturally would have a bent towards the *nouveau roman*.' [20]

Robbe-Grillet defines some of these common thoughts, and the atmosphere or 'air' of postwar scepticism generally, when describing the convictions of fellow authors of the *nouveau roman* in his 1956 essay 'A Future for the Novel':

> we had thought to control it [the world around us] by assigning it a meaning, and the entire art of the novel, in particular, seemed dedicated to this enterprise. But this was merely an illusory simplification [. . .] We no longer consider the world as our own, our private property, designed according to our needs and readily domesticated. [21]

Reading postwar fiction in terms of loss of confidence as general and fundamental as described by Robbe-Grillet offers distinct critical advantages, including a fuller understanding of Spark's relations with the postmodern. Willy Maley shows these relations developing in later novels such as *The Public Image* (1968) and *Not to Disturb* (1971), each reflecting what he describes as the 'mediatization of the culture at large [. . .] emerging with postmodernity' and summarily criticised by Jean Baudrillard. But it is the early fiction, the principal focus of this chapter, which may be still more valuable in vindicating or even extending Maley's claim for Spark as 'postmodernist before her time'.[22] In the literary sense she is. Her fiction in the 1950s and 1960s displayed postmodern characteristics some time before these had become commonplace in anglophone writing. In other ways, though, Spark is a postmodernist exactly *of* her time and *because* of her time, embodying in her work specific stresses which events in the mid-twentieth century had forced upon the imagination of European authors.

Reading Spark's work in this way, and alongside her contemporaries', also allows developments in the mid-century novel to be observed illuminatingly in parallel – breathing, or gasping, in the same air – without necessarily seeking over-complicated relations of precedence, influence or complete identity between them. Concerns with art's 'illusory simplification' or language's 'flimsy superstructure' might take the form of Robbe-Grillet's own austerely self-reductive fictions. Or in work by another writer Spark admired, Samuel Beckett, they might appear in reasserted needs for art's consoling configurations of life, along with recognition of the impossibility of realising them: concerns, along with the unreliability of language, apparent throughout Beckett's trilogy *Molloy*, *Malone Dies* and *The Unnamable* (1950–2; tr. 1956–9). Or, like Spark and Murdoch, and closer to domestic British traditions, postwar fiction might retain strong components of realism, even while challenging, at a level of parable or metaphor, the reliability of art's representation and ordering of reality.

Seeing such fictions in parallel, as siblings in a spectrum of scepticism, also helps account for apparently odd generic transgressions in postwar fiction. Graham Greene, for example, is generally a conventional writer, even, for the most part, in *The End of the Affair*. Yet the diverse accounts of the same events in that novel, along with metafictional commentary about the practices of realist writing (some quoted earlier) seem to belong to the self-reflexive, experimental idiom of postmodernism. The same idiom reappears briefly but strikingly in Greene's near-contemporary novel *The Third Man* (1949), in which, in the course of a British Council lecture on 'The Crisis of Faith', the protagonist claims to be engaged in writing a novel called *The Third Man*. This kind of momentary or occasional change of idiom seems less surprising if uneasy self-consciousness and self-questioning – shaken confidence in art – is recognised as a fundamental consequence of the war, variously expressed in different strands of contemporary writing, and with some scope for movement between them. Spark herself, after all, changes idiom fairly freely between novels, or sometimes even within them. Though *The Driver's Seat* is close to the puzzling, self-questioning idiom of the *nouveau roman*, in many other novels Spark's style is more conventional. Murdoch's work ranges across a similar arpeggio of stylistic and generic possibilities. Occasionally, as in *The Black Prince* (1973), these include a strongly postmodern, self-reflexive element. Generally, Murdoch remains a realist, even in presenting implausible characters or relationships, and sometimes as a stylistic extension of her moral vision. The carefully detailed observation of *The Sea, the Sea* (1978), for example, helps underwrite its narrator's acceptance that raw particularities of lived experience inevitably negate his imperious visions. Like Jake in *Under the Net* (1954), or many other Murdoch protagonists, he learns that 'all theorizing is flight. We must be ruled by the situation itself and this is unutterably particular'.[23]

One of the reasons comparisons of Murdoch and Spark are so illuminating, though, is that the latter seems so much more relaxed about transitions of idiom – transfigurations of the commonplace, perhaps – within individual novels. The marine monster that may (or may not) appear in *The Sea, the Sea* (1978), or the bizarre relationships of *A Severed Head* (1961), seem rather an embarrassment to the respective narrators of these novels. 'Principalities and powers [. . .] demons' tend to remain only on the fringes of other Murdoch novels, such as *A Fairly Honourable Defeat* (209). Though 'the angels and the demons of earlier times' make such a strong comeback more generally in postwar fiction, it is likewise often in oblique, furtive or metaphoric roles. Spark seems more frank and flexible. Critics have often sensibly attributed this to her Scottish background and to Scottish literature's tradition of free transition between the supernatural and the everyday. If the devil, or a figuration of him, can plausibly turn up on the streets of Edinburgh and the slopes of Arthur's Seat in James Hogg's *Confessions of a Justified Sinner*, why not also in the factories, parks and dance-halls of postwar Peckham Rye? Yet Ian Rankin has also claimed Spark as 'surely the most "European" writer whom Scotland has produced'.[24] In assessing Spark alongside her English and European contemporaries, part of this chapter's purpose has been to emphasise varied and cosmopolitan backgrounds to her work. Religious conversion may have been as much an influence as her Scottish background on her writing's double vision – realist and fantastic; metaphysical and mundane. A partly Jewish background may have particularly alerted her to 'the empty hole in the earth' yawning beneath the postwar years. Many currents coalesce in Spark's writing, and they are often more specific historically than geographically or nationally. Many of the world's nerves in the quarter-century after the war cross and pattern her fiction. Part of the value of this apparently slight writer is the comprehensive insight her work offers into that uneasy period, and the darkening pressures shaping its shaken imagination.

CHAPTER TEN

Muriel Spark's Crimes of Wit

Drew Milne

Muriel Spark's novels are not often read as contributions to the socialist critique of bourgeois capitalism. The opening paragraph of *The Girls of Slender Means* (1963) nevertheless suggests that there is something paradoxical about this apparent distance from socialist tendencies: 'Long ago in 1945 all the nice people in England were poor, allowing for exceptions. [. . .] All the nice people were poor; at least, that was a general axiom, the best of the rich being poor in spirit.'[1] There is a pointed local disturbance in play here, and not just in the uprooting of the distinctions between *rich* and *poor*, and what might be inferred as the question of *spirit*. Spark's readers learn to distrust general axioms. The quality of the 'nice' is nicely doubted, and the novel as a whole makes much of the slenderness of such means. Despite the various dubious machinations of otherwise well-bred girls knowingly in pursuit of more substantial means, *The Girls of Slender Means* concludes by framing the book's story as one of 'meek, unselfconscious attitudes of poverty'.[2] How might meekness avoid self-consciousness so as to inherit the earth? The novel's story of the May of Teck club can be read as an allegorical representation of the emergent Welfare State and the postwar Labour government. Spark certainly encourages readers to probe the differences between economic and spiritual poverty, but lightness of touch deflects any too earnest attempt to ask directly what the novel has to say about postwar blessings and the inheritances that might be visited upon peacemakers and meek souls. Against the desire to map the historical context, socio-political context is displaced by an amusingly disruptive play on words and means. Her witty displacement of politics is itself political, however, part of the hegemony of common sense in British culture that tends to outlaw words like *hegemony*.

Attempts to frame Spark's works ideologically – as representations, for example, of the politics of Scottish, British, Jewish or Catholic identity – scarcely capture the pleasure or interest of her fictions. Brian Cheyette rightly suggests a more playful, almost anarchic disruption of stable identities.[3] Her novels strike even her most ardently politicised readers as being politically canny to the point of making ideological framing appear clumsy or contrived.

Her novels are nevertheless sensitive to the merest inklings of socio-political hypocrisy, to the delusions of class-consciousness and to the reality of existing inequalities of class and gender. Attempts to specify the politics of her writing have to reckon with the inadequacy of such categories in understanding her modes of representation. Willy Maley cites a characteristic statement from Spark herself – 'I can never now suffer from a shattered faith in politics and politicians, because I never had any' – as evidence of her anti-establishment stance,[4] but is the stance of the anti-establishment writer not also the refuge of the conservative scoundrel? Insofar as her fictions have realist qualities in their address to contemporary realities, her realism is not sociological or naturalist in its ambitions and techniques. Indeed, the perils of pretensions to omniscience figure prominently among the delusions afflicting her narrators. Playing god with narration or the claims of objectivity, especially objectivity in the form of writing, is represented through her fiction as a kind of criminal sin. Central to both the experience of reading her work, then, and to the techniques of its composition, is the variousness of her writing's knowingness, its satirical and witty resistance to socio-political paraphrase.

Qualities of satirical wit are critical to the way her writing is entertaining, delightful and intelligent. The burden of socio-political concerns is somehow lifted from the shoulders of her readers, as if such concerns made heavy work of the amusing surfaces of life, while also neglecting more metaphysical concerns, such as the sins of omission constitutive of daily life and the all too human neglect of death and of God. In achieving this knowing suspension of the socio-political, the wit of her fiction carries within its elaboration an implicit poetics of the novel, a poetics with a deep debt to English poetry: 'I always tell students of my work, and interviewers, that I think of myself as predominantly a poet.'[5] Her development into a novelist out of her interest in poetry is well known and is evident in the persistent and sometimes obtrusive range of allusions to poetry made by her novels. *The Girls of Slender Means* makes continual play with Gerard Manley Hopkins' poem *The Wreck of the Deutschland*, but not so as to trouble or disable readers for whom the literary allusion is not already part of the pleasures of her text. *The Ballad of Peckham Rye* (1960) owes something to the poetry of Robert Burns and the border ballads, even if it is hard to specify quite what that debt amounts to. *The Takeover* (1976) takes on Ovid, Virgil and Byron, but not so directly that her readers have been detained while heading in a scholarly direction. Recognition of the principal poetic antecedents of Spark's fiction might appear to constitute a badge of readerly competence, but readers are rarely given the impression that they need embark on further study to make sense of Spark's work. Her novels, moreover, are not written in a poetic prose, so much as through investigations into narrative patterns and tones, and through a poetics of the novel that prefers not to wear its theory on its sleeve.

Rather than being poetically elusive, allusive or imagistic, then, Spark's sentences offer a pithier, neoclassical kind of wit, a wit of crystalline and explicit statement that is rich with implied judgements. Less clear, however, is the social perspective or Olympian vantage from which the richness of such witty observation and sentence-making is pronounced or observed. Spark deflects readers from discerning anything as grand as a theory of the novel, but her books are formalised such that the artifice of construction is clear, playful and reflexive, often appearing to generate itself out of a pithy, synoptic and knowingly proleptic title.[6] The back and forth of flashbacks and proleptic leaps is but one understated feature of the way her poetics of fiction is schooled in the fiction of Marcel Proust. The way implicit puns in titles unfold their potential can become almost scandalously tidy, putting too much into such conceits over the conventions of a more organic realism. Biblical parallels of various kinds, notably to The Book of Job, sustain many of her fictions. It could be argued, accordingly, that the model for the way her work maps contemporary stories onto literary classics is suggested by the use James Joyce makes of Homer in *Ulysses*, but whereas Joyce appears to invite readers to engage in the comedy of literary scholarship, Spark's work frames such scholarship as a kind of trivial pursuit. The literary scholarship of her work is worn lightly, albeit with a persistence that secures from her learned and knowing readers a delighted recognition of ironic wit. The effect is to disable scholarly interpretation rather than to encourage its elaboration. The pleasures of textual wit and narrative artifice are developed and defended, however, against the playful sins of their literary construction, turning reflexively back against the crimes of authorship through the representation of various analogous crimes of wit.

Sustained knowingness in the face of both socio-political critique and literary scholarship is achieved in her novels through an intelligence of compositional technique. Such intelligence is resistant to what has become known as literary theory, but in Spark is developed as a self-critical and almost metacritical quality of the way her stories are told. *Symposium* (1990) borrows Plato's *Symposium* for its epigraphs, but records how her characters agree: 'no more Greek food. Never again.'[7] Criticism and writing about her work that attempts more than admiring praise often seems over-theorised or simply naive by comparison with the pith, irony and sophisticated restraint of her writing. There is something implausible about attempts to position Spark's work in direct dialogue with critical theory.[8] To the extent that her fiction scarcely needs explanation or critical interpretation, her novels are elegantly self-contained. This containment, however, has affinities with the patrician, conservative, neoclassical tendencies of English literary wit that threaten to restrict recognition of the work's interest and its structuring poetics. Put differently, her work's resistance to socio-political interpretation, to literary

scholarship and to literary theory mark out the limits of the historical formation of literary taste her work exemplifies. Her work can nevertheless be
read as offering critical perspectives on the qualities of bourgeois ideology
constitutive of her writing's wit.

A deep fault line runs through British culture in the hegemonic association of wit with an ironic or cynical contempt for the earnestness of critique,
whether critique takes the form of liberal moralism, puritan sermonising or
socialist critical theory. From within a prevailing anti-intellectual cynicism,
abstract or conceptual language is often derided and satirised as jargon. Such
cynicism takes its place amid pragmatic resistances to abstraction and conceptual thinking, resistances that help to preserve a circumscribed ideology of
common sense. The satirical texture of Spark's novels makes a virtue out of
remaining within the prevailing discourses of common sense, while seeking
to disturb the complacency of common sense from within. Such disturbances
insulate the narrative framing from the accusation that it is as complacent as
the complacency of the characters described. Such disturbances are also con-
tained, however, both within resonances particular to the frames supplied by
individual novels and within a conservative, religious or Catholic scepticism.
Scepticism in the face of worldly values positions itself outside or above the
worldly critique of existing capitalist relations. For all the disturbing implications of her work, her readers are nevertheless allowed to enjoy the privileges
of their complicity with the values satirised. Despite the implicit theoretical
and conceptual intelligence with which Spark develops her poetics of the
novel form, then, her readers are allowed to remain amused and sceptically
indifferent before the claims of critique, critical theory and more explicit
theoretical poetics.

Spark's work could be read, accordingly, as a continuation of a conservative tradition of witty fiction that satirises middle-class values in a neoclassical vein, mocking bourgeois culture, but without going as far as to suggest the
need for a revolutionary break with such values. Often compared with Evelyn
Waugh, a literary tradition for her poetics of the novel could be extended to
include some of the novels of Wyndham Lewis, the early satirical novels of
Aldous Huxley or the comedies of Nancy Mitford. And yet such genealogies
and comparisons do not quite capture the more darkly structural and critical
qualities of Spark's wit as a carefully but implicitly theorised poetics of fiction.
Recognition of the literary and intellectual sophistication of her writing is
hindered, moreover, by the way the wit of her novels wears its knowingness –
its poetics and theory of writing – so lightly. Such playful literary wit scarcely
disguises her writing's engagement with evil and crime. The self-critical
poetics of her writing is well defended against accusations of complicity: the
evils humans perpetrate on each other are foregrounded. However critical
of bourgeois values, the wit of her writing, its knowing suspension of the

socio-political, nevertheless suggests a profoundly ideological shrug of the shoulders, cynical indifference even, when confronted with the socialist critique of the way bourgeois values efface the realities of contemporary capitalism.

The implication that socio-political critique is some kind of *lumpen* moralism works in tandem with the suggestion that the mark of lively intelligence, not least as it is expressed in the art of writing, is its difference from the kinds of moralising associated with the politicisation of writing.[9] Writing, intelligence and wit are nevertheless predetermined by social and political conditions that are not so easily negated or moralised. The critical question to emerge, accordingly, is the extent to which Spark's writing remains complicit with the bourgeois values so knowingly and amusingly dissected by her work. One symptom of such complicity is the mysterious presence in Spark's work of the underlying forces and relations of social production. Spark's writing is, as Peter Kemp puts it, 'extremely economic',[10] but economic to the point of silence on the politics of economic structures. The complexities of economic processes are figured more as paradoxes of inherited wealth and as sites of narrative comedy. Spark implies distrust of the wealthy and their wealth, but the generation and production of wealth, and especially the forms and relations legitimised as *capitalist* wealth, remain mysterious. Central to the reflexively intelligent quality with which Spark's writing negotiates its symptomatic complicities is the way both the dubiousness of inherited wealth and the duplicity of those who would steal such wealth are represented as criminal or sinful. Capitalism, however, despite the efforts of moralising critics intent on demonising it as a thing or a system, is not reducible to a narrative of crime or of sin. Is Spark, then, an apologist for capitalism, despite or even because of her writing's attempts to suspend socio-political moralism?

The opening paragraphs of Spark's last novel, *The Finishing School* (2004), provide a microcosm of the texture of such difficulties. The dubious pedagogical benefits of Rowland Mahler's finishing school are given an immediate economic subtext: 'Rowland took off his reading glasses to stare at his creative writing class whose parents' money was being thus spent' (1). The creation of the wealth thus spent, and how it is being made, is scarcely glimpsed in the rest of the novel, and where glimpsed, such wealth appears shady if not simply criminal. The finishing school described in the novel is itself scarcely viable and more a question of fooling parents into believing that 'they were getting good money's worth' (3). It is implied that the economics of finishing schools and creative writing classes might amount to little more than con tricks in which the blind pursue the children of the blinded. The precision with which Spark undermines Mahler's take on how to use the word 'fucking' in a literary context suggests an ironic swipe at the texture of novelists such as Irvine Welsh and James Kelman. But if the vanity of would-be novelists and the

delusions of publishing are given a satirical gloss, the question of the perspective from which Spark mocks the efforts of teachers and novelists can scarcely
avoid raising the question as to the money's worth Spark gives her readers. In
A Far Cry from Kensington (1988) Spark's narrator boldly states the paradox
of fiction's worth: 'I offer this advice without fee; it is included in the price of
this book.' [11] The economic independence Spark achieved through her work
as a novelist, part of the contract developed between Spark and her reader-
ship, is continually figured so as to question literary fiction's similarity to the
work of con artists and professional blackmailers.[12] The wealth readers give
writers as buyers of their work remains mysterious, however, part of a world
of economic production and exchange that Spark's literary independence
lived off, but represents more as a surface of delusions than as a socio-political
process. The English literary novel since 1945 has rarely foregrounded self-
critical representations of its own economics beyond genteel satire of its
gentlemen's clubs and networks. Spark offers some of the more explicit and
mordant satires of publishing and publishers, but her work is thereby all the
more revealing in the way it observes the prevailing bourgeois literary taboo
against more explicit representations of the underlying capitalist relations.

Rather than attempting to fathom the mysteries of capitalist wealth creation, and of publishing as a predominantly capitalist set of social relations,
Spark's representations of writers, publishers and con artists tend to adopt
a more detached, almost aristocratic or neoclassical perspective. *A Far Cry
from Kensington* offers some of Spark's more satirical and critical representations of the class dynamics of English literary publishing through the first-
person narrative perspective of a Mrs Hawkins, or Nancy. Nancy comments
in passing, for example, that 'he [Martin York] felt that men or women of
upper-class background and education were bound to have advantages of
talent over writers of modest origins. In 1954 quite a few bright publishers
secretly believed this' (44–5). Nancy is no Muriel Spark, however, even if
there is a strong hint of authorial self-reflection built into the character. Her
perceptions of publishing are no more reliable than her attitudes to homo-
sexuality: 'Perhaps it was the fact that homosexual practices were still against
the law that made homosexuals in those days much more hysterical than they
are now' (185). Indeed, the framing of *A Far Cry from Kensington* highlights
the sense of historical difference between the novel's setting in 1954 and its
moment of production in the 1980s.[13] Mrs Hawkins remarks that 'The term
"upper class" in those days meant more than it does now' (45). But although
the novel has an epilogue which situates her narrative point of retrospection
in the mid-1980s, neither Nancy nor Spark offer much sense of the different
world of Thatcherism and of the more nakedly capitalist publishing corpo-
rations in which the novel was written and published. The book remains
engaging as a study in the criminality of writers and publishers, but through

its setting in the past it nevertheless suggests nostalgia for the ungentlemanly
world of gentlemen publishers. The literariness of 1950s London and the
Highgate Review is criticised, among other things, in terms of its deluded
class dynamics, but the world of 1980s literary London, amid the conflicts of
Rupert Murdoch's *Sun* and the battle of Wapping, is scarcely acknowledged.

Rather than offering representations of contemporary capitalism, Spark's
poetics of the novel leans heavily on crime fiction and its potential for literary play. In 2003, for example, Spark was drawn into writing an article on a
book by Duncan MacLaughlin and William Hall entitled *Dead Lucky: Lord
Lucan: The Final Truth*.[14] MacLaughlin, a former Scotland Yard detective,
claimed to have tracked down Lord Lucan, the aristocrat who vanished
in 1974 after the brutal murder of his children's nanny, Sandra Rivett, at
Lucan's home in Belgravia. With pictures claiming to identify Lord Lucan
accompanied by general journalistic nodding, the truth of MacLaughlin's
story was nevertheless quickly called into doubt. MacLaughlin's investigative
claims were unconvincing, leaving the book generically stranded between
inconclusive investigative journalism and an unknowingly fictional crime
story. Such shifts of form and recognition, shifts between truth, crime and
fiction, provide materials for Spark's novels. The quality of entertainment in
her novels, however, is generated by the sharp wit with which such materials
are shaped and told. Spark, perhaps provoked by the potential damage to her
own fictional representation of Lucan, suggested that Lucan was too dull to
fit MacLaughlin's account. She remarked of her own fictional account of him
in *Aiding and Abetting* (2000) that she had been faced with a specific problem:
'To depict a boring person as such, without being boring, was, incidentally,
quite difficult.' [15] This sketch of a technical interest points to the compositional sophistication with which Spark's novels rework crime narratives. The
con tricks of literary fiction are mapped onto analogous criminal practices,
from sleights, misdirection and lying to fraud, murder and terrorism. *The
Abbess of Crewe*, for example, draws direct satirical parallels between the
fictional affairs of a nunnery and the political corruption of the Watergate
scandal. *Aiding and Abetting* makes no real attempt to identify the true Lucan
or the truth of the Lucan story. Her book gambles, rather, that the Lucan
story will remain unsolved and available for fictional exploration, such that
narrative speculations associated with Lucan can generate literary paradoxes
and entertaining religious and metaphysical inquiry. If *Dead Lucky* had solved
the mystery of Lucan's story, *Aiding and Abetting* might have come to seem
merely historical, rather than witty and speculative. The continuing mystery
of Lucan's story points to fiction's affinity with the unresolved historical
potential of true but unsolved crimes.

Criminal acts that remain fictional allow Spark to trace analogies between
legal understandings of crime and religious conceptions of sin, while her

knowing narrators manipulate the judgements of readers in ways that have more than a hint of devilish charm. Her use of the broadly familiar and populist narrative patterns associated with crime breaks with crime as a genre to suggest a deeper, but wittily understated critique of human fallenness. Most of her novels make some play with the patterns and structures of crime fiction, if only to overturn or play with them. The tropes and patterns of crime fiction offer a popular framework through which her sceptical wit and literary texture can be woven. While the surface of the narrative texture is overdetermined by allegories, social parallels and implied depths, the guiding tone and style of Spark's writing is guardedly brisk and light, self-critically witty, rather than portentous. Witty narrative framing is mapped onto the witty portrayal of characters and narrators. Her self-critical articulation of literary wit knowingly turns back on its own wit, bringing the resources of wit before a sustained process of trial, at once legal and spiritual, and yet profoundly unsociological in its representation of the sociality of wit. For all its sensitivity to class dynamics, Spark's fiction scarcely involves itself with investigations into the sociology and economics of wit's production, the political economy of crime fiction or indeed the economics of production more generally. Money in her stories is more often an ill-gotten gain than the fruit of anything resembling honest labour. *The Takeover* (1976) is perhaps the exception that proves the rule, offering descriptions of bourgeois illusions as to property relations that are especially explicit:

> They talked of hedges against inflation, as if mathematics could contain actual air and some row of hawthorn could stop an army of numbers from marching over it. They spoke of the mood of the stock-market, the health of the economy as if these were living creatures with moods and blood. And thus they person-alized and demonologized the abstractions of their lives, believing them to be fundamentally real, indeed changeless. But it did not occur to one of those spirited and in various ways intelligent people around Berto's table that a com-plete mutation of our means of nourishment had already come into being where the concept of money and property were concerned, a complete mutation not merely to be defined as a collapse of the capitalist system, or a global recession, but such a sea-change in the nature of reality as could not have been envisaged by Karl Marx or Sigmund Freud.[16]

False personification of real social abstractions is evidently criticised, but what critical vocabulary might be adequate to a description of capital-ist crisis that goes beyond both Marx and Freud? From whence comes the theoretical judgement that Marx and Freud have been surpassed by the apparently autodidactic narrator of Spark's worldview? The allegorical plot rather reduces the mysteries of surplus value to the fraudulent reproduction of Louis XIV chairs, but is nevertheless explicitly addressed to the problems of international finance, banking and property relations. Such passages are rare, but symptomatic. Even here, however, the sociality of wit, its play with recognition, social perspectives and knowingness, is under suspicion. The cost of wit is often achieved through assumptions of familiarity and quickness of recognition that run the risk of suggesting a kind of class condescension. Spark, accordingly, goes to some trouble to delimit the sins of her narrators. There is a persistent sense of the pressure of judgements from above, a kind of criminality that associates itself with the wit of omniscience.

Spark's poetics of the novel weaves narrative textures out of crime fiction materials, then, but also deflects the pleasures associated with crime and detection genres into a sense of the novel as a form tempted into crimes of wit. Rather than suggesting any substantive interest in the sociology of crime, her use of crime fiction forms is evidently determined as a 'literary' strategy. The crime novels of Ian Rankin, by contrast, use crime fiction as a vehicle for sociological naturalism leavened by the sensationalism of the criminal processes depicted. Spark's use of crime fiction offers sharp and witty metaphysical inquiries into the meaning and paradoxes of fiction, a poetics of fiction that obliges her readers to resist the generic drift of crime fiction. Rankin's novels are more amenable to readerly consumption or sociological interpretation, or both. The interest and difficulty of Spark's novels is the way the artifice of narrative construction is worked back through the wit of the narrative tone.

A number of Spark's novels, perhaps most famously *The Prime of Miss Jean Brodie* (1961), have elements that can be read referentially, as if some of the fiction's truth could be tracked down by literary detectives to representations of real people. The points of reference to 'real' people and places are not usually as direct as her portrayal of Lord Lucan, but while offering 'realist' referentiality Spark's writing is far from realist in its sense of wit and style. In *Curriculum Vitae* (1992) Spark herself sketches autobiographical frameworks that encourage readers to believe that her fiction's plausibility owes something to its awkward dance with elements of lived experience recognisable as 'reality'. This impression is confirmed by Martin Stannard's 2009 biography.[17] While Spark's life story appears to support autobiographical layers in her fictions, the novels themselves offer an ongoing play of ideas without labouring anything resembling theory, appearing to mock tendencies in critical and literary theory. Though rarely read, the template for knowing mockery of academic intellectuals is evident in Spark's play *Doctors of Philosophy* (1963), even if the dramatic form makes the satire appear clumsily populist. Spark's work is explicit and explicitly intelligent, but inclined to mock the illusions of intellectuals rather than lend itself to theoretical interpretation. Her writing works within a conception of literary fiction that is intellectually conservative, part of a wider historical formation in professional middle-class writing that prefers 'literary' ideas to be packaged wittily rather than as something demanding intellectual work. Spark is at one with the tastes of the English literary bourgeoisie in preferring to steer clear of writing that too closely engages with what, after Hegel, might be called a labour of the concept.

Literary appropriations of true crime and detective narratives have a long history, from *Oedipus Tyrannus* to Paul Auster's *New York Trilogy* (1987), via Franz Kafka's *The Trial*, Gertrude Stein's *Blood on the Dining-Room Floor: A Murder Mystery*, Samuel Beckett's *Molloy* (1950), and Thomas Pynchon's *The Crying of Lot 49* (1966). Spark's poetics of the novel resists such extremities and limit texts, and remains more conventional in its use of generic forms. Aside from analogous interests in unsolved fictions of crime and the narration of lies as ruses for metaphysical inquiry, Spark's poetics of fiction combines qualities of formal reflexivity and technical dexterity associated with the French *nouveau roman*,[18] while maintaining an accessible, readable and witty textual surface that is inviting for many different sorts of readers. The textual surface of her novels adapts itself to the demand for page-turning pace associated with crime fiction, but her short or sharp sentences are not 'hard-boiled' so much as glitteringly poetic and sprightly. The various kinds of crime and criminality that motivate so many of her stories, moreover, are often shaped around homages to specific poets, poetic texts and religious fables. Such structural and formal types of reference and allusion do not become a burden for readers who do not recognise them. In effect, Spark succeeded in disguising more poetic, literary and structural concerns associated with allusion and intellectual inquiry, articulating the novel as a reflexive medium, while writing in a mode sufficiently easy in its overlapping levels of wit to be both literary and popular. Seen from a different angle, Spark's work is part of the wider exploration of narrative theories through the literariness of crime fiction.[19]

Spark's witty use of detective fiction encourages her readers to wonder about the literary crimes associated with the genres of crime. Is there something inherently criminal about readerly enthusiasm for the processes and contents of crime fiction? Is there something immoral, amoral or unethical about the violence of literary form and construction associated with the characteristic prose style and socio-political assumptions associated with crime as a literary genre? In parallel with the characteristic misogyny and gendered sensationalism of crime fiction, Spark's novels often represent violence against women, but through various literary displacements of generic expectations, displacements that are both formal and ideological, perhaps most notably in *The Public Image* (1968) and *The Driver's Seat* (1970). Such novels can be read as proto-feminist representations of femininity, but Spark makes an unlikely feminist, not least because she so clearly distanced herself from offering 'representations of the victim-oppressor complex'.[20] Breaking with generic character conventions, her women are neither objects nor victims, but strangely willing agents and accomplices. Although women figure prominently in her novels, then, and often as criminals, Spark's feminism is delimited and figured as the feminism of intelligent common sense rather than as feminist ideology critique. Against the tendencies of hard-boiled fiction, with its serial punch-ups, victims and murders, there is something more difficult, conceptually murky and uneasily generic about *The Driver's Seat* (1970), not least the questions posed to the agency of the reader as a driver. Spark opens up the crimes of wit as a double-bind. Criminal tendencies lurk beneath the airs and graces of the well-heeled in Spark's novels. Without prescribing austerity or a new puritanism, her pages wittily dissect both the superficial and more deeply sinful criminality of characters who might appear better off. Although her novels imply ways of mapping secular criminality onto religious narratives of sin, the author herself scarcely claims that her poetics of fiction is innocent. Amid her gallery of criminals, from rogues and fraudsters to thieves, blackmailers and murderers, there is usually a special circle of hell reserved for liars, artists and makers of fiction alike. Novelists, too, are con artists. While her narrative genres overlap with those of crime fiction, her characteristic narrative voice is that of an omniscient narrator who is not so much unreliable as criminally witty.

Amid more than superficial resemblances with, say, the films of Alfred Hitchcock or *film noir*, Spark's novels delight in the potentially criminal wit of plot construction, characterisation and knowingly judgemental commentary. Readers can enjoy Spark's novels without taking the full force of their self-critically devilish affinities. But the precision with which she articulates the pleasures of narrative wit nevertheless implicates readers in uncomfortable judgements of her characters and, more critically, of her narrators. Descriptions of Spark's writing invariably recognise that her narrative textures are playful, ironic or satirical, as if the pleasures of levity might afford some dance of the intellect over dark matter. The intellectual reflexivity running through Spark's work frequently distinguishes it as 'literary',[21] moreover, warily engaged with the pleasures of crime fiction. Spark reserves her deepest critique for the crimes of wit associated with her characteristic superiority of tone and style. Comparable novelists tend to confirm the fascinating superiority of an aristocratic tone, offering a brightly judgemental nonconformity that can mock the foibles of property from the perspective of class superiority. Spark plays with such tones, but also suggests the criminality of such witty nonconformity.

It is not just Spark's Scottishness that informs the distance she puts between herself and the wits of English fiction. The *hauteur* of Spark's most famous character – Miss Jean Brodie – is evidently flawed. The very aspiration to a kind of glamorous superiority of tone is complicit with a deluded and corrupt pedagogy that is tragically misplaced and distantly complicit with fascism. Neoclassical literary forms, not least satire, can imply an aloof, patrician or Olympian disdain that coexists too easily with snobbery. Spark's writing offers numerous critical representations of snobbery. In 'The Snobs' (1998), for example, her narrator comments: 'Snobs are really amazing. They mainly err in failing to fool the very set of people they are hoping to be accepted by, and above all, to seem to belong to, to be taken for. They may live in a democratic society – it does nothing to help. Nothing.' [22] There is something democratic about the energy and independence of spirit in Spark's conception of the art of writing, the art of a democratic intellect rather than an anti-intellectual social complacency. Her work could hardly be mistaken for socialist realism, but her writing is persistently distrustful both of the *hauteur* of witty superiority and of the abuse of wit by social climbers. But if her writing is nevertheless engagingly witty, her literary wit resists the temptation to locate itself complacently in an existing social or class perspective. Spark's work, wary of anything resembling the superciliousness of false airs and graces, can nevertheless appear too knowing, written from the perspective of the high and mighty, rather than meekly hoping to inherit the earth. Given the difficult choices facing any attempt to sustain social perspectives that are both self-critical and formally reflexive, both democratic and socially engaged, Spark challenges her readers to the difficult art of maintaining some poise amid the crimes of wit. Readers of Spark need to have their wits about them.

Endnotes

Introduction – Gardiner and Maley

1. See, for example, 'The Golden Fleece' in the journal of the National Jewellers' Association, *Argentor* 3: 1 (1948), 29–32, 70.
2. Martin Stannard, *Muriel Spark: The Biography* (London: Weidenfeld & Nicolson, 2009), 2.

Chapter 1 – Goldie

1. Muriel Spark, *Memento Mori* (Harmondsworth: Penguin Books, 1961), 57.
2. Ibid., 58.
3. Ibid., 187. Muriel Spark, *Loitering with Intent* (London: Bodley Head, 1981), 105.
4. Bryan Cheyette, *Muriel Spark* (Tavistock: Northcote House, 2000), 32–3.
5. Muriel Spark, *Robinson* (Harmondsworth: Penguin Books, 1964), 84.
6. Ibid., 109.
7. Muriel Spark, *The Girls of Slender Means* (Harmondsworth: Penguin Books, 1966), 140.
8. Ibid., 65.
9. Muriel Spark, *The Hothouse by the East River* (London: Macmillan, 1973), 129.
10. Muriel Spark, *John Masefield* (London: Peter Nevill, 1953), 26.
11. See, for example, the discussion of the relationship between Masefield and his protagonist, Saul Kane, in *The Everlasting Mercy*. Ibid., 96.
12. Ibid., x.
13. Ibid., 42.
14. Muriel Spark (ed.), *The Brontë Letters* (London: Peter Nevill, 1954), 11–12.
15. Muriel Spark, 'My Conversion', in Joseph Hynes, *Critical Essays on Muriel Spark* (New York: G. K. Hall & Co., 1992), 24. Derek Stanford and Muriel Spark (eds.), *Letters of John Henry Newman: A Selection* (London: Peter Owen, 1957), 143, 58.

16. Muriel Spark and Derek Stanford (eds.), *Tribute to Wordsworth: A Miscellany of Opinion for the Centenary of the Poet's Death* (London: Wingate, 1950), 129. Muriel Spark, *The Essence of the Brontës: A Compilation with Essays* (London: Peter Owen, 1993), 9.

17. She had as editor of *Poetry Review* published Agius's 'The Psychology of Poetry' in 1947. See Valerie Shaw, 'Fun and Games with Life-stories', in Alan Bold (ed.), *Muriel Spark: An Odd Capacity for Vision* (London: Vision, 1984), 59–60.

18. Muriel Spark, *Mary Shelley* (London: Constable, 1988), 232.

19. Stanford and Spark (eds.), *Letters of John Henry Newman*, 159.

20. Muriel Spark and Derek Stanford, *Emily Brontë: Her Life and Work* (London: Peter Owen, 1953), 16.

21. Ibid., 15.

22. Stanford and Spark (eds.), *Letters of John Henry Newman*, 152.

23. Spark (ed.), *The Brontë Letters*, 16, 21.

24. Muriel Spark, *Child of Light: A Reassessment of Mary Wollstonecraft Shelley* (Hadleigh: Tower Bridge, 1951), 6. Spark softened this argument in the revised edition, suggesting there that she had been beguiled by the prevailing and over-simplistic view that 'after the death of Shelley she [Mary] gradually craved more and more for bourgeois respectability'. Spark, *Mary Shelley*, x.

25. 'Wordsworth the Person', in Spark and Stanford (eds.), *Tribute to Wordsworth*, 15–16.

26. Peter Kemp, *Muriel Spark* (London: Paul Elek, 1974), 37.

27. See Derek Stanford, *Muriel Spark: A Biographical and Critical Study* (Fontwell: Centaur, 1963), 52.

28. Spark, *Loitering with Intent*, 84.

29. See ibid., 222; and Muriel Spark, *Curriculum Vitae: Autobiography* (London: Constable, 1992), 213.

30. Spark, *Loitering with Intent*, 41.

31. Quoted in Dorothea Walker, *Muriel Spark* (Boston, MA: Twayne, 1988), 105.

32. Spark, *Curriculum Vitae*, 11.

33. A. S. Byatt, quoted by Tim Walker, 'Companion Puts Hold on "Unfair" Spark Biography', *Sunday Telegraph* (22 April 2007), 9.

34. 'Control Your Reputation from beyond the Grave', *Evening Standard*, 24 April 2007, 1. See also Gareth Rose, 'Friend of Spark Halts Biography', *Scotland on Sunday* (22 April 2007), 6.

Chapter 2 – Kolocotroni

1. As editor of the *Poetry Review*, Spark published two short compilations of political poems in the journal *Parliamentary Affairs*: 'Poetry and Politics', I

(Autumn 1948), 12–23; and 'Poetry and the American Government', III (Winter 1949), 260–72.

2. 'Keeping it Short: Muriel Spark Talks about Her Books to Ian Gillham', *The Listener* (24 September 1970), 411–13, p. 412.

3. Muriel Spark, *Loitering with Intent* ([1981] London: Virago, 2007), 16.

4. Muriel Spark, *The Girls of Slender Means* ([1963] Harmondsworth: Penguin Books, 1966), 11.

5. Ibid., 12.

6. For a discussion of the aptness of the Hopkins poem, see Jude V. Nixon, '"[A] Virginal Tongue Hold": Hopkins's *The Wreck of the Deutschland* and Muriel Spark's *The Girls of Slender Means*', *Renascence* 57: 4 (Summer 2005), 299–322.

7. Spark, *The Girls of Slender Means*, 44. Interestingly, this is exactly what happens to Lise in Spark's *The Driver's Seat*: 'he actually raped her, she was amazed'.

8. Ibid., 50.

9. See Nina Auerbach, *Communities of Women: An Idea in Fiction* (Cambridge, MA and London: Harvard University Press, 1978).

10. Spark, *The Girls of Slender Means*, 11.

11. Ibid., 22.

12. Ibid., 24, 25.

13. Ibid., 25.

14. V. N. Voloshinov, *Marxism and the Philosophy of Language* (1929), in Pam Morris (ed.), *The Bakhtin Reader: Selected Writings of Bakhtin, Medvedev and Voloshinov* (London and New York: Edward Arnold, 1994), 52.

15. Mikhail Bakhtin, 'Discourse in the Novel' (1934–5), *The Dialogic Imagination: Four Essays*, ed. Michael Holquist, trans. Caryl Emerson and Michael Holquist (Austin, TX: University of Texas Press, 1981), 259–422, p. 344.

16. Bakhtin, 'Discourse in the Novel', 342.

17. Spark, *The Girls of Slender Means*, 80.

18. Mark Morrison, 'Performing the Pure Voice: Elocution, Verse Recitation, and Modernist Poetry in Prewar London', *Modernism/Modernity* 3: 3 (1996), 25–50, p. 26.

19. Muriel Spark, *Doctors of Philosophy: A Play*, Act 1, scene 2 (London: Macmillan, 1963), 29.

20. Morrison, 'Performing the Pure Voice', 26.

21. Abby Arthur Johnson, 'The Politics of a Literary Magazine: A Study of *The Poetry Review*, 1912–1972', *Journal of Modern Literature* 3: 4 (April 1974), 951–64, p. 953.

22. For an account of Spark's brief but eventful period of employment (or 'embroilment', as she called it) in the post of general secretary of the Poetry Society and editor of the *Poetry Review*, see Spark's autobiography *Curriculum Vitae* (London: Constable, 1992), 165–84. Derek Stanford's reminiscences, *Muriel Spark: A Biographical and Critical Study* (Fontwell: Centaur, 1963) and *Inside the Forties: Literary Memoirs 1937–1957* (London: Sidgwick & Jackson,

1977), Abby Arthur Johnson's, 'The Politics of a Literary Magazine: A Study of *The Poetry Review*, 1912–1972', *Journal of Modern Literature* 3:4 (April 1974), 951–64', and Susan Sheridan's 'In the Driver's Seat: Muriel Spark's Editorship of the *Poetry Review*', *Journal of Modern Literature* 32: 2 (Winter 2009), 133–42, provide further details and insights.

23. Morrison, 'Performing the Pure Voice', 32.
24. Ibid., 39–40.
25. Cited in Sheridan, 'In the Driver's Seat', 957, 958.
26. Spark, *The Girls of Slender Means*, 12.
27. Ibid., 86.
28. Ibid., 80.
29. Ibid., 86–7.
30. Ibid., 87.
31. Ibid., 63.
32. Muriel Spark, *The Comforters* (New York: New Directions, 1994), 142.
33. Muriel Spark, *The Bachelors* (Harmondsworth: Penguin Books, 1963), 140.
34. Ibid., 108.
35. For a theorised account of Annabel's spectacularly constructed femininity, see Fotini Apostolou, 'Seduction, Simulacra and the Feminine: Spectacles and Images in Muriel Spark's *The Public Image*', *Journal of Gender Studies* 9: 3 (2000), 281–97.
36. Spark, *The Girls of Slender Means*, 25.
37. Muriel Spark, *The Public Image* ([1968] New York: New Directions, 1993), 105. Emphasis in the original.
38. Peter Kemp, *Muriel Spark* (London: Paul Elek, 1974), 119.
39. Spark, *The Public Image*, 144.
40. For an encyclopaedic account of the figurations of the Virgin Mary through the ages, see Marina Warner, *Monuments and Maidens: The Allegory of the Female Form* (London: Weidenfeld & Nicolson, 1985).
41. Muriel Spark, 'The Religion of an Agnostic: A Sacramental View of the World in the Writings of Proust', *The Church of England Newspaper* (27 November 1953), 1.
42. Ibid., 1.
43. Ibid., 1.
44. Muriel Spark, 'My Conversion', in Joseph Hynes (ed.), *Critical Essays on Muriel Spark* (New York, Oxford, Singapore and Sydney: Maxwell Macmillan International, 1992), 24–8, p. 27.
45. Spark, *The Bachelors*, 84, 85.
46. Muriel Spark, *Reality and Dreams* (London: Constable, 1996), 55.
47. Spark uses the phrase to pin down a particular species of believer, as opposed to the convert to the faith. Ian Brodie is a typical example, as is Georgina Hogg in *The Comforters*, about whom the term is first used (40).
48. Spark, *Robinson*, 78–80.

49. Ibid., 30.
50. Ibid., 42.
51. Ibid., 84.
52. Ibid., 137.
53. The Black Madonna makes its first appearance in *The Comforters*, as a miracu-
lous icon (175). It features largely in the 1958 story 'The Black Madonna'
(*The Complete Short Stories*, 417–37), as a statue gifted to the local church by a
Catholic convert, a focal point for the community's hypocrisy and confusion
about racial purity and, ultimately, as Gerard Carruthers puts it, as 'a dis-
penser of oxymoronic identity' ('"Fully to savour her position": Muriel Spark
and Scottish Identity', *Modern Fiction Studies* 54: 3 (Fall 2008), 487–504,
p. 503). It is also a signifier for ambiguity and apocryphal interpretation in
Territorial Rights (1979), through Robert Leaver's theory about the hidden
meaning of the biblical phrase *Nigra sum sed formosa*, normally a reference to
the Madonna's purity: 'Now as it happens I have discovered that the ancient
Hebrew could mean "black but comely" [. . .] and it could also mean "black
and comely", or again it could mean "black, *therefore* comely". So I intend to
write a thesis . . .' (London: Penguin Books, 1991), 23.
54. In 'The First Christmas Eve', a 1984 piece originally commissioned by *Vanity
Fair*, Spark wrote about a Renaissance fresco by the Tuscan artist Piero della
Francesca in terms reminiscent of Annabel's 'predicament'.
55. Muriel Spark, *The Abbess of Crewe* ([1974] Harmondsworth: Penguin Books,
1975), 25.
56. See, for instance, 'The Golden Fleece', her arduously researched piece on the
mythological provenance of the insignia of the Order of the Golden Fleece
for *Argentor*, the 'beautifully produced' journal of the National Jewellers'
Association, of which she was very proud (*Argentor* III: I (1948), 29–32, 70;
Curriculum Vitae, 163–4).
57. Muriel Spark, *The Takeover* ([1976] London: Penguin Books, 1978), 99.
58. Ibid., 153.
59. As Spark put it to John Tusa, 'Reversal of circumstances is what Aristotle
called Peripeteia. I like that very much, towards the end, a reversal of circumstances'.   http://www.bbc.co.uk/radio3/johntusainterview/spark_transcript.
shtml. Accessed 25 May 2009; Fleur Talbot echoes that view: 'I do dearly
love a turn of events' (*Loitering with Intent*, 157).
60. Muriel Spark, 'Emily Brontë: Her Life' [1953], Muriel Spark and Derek
Stanford, *Emily Brontë: Her Life and Work* (London: Peter Owen, 1960), 259,
260, 262.
61. Spark, *The Abbess of Crewe*, 24–5.
62. Spark, *Emily Brontë: Her Life and Work*, 314.
63. Jennifer Lynn Randisi, *On Her Way Rejoicing: The Fiction of Muriel Spark*
(Washington, DC: The Catholic University of America Press, 1991),
79–102.

64. Spark, *Symposium* ([1990] London: Penguin Books, 1991b), 186.
65. 'No Need for the Grill: Hell is Other People', Jean-Paul Sartre, *Huis Clos: Pièce en un acte*, ed. Keith Gore (London: Methuen, 1987), 95. My translation.
66. http://www.bbc.co.uk/radio3/johntusainterview/spark_transcript.shtml. Accessed 25 May 2009.
67. Spark, 'Come Along, Marjorie', *The Complete Short Stories*, 315.
68. Muriel Spark, *The Driver's Seat* ([1970] Harmondsworth: Penguin Books, 1974), 107.
69. Spark, 'Come Along, Marjorie', 314.
70. Spark, *The Driver's Seat*, 107.
71. Ibid., 106.
72. Spark, 'Come Along, Marjorie', 311.
73. Spark, *The Girls of Slender Means*, 126, 130.
74. Judy Sproxton, *The Women of Muriel Spark* (London: Constable, 1992), 13.
75. Allan Pero, '"Look for One Thing and You Find Another": The Voice and Deduction in Muriel Spark's *Memento Mori*', *Modern Fiction Studies* 54: 3 (Fall 2008), 558–73, p. 559.
76. 'Muriel Spark between the Lines', *The New Yorker* (24 May 1993), 41–2.
77. Spark, 'Come Along, Marjorie', 314.
78. Examples include typewriters (*The Comforters*), telephones (*Memento Mori*), wirelesses (*The Girls of Slender Means*), tape recorders (*The Comforters*; *The Girls of Slender Means*), cameras (*Not to Disturb*; *The Public Image*), bugging devices (*The Abbess of Crewe*) and various contraptions derived from plausible and implausible fields of research, such as bionics (*Symposium*) and radionics (*A Far Cry from Kensington*).
79. Spark, *Curriculum Vitae*, 148.
80. 'Against the Transcendentalists' (*c.* 1952), *All the Poems* (Manchester: Carcanet, 2004), 58.

Chapter 3 – Gardiner

1. Alain Robbe-Grillet, 'A Future for the Novel', repr. in David Lodge (ed.), *Twentieth Century Literary Criticism: A Reader* (London: Longman, 1972), 467–74, 471.
2. Ruth Whittaker, *The Faith and Fiction of Muriel Spark* (London: Macmillan, 1982), 9; cf. *Iris Murdoch, Muriel Spark, and John Fowles: Didactic Demons in Modern Fiction* (London: Fairleigh Dickinson University Press, 1988); cf. R. C. Kane, 'Didactic Demons in Contemporary British Fiction', *University of Mississippi Studies in English* 8 (1990), 36–57.
3. Evelyn Waugh, 'Something Fresh: *The Comforters*', *The Spectator* (22 February 1957), 256.
4. Cf. Judy Little, *Comedy and the Woman Writer: Woolf, Spark, and Feminism* (Lincoln, NB: University of Nebraska Press, 1983), 110.

5. Joseph Hynes, *The Art of the Real: Muriel Spark's Novels* (Cranbury, NJ: Associated University Presses, 1988), 19.
6. Whittaker, *The Faith and Fiction of Muriel Spark*, 50.
7. Daniel Defoe, *History of the Union* (Dublin: J. Exshaw, 1799 [1709]), 50.
8. Cf. Norman Page, *Muriel Spark* (London: Macmillan, 1990), 13.
9. Virginia Woolf, *The Common Reader*, second series, chapter 4 (1935), consulted at: http://ebooks.adelaide.edu.au/w/woolf/virginia/w91c2/chapter4.html, Accessed 12 November 2008.
10. Whittaker, *The Faith and Fiction of Muriel Spark*, 4.
11. Cf. Lewis MacLeod, 'Matters of Care and Control: Surveillance, Omniscience, and Narrative Power in *The Abbess of Crewe* and *Loitering With Intent*', *Modern Fiction Studies* 54: 3 (2008), 574–94.
12. Cairns Craig, *The Modern Scottish Novel* (Edinburgh: Edinburgh University Press, 1999), 167–99.
13. Cf. Nicholas Royle, 'Memento Mori', in Martin McQuillan (ed.), *Theorizing Muriel Spark: Gender, Race, Deconstruction* (Basingstoke: Palgrave Macmillan, 2001), 189–203.
14. Alan Bold, *Muriel Spark* (London: Methuen, 1986), 20.
15. Page, *Muriel Spark*, 50.
16. Alasdair Gray, *The Fall of Kelvin Walker* (Glasgow: Morag McAlpine, 1985).
17. See Gerard Carruthers, 'Muriel Spark as Catholic Novelist', this volume, Chapter 7.
18. G. Gregory Smith, *Scottish Literature: Character and Influence* (London: Macmillan, 1919).
19. Cf. Julian Wolfreys, 'Muriel Spark's *Mary Shelley*: A Gothic and Liminal Life', in McQuillan (ed.), *Theorizing Muriel Spark*, 155–69.
20. Christopher MacLachlan, 'Muriel Spark and Gothic', in Susanne Hagemann (ed.), *Studies in Scottish Fiction: 1945 to the Present* (Frankfurt am Main: Peter Lang, 1996), 125–44, p. 140.
21. James Hogg, *The Private Memoirs and Confessions of A Justified Sinner* (London: Penguin Books, 1987 [1824]), 132.

Chapter 4 – Reizbaum

1. See 'Edinburgh-born', first published in *The New Statesman* in 1964, in *Critical Essays on Muriel Spark*, ed. Joseph Hynes (New York: G. K. Hall & Co., 1992)..
2. Spark refers to artistic inspiration in this way in *Curriculum Vitae*, (London: Constable, 1992), 115.
3. See Allan Pero, '"Look For One Thing and You Find Another": The Voice and Deduction in Muriel Spark's *Memento Mori*', *Modern Fiction Studies* 54: 3 (Fall 2008), 558–635.

4. Ibid., 562. Also, Roland Barthes' discussion of 'the writerly' can be found in *S/Z* (1970). Trans. Richard Miller (London: Jonathan Cape, 1975).

5. Muriel Spark, *The Prime of Miss Jean Brodie* (New York: HarperCollins, 1961), 8; Gerard Carruthers discusses Brodie's practices of 'linguistic transformation': 'While objecting to her girls using the words "comic" [sic] and "social" [sic] as nouns when these should be adjectives, Brodie utilizes the word "prime" [sic] to describe her abstract state of maturity and so performs the same act of transmutation'. In Gerard Carruthers, '"Fully to Savour Her Position": Muriel Spark and Scottish Identity', in *Modern Fiction Studies* 54: 3 (Fall 2008), 487–504, p. 498.

6. Spark, *The Prime of Miss Jean Brodie*, 129.

7. Ibid., 8, 47.

8. Ibid., 31.

9. Ibid., 8.

10. Muriel Spark, *Memento Mori* (New York: New Directions, 2000), 39.

11. Ibid., 154.

12. Jacques Derrida, '*Ulysses* Gramophone: Hear Say Yes in Joyce', trans. Tina Kendall, revised Shari Benstock, *Acts of Literature*, ed. Derek Attridge (New York: Routledge, 1992), 253–309, p. 39.

13. Spark, *Memento Mori*, 38–9.

14. Ibid., 155.

15. Ibid., 154.

16. Derrida, '*Ulysses* Gramophone', 38.

17. Nicholas Royle, 'Memento Mori', in Martin McQuillan (ed.), *Theorizing Muriel Spark: Gender, Race, Deconstruction* (Basingstoke: Palgrave Macmillan, 2001), 189–203, p. 193. Hélène Cixous also discusses the telephone as the technological apparatus of the medium in 'Grimacing Catholicism', H. Cixous, 'Grimacing Catholicism: Muriel Spark's Macabre Farce and Muriel Spark's Latest Novel: *The Public Image*'. *Theorizing Muriel Spark* (2002), pp. 204–9, 206.

18. Nicholas Royle, 'Memento Mori', in Martin McQuillan (ed.), *Theorizing Muriel Spark: Gender, Race, Deconstruction* (Basingstoke: Palgrave Macmillan, 2002)193–4.

19. See Mladen Dolar, *A Voice and Nothing More* (Cambridge, MA: MIT Press, 2006), 61, 67.

20. Spark, *The Prime of Miss Jean Brodie*, 16, 21, respectively.

21. Ibid., 30.

22. Ibid., 43.

23. Ibid., 116.

24. Ibid., 137.

25. Dolar's questions about the source of the voice in Hitchcock's *Psycho* are useful to a consideration of Sandy's identificatory relation to Jean Brodie and the reader's efforts to identify narrative voices in *Brodie*: 'Where does the

mother's voice come from? To which body can it be assigned?' (Dolar, *A Voice and Nothing More*, 61).

26. Spark, 'Edinburgh-born', and in Martin McQuillan, 'An Interview with Muriel Spark', *Theorizing Muriel Spark: Gender, Race, Deconstruction* (Basingstoke: Palgrave Macmillan, 2001), 226–7, Spark tells him: 'I'm Scottish as far as I can claim to be anything' and 'I never liked it, I don't like nationalism as an idea'.

27. See Bryan Cheyette, 'Writing Against Conversion: Muriel Spark the Gentile Jewess' and Willy Maley, 'Not to Deconstruct? Righting and Deference in *Not to Disturb*', both in McQuillan, *Theorizing Muriel Spark*, 93–112; and Carruthers, '"Fully to Savour Her Position"', 490–1.

28. In Carruthers, '"Fully to Savour Her Position"', 488. On the subject of Scottish literature and cosmopolitanism, see the recent discussion by Berthold Schoene in 'Going Cosmopolitan: Reconstituting "Scottishness" in Post-devolution Criticism', in Berthold Schoene (ed.), *The Edinburgh Companion to Contemporary Scottish Literature* (Edinburgh: Edinburgh University Press, 2007), pp. 7–16.

29. Spark, 'Edinburgh-born', 21. Stannard glosses this comment: 'Now that he was dying, she would soon, metaphorically speaking, be homeless. She had cast herself out as a young woman and had never wished to return. Nevertheless, Edinburgh was the home which had made her independence possible, and, for her, all the positive qualities of "home" centred on her father.' Martin Stannard, *Muriel Spark: The Biography* (London: Weidenfeld & Nicolson, 2009), 3. My thanks to Willy Maley for this reference.

30. Muriel Spark, 'My Conversion', in Joseph Hynes (ed.), *Critical Essays on Muriel Spark* (New York: G. K. Hall & Co., 1992) 27: 'But the Catholic Faith really has enormous scope'.

31. Spark, 'Edinburgh-born', 22.

32. Ibid.

33. Ibid., 23.

34. Carruthers, '"Fully to Savour Her Position"', 491.

35. Spark, *Brodie*, 33.

36. Ibid., 32.

37. Ibid., 33. The figure of Mary Queen of Scots, as Stannard reveals, held a particular fascination for Spark (Stannard, *Muriel Spark*, 74). Again, my thanks to Willy Maley for this reference.

38. Muriel Spark refers to her Proustian methods in the 'Foreword' to *All the Stories of Muriel Spark* (New York: New Directions, 2001), for instance, and in 'My Conversion'.

39. Spark, *Brodie*, 72.

40. Ibid., 76.

41. Ibid., 116.

42. Spark, *Memento Mori*, 72.

43. See Bryan Cheyette, *Muriel Spark: Writers and the Work* (Tavistock: Northcote House, 2000). Also in McQuillan, 'Interview with Muriel Spark', 96.

44. See, for example, Liam McIlvanney, 'The Politics of Narrative in the Post-war Scottish Novel', in *On Modern British Fiction*, ed. Zachary Leader (Oxford: Oxford University Press, 2002), p. 187.

45. Sigmund Freud, *Beyond the Pleasure Principle* (1920), in J. Strachey, *The Standard Edition of the Complete Psychological Works of Sigmund Freud* (London: Hogarth Press, 1953–74). pp. 32–49.

46. In 'The Desegregation of Art' Spark discusses the use of ridicule as an antidote to conformity in art and politics. See also her address to this in the McQuillan interview.

47. Peter Brooks, *Reading For the Plot* (New York: Vintage Books, 1985), 102–3.

48. Spark, *Brodie*, 7.

49. See Spark in 'Desegregation' on these ideas of character formations and also Ellmann about naming and memory. M. Ellmann, 'The Ghosts of *Ulysses*', in D. Attridge (ed.), *James' Joyce's 'Ulysses': A Casebook* (Oxford: Oxford University Press, 2004).

50. See Marina MacKay, 'Muriel Spark and the Meaning of Treason', *Modern Fiction Studies* (2008): 505–22; and Peter Robert Brown, '"There's Something about Mary": Narrative and Ethics in *The Prime of Miss Jean Brodie*'. *Journal of Narrative Theory* 36, 2 (2206): 228–53.

51. Royle, 'Memento Mori', 199–200.

52. Pero, '"Look For One Thing and You Find Another"', 563.

53. Ibid., 561. See also Roland Barthes' discussion of consecution and causality in 'Structural Analysis of Narratives', in Susan Sontag (ed.), *A Barthes Reader* (New York: Hill and Wang, 1982), 266.

54. Spark, *Curriculum Vitae*, p. 208.

55. Anthony Burgess famously entitled his work on James Joyce *ReJoyce*, in a partial reference to Joyce's 'commodious recirculations'. A. Burgess, *Re Joyce* (New York: W. W. Norton, 1965); Carruthers, '"Fully to Savour Her Position"', 490, along with others, has pointed to 'rejoicing' as an 'important Sparkian word'.

Chapter 5 – Piette

1. Muriel Spark, *The Mandelbaum Gate* (London: Penguin Books, 1967 [1965]), 60.

2. 'I see it happening – in families – terrorism and blackmail. [. . .] There's lots of blackmail in my work and unspoken blackmail.' In Martin McQuillan (ed.), *Theorizing Muriel Spark: Gender, Race, Deconstruction* (Basingstoke: Palgrave Macmillan, 2001), 224–5.

3. Mikhail Bakhtin, *The Dialogic Imagination: Four Essays*, ed. Michael Holquist, trans. Caryl Emerson & Michael Holquist (Austin: University of Texas Press, 1981), p. 84.

4. *The Hothouse by the East River* (Harmondsworth: Penguin, 1973), p. 140.
5. And at the end of *The Ballad of Peckham Rye* where the town looks 'like a cloud of green and gold, the people seeming to ride upon it, as you might say there was another world than this' (143).
6. Cf. Mary McGregor and the fire in Muriel Spark, *The Prime of Miss Jean Brodie* (15).

Chapter 6 – Wickman

1. Muriel Spark, *Symposium* (New York: New Directions, 1990), 16, 64. Subsequent references will be cited in the text.
2. Muriel Spark, *Curriculum Vitae* (Boston, MA: Houghton Mifflin, 1993), 83, 199.
3. 'I advocate the arts of satire and ridicule . . . Ridicule is the only honourable weapon we have left.' Muriel Spark, 'The Desegregation of Art', *Proceedings of the American Academy of Arts and Letters* (1971), 20–7, p. 24.
4. See Liam McIlvanney, 'The Politics of Narrative in the Post-War Scottish Novel', in *On Modern British Fiction*, ed. Zachary Leader (Oxford: Oxford University Press, 2002), 181–208.
5. See Martin McQuillan, 'Introduction: "I Don't Know Anything about Freud": Muriel Spark Meets Contemporary Criticism', in Martin McQuillan (ed.), *Theorizing Muriel Spark: Gender, Race, Deconstruction*, (Basingstoke: Palgrave Macmillan, 2001), 1–31.
6. See Ihab Hassan, *The Postmodern Turn: Essays in Postmodern Theory and Culture* (Columbus: Ohio State University Press, 1987), 91–2.
7. See, for instance, Helmut Lethen's relatively early (1984) essay on this subject, 'Modernism Cut in Half: The Exclusion of the Avant-garde and the Debate on Postmodernism', in *Approaching Postmodernism*, ed. Douwe Fokkema and Hans Bertens (Amsterdam: John Benjamins, 1986), 233–8.
8. Bryan Cheyette, *Muriel Spark* (Tavistock: Northcote House, 2000), 10.
9. Allan Massie, *Muriel Spark* (Edinburgh: Ramsay Head, 1979), 9.
10. This conclusion runs contrary in some ways to Spark's sensibilities. For her, 'labels are very useful because they're a kind of guideline'. This was partly her logic in explaining her conversion to Catholicism. See James Brooker and Margarita Estévez Saá, 'Interview with Dame Muriel Spark', *Women's Studies* 33: 8 (2004), 1035, and Sara Frankel, 'An Interview with Muriel Spark', *Partisan Review* 54 (1987), 443–57.
11. The term 'crystal' is from Iris Murdoch, who broke modern novels into categories of the 'journalistic' and the 'crystalline'. On the relationship between these categories and Spark's fiction, see Richard Todd, 'The Crystalline Novels of Muriel Spark', *Essays on the Contemporary British Novel*, ed. Hedwig Bock and Albert Wertheim (München: M. Hueber, 1986), 175–92.
12. Cheyette, *Muriel Spark*, 85.

13. Ruth Whittaker, *The Faith and Fiction of Muriel Spark* (London: Macmillan, 1982), 86.

14. Todd, 'The Crystalline Novels of Muriel Spark', 189.

15. For a lucid and far more detailed account of the novel's characters and plot twists, see Alan Bold, *Muriel Spark* (London: Methuen, 1986), 107–10.

16. Muriel Spark, *Territorial Rights* (New York: Perigee, 1979), 5. Subsequent references will be cited in the text.

17. Ian Rankin, 'The Deliberate Cunning of Muriel Spark', *The Scottish Novel Since the Seventies: New Visions, Old Dreams*, ed. Randall Stevenson and Gavin Wallace (Edinburgh: Edinburgh University Press, 1993), 41–53.

18. See Søren Kierkegaard, 'Repetition', trans. Howard V. Hong and Edna H. Hong, *Fear and Trembling; Repetition: Kierkegaard's Writings*, vol. VI (Princeton, NJ: Princeton University Press, 1983), 125–231; Friedrich Nietzsche, *Thus Spoke Zarathustra*, trans. Walter Kaufmann (New York: Penguin Books, 1966), 323–4; and Jacques Derrida, 'Différance', in *Margins of Philosophy*, trans. Alan Bass (Chicago: University of Chicago Press, 1982), 1–27.

19. Spark had grown accustomed to such doubling and disfiguration in her wartime experience working in a counter-intelligence office. See *Curriculum Vitae*, 147–53.

20. Todd, 'The Crystalline Novels of Muriel Spark', 180.

21. Muriel Spark, *The Driver's Seat* (New York: New Directions, 1994), 18.

22. Fredric Jameson, *Postmodernism, or, The Cultural Logic of Late Capitalism* (Durham, NC: Duke University Press, 1991), 14. Subsequent references are cited in the text.

23. See Harold Bloom's famous model of literary transformation, most succinctly summarised in *The Anxiety of Influence: A Theory of Poetry* (London: Oxford University Press, 1973).

24. For an extended discussion of Gordon's work in light of critical theory, see Mark Hansen, 'The Time of Affect, or Bearing Witness to Life', *Critical Inquiry* 30: 3 (2004), 584–626.

25. See, for instance, Alex Callinicos, *Against Postmodernism* (Cambridge: Polity Press, 1989) and, more recently, Christopher Nash, *The Unravelling of the Postmodern Mind* (Edinburgh: University of Edinburgh Press, 2001), 261.

26. Bruno Latour, *We Have Never Been Modern*, trans. Catherine Porter (Cambridge, MA: Harvard University Press, 1993), 10.

27. For a reading of Spark's interest in border ballads in light of literary theory, see Michael Gardiner, *From Trocchi to Trainspotting: Scottish Critical Theory Since 1960* (Edinburgh: Edinburgh University Press, 2006), 55–61.

28. Muriel Spark, *All the Poems* (Manchester: Carcanet, 2004), 50.

29. On the uncanny effects of repetition, see Jacques Derrida, 'Ulysses Gramophone: Hear Say Yes in Joyce', trans. Tina Kendall, revised Shari

Benstock, *Acts of Literature*, ed. Derek Attridge (New York: Routledge, 1992), 253–309.

30. On the 'paramodern', see Stephen Barker, *Autoaesthetics: Strategies of the Self after Nietzsche* (Atlantic Highlands, NJ: Humanities Press, 1992), 214–59.

31. Bryan Cheyette, *Muriel Spark* (Tavistock: Northcote House, 2000), 119.

32. On Hamilton Finlay's art, see Alec Finlay (ed.), *Wood Notes Wild: Essays on the Art and Poetry of Ian Hamilton Finlay* (Edinburgh: Polygon, 1995).

Chapter 7 – Carruthers

1. For an illuminating survey of Spark's Scottish literary context and also for her reading in the Psalms, see Valerie Shaw, 'Muriel Spark', in Cairns Craig (ed.), *The History of Scottish Literature* vol. 4 (Twentieth Century) (Aberdeen: Aberdeen University Press, 1987), 277–90; see also Gerard Carruthers, '"Fully to Savour Her Position": Muriel Spark and Scottish Identity', in *Modern Fiction Studies* 54-3 (Fall 2008), 487–504. Bryan Cheyette has much of interest to say in regard to Spark's relationship to Judaism, see *Muriel Spark*. (Tavistock: Northcote House, 2000), especially 16–19, 26–7, 63–6.

2. Martin McQuillan, *Theorizing Muriel Spark: Gender, Race, Deconstruction* (Basingstoke: Palgrave Macmillan, 2001).

3. McQuillan, 'Introduction', in ibid., 5–6.

4. See, for instance, Christopher Whyte, 'Queer Readings, Gay Texts: From *Redgauntlet* to *The Prime of Miss Jean Brodie*', in Marco Fazzini (ed.), *Resisting Alterities: Wilson Harris and Other Avatars of Otherness* (Amsterdam: Rodopi: 2004), 159–75; also Jonathan Kemp, '"Her lips are slightly parted": The Ineffability of Erotic Sociality in Muriel Spark's *The Driver's Seat*', in *Modern Fiction Studies* 54: 3 (Fall 2008), 544–57.

5. 'My Conversion' is reprinted in Joseph Hynes (ed.), *Critical Essays on Muriel Spark* (New York: G. K. Hall & Co., 1992), 25.

6. Muriel Spark, *The Comforters* (London and New York: Penguin Books, 1963), 63.

7. Muriel Spark, *The Mandelbaum Gate* (London: Penguin Books, 1967), 198.

8. Muriel Spark, *The Collected Stories* (London: Penguin Books, 1994), 315.

9. See her autobiography, Muriel Spark, *Curriculum Vitae* (London: Constable, 1992), 202.

10. Bryan Cheyette, *Muriel Spark* (Tavistock: Northcote House, 2000), 9.

11. Muriel Spark, *The Prime of Miss Jean Brodie* (London: Penguin, 1965), 120.

12. Ibid., 111.

13. Ibid., 123.

14. Ibid., 42.

15. Ibid., 123.

16. Ibid., 120.

17. Ibid., 43.

18. Spark, *Curriculum Vitae*, 174.
19. Spark, *The Prime of Miss Jean Brodie*, 43.
20. Muriel Spark, *The Girls of Slender Means* (London: Reprint Society, 1965), 222.
21. Spark, *The Prime of Miss Jean Brodie*, 127–8.
22. Muriel Spark, *Collected Stories*, vol. 1 (London: Macmillan, 1985), 53.
23. Ibid., 76.
24. Muriel Spark, *The Driver's Seat* (London: Penguin Books, 1974), 106.

Chapter 8 – Lyons

1. Muriel Spark, *A Far Cry from Kensington* (London: Constable, 1988), 102.
2. D. H. Lawrence, *Studies in Classic American Literature* (London: Penguin Books, 1971 [1923]), 8.
3. Doris Lessing, *The Diaries of Jane Somers* (London: Michael Joseph, 1984), 7.
4. Muriel Spark, *Curriculum Vitae* (London: Constable, 1992), 11.
5. Alain Badiou, *The Century*, trans. Alberto Toscano (London: Polity, 2007: original French edn 2005), 153.
6. Muriel Spark and Derek Stanford, *Emily Brontë: Her Life and Work* (London: Arrow, 1985 [1953]), 81.
7. Ibid., 93.
8. Ibid., 94.
9. Ibid., 95.
10. Badiou, *The Century*, 153.
11. Muriel Spark, *Mary Shelley* (London: Constable, 1988; revised from *Child of Light*, 1951), 162–4.
12. Badiou, *The Century*, 154.
13. Evelyn Waugh, 'Something Fresh', *Spectator* (22 February 1957), 256; cited in Martin Stannard, *Muriel Spark: The Biography* (London: Weidenfeld & Nicolson), 179.
14. Muriel Spark, *The Comforters* (New York: HarperCollins, 1961), 184.
15. Ibid., 117.
16. Ibid., 154–5.
17. Badiou, *The Century*, 155.
18. Spark, *The Comforters*, 233.
19. Muriel Spark, 'My Conversion', first published in *The Twentieth Century*, 1961; reprinted in Joseph Hynes (ed.), *Critical Essays on Muriel Spark* (New York: G. K. Hall & Co., 1992), 27.
20. Muriel Spark, *The Prime of Miss Jean Brodie* (London: Macmillan, 1961), 94–5.
21. Muriel Spark, *The Public Image* (London, Macmillan, 1969 [1968]), 141.
22. Peter Kemp, *Muriel Spark* (London: Paul Elek, 1974), 119.

23. Spark, *The Public Image*, 192.
24. Kemp, *Muriel Spark*, 113.
25. Muriel Spark, *The Driver's Seat* (London: Macmillan, 1970), 35.
26. Ibid., 37.
27. Ibid., 72–4.
28. Roland Barthes, *Writing Degree Zero*, trans. Annette Lavers and Colin Smith (London: Jonathan Cape, 1967; original French edn. 1953), 36–7.
29. Spark, *The Driver's Seat*, 156.
30. Ibid., 157.
31. Ibid., 158–9.
32. Ibid., 158.
33. Ibid., 160.
34. Malcolm Bradbury, 'Muriel Spark's Fingernails', *Critical Quarterly* 14 (1972), 250.
35. Lorna Sage, *Women in the House of Fiction* (London: Macmillan, 1992), 142.
36. Muriel Spark, *The Abbess of Crewe* (London: Macmillan, 1974), 9.
37. Ibid., 114.
38. Ibid., 128.
39. Ibid., 128.
40. Ibid., 106.
41. Ibid., 9, 10, 11, 117.
42. Spark, *A Far Cry from Kensington*, 62.
43. Ibid., 87.
44. Ibid., 178.

Chapter 9 – Stevenson

1. Graham Greene, *The End of the Affair* (Harmondsworth: Penguin Books, 1976 [1951]), 186, 173, 147.
2. Muriel Spark, *The Comforters* (Harmondsworth: Penguin Books, 1982 [1957]), 39. Subsequent references are to this edition.
3. Muriel Spark, *The Ballad of Peckham Rye* (Harmondsworth: Penguin Books, 1999 [1960]), 77.
4. Muriel Spark, *The Mandelbaum Gate* (Harmondsworth: Penguin Books, 1967 [1965]), 264.
5. Brian McHale, *Postmodernist Fiction* (London: Methuen, 1987), 120.
6. Muriel Spark, *Robinson* (London: Macmillan, 1972 [1958]), 185, 36.
7. Muriel Spark, *The Prime of Miss Jean Brodie* (Harmondsworth: Penguin Books, 1982 [1961]), 120. Subsequent references are to this edition.
8. Valerie Shaw, 'Muriel Spark', in Cairns Craig (ed.), *The History of Scottish Literature*, vol. 4, *Twentieth Century* (Aberdeen: Aberdeen University Press, 1987), 279; Malcolm Bradbury, 'Muriel Spark's Fingernails', in Joseph Hynes

(ed.), *Critical Essays on Muriel Spark* (New York, Oxford, Singapore and Sydney: Maxwell Macmillan International , 1992), 187.

9. Dominic Head, *The Cambridge Introduction to Modern British Fiction, 1950–2000* (Cambridge: Cambridge University Press, 2002), 152.

10. Brian Cheyette, *Muriel Spark* (Tavistock: Northcote House/British Council, 2000), 9, 8. His comments on conversion draw on the work of Gauri Viswanathan. Spark, of course, encountered forms of strategic 'doubleness' in supposedly official discourse long before her conversion, when working in the Intelligence service during the war.

11. Quoted in Neil Corcoran, *English Poetry since 1940* (London: Longman, 1993), 116.

12. Muriel Spark, *A Far Cry from Kensington* (London: Constable, 1988), 104.

13. Elaine Feinstein, *The Survivors* (London: Hutchinson, 1982), 297.

14. Iris Murdoch, 'Against Dryness' (1961), rpt. in Malcolm Bradbury (ed.), *The Novel Today: Contemporary Writers on Modern Fiction* (Glasgow: Fontana, 1977), 23, 30.

15. Virginia Woolf, *To the Lighthouse* (Harmondsworth: Penguin Books, 1973 [1927]), 236–7, 170.

16. Malcolm Lowry, *Under the Volcano* (Harmondsworth: Penguin Books, 1983 [1947]), 15, 107.

17. Stephen Spender, 'Books and the War – VII', in John Lehmann (ed.), *The Penguin New Writing*, no. 8 (London: Penguin Books, July 1941), 130.

18. Martin McQuillan, 'The Same Informed Air: An Interview with Muriel Spark', in Martin McQuillan (ed.), *Theorizing Muriel Spark: Gender, Race, Deconstruction* (Basingstoke: Palgrave Macmillan, 2001), 216.

19. Aidan Day, 'Parodying Postmodernism: Muriel Spark (*The Driver's Seat*) and Robbe-Grillet (*Jealousy*)', *English*, 56: 216 (Autumn 2007), 321, 326.

20. McQuillan, 'The Same Informed Air', 216 n. 20.

21. Alain Robbe-Grillet, 'A Future for the Novel' (1956); rpt. in David Lodge (ed.), *Twentieth-Century Literary Criticism* (London: Longman, 1972), 471–2.

22. Willy Maley, 'Not to Deconstruct? Righting and Deference in *Not to Disturb*', in *Theorizing Muriel Spark*, 175, 173(n. 20).

23. Iris Murdoch, *Under the Net* (London: Granada, 1983 [1954]), 82.

24. Ian Rankin, 'The Deliberate Cunning of Muriel Spark', in Gavin Wallace and Randall Stevenson (eds.), *The Scottish Novel since the Seventies* (Edinburgh: Edinburgh University Press, 1993), 52.

Chapter 10 – Milne

1. Muriel Spark, *The Girls of Slender Means* (1963) (Harmondsworth: Penguin Books, 1966), 7.

2. Ibid., 142.

3. Brian Cheyette, *Muriel Spark* (Tavistock: Northcote House, 2000), xi.

4. Muriel Spark, 'Edinburgh-born', *Critical Essays on Muriel Spark*, ed. Joseph Hynes (New York: G. K. Hall & Co., 1992), 23.

5. Muriel Spark, *Curriculum Vitae* (London: Penguin Books, 1993), 206.

6. On fictional prolepsis, see Mark Currie, *About Time: Narrative, Fiction and the Philosophy of Time* (Edinburgh: Edinburgh University Press, 2007).

7. Muriel Spark, *Symposium* (London: Penguin Books, 1991), 27.

8. Martin McQuillan (ed.), *Theorizing Muriel Spark: Gender, Race, Deconstruction* (Basingstoke: Palgrave Macmillan, 2001).

9. See, for example, Muriel Spark, 'The Desegregation of Art', in *Critical Essays on Muriel Spark*, ed. Joseph Hynes (New York: G. K. Hall & Co., 1992), 33–7.

10. Peter Kemp, *Muriel Spark* (London: Paul Elek, 1974), 14.

11. Muriel Spark, *A Far Cry from Kensington* (London: Constable, 1988; Harmondsworth: Penguin Books, 1989).

12. On affinities of writing and blackmail, see Cheyette, *Muriel Spark*; and Alan Bold, *Muriel Spark* (London: Methuen, 1986).

13. For some discussion of the intervening history of literary publishing, see John Sutherland, *Fiction and the Fiction Industry* (London: Athlone, 1978).

14. Duncan MacLaughlin and William Hall, *Dead Lucky: Lord Lucan, The Final Truth* (London: Blake, 2003).

15. Muriel Spark, 'Loser Lucan was too Dull for Goa', *The Guardian* (9 September 2003). http://www.guardian.co.uk/books/2003/sep/09/biography.murielspark. Accessed 9 November 2009.

16. Muriel Spark, *The Takeover* (London: Penguin Books, 1978 [1976]), 90–1.

17. Martin Stannard, *Muriel Spark: The Biography* (London: Weidenfeld & Nicolson, 2009).

18. See, for example, Alain Robbe-Grillet, *Snapshots; and Towards a New Novel* (London: Calder & Boyars, 1965); and Stephen Heath, *The Nouveau Roman: A Study in the Practice of Writing* (London: Paul Elek, 1972).

19. Laura Marcus, 'Detection and Literary Fiction', *The Cambridge Companion to Crime Fiction*, ed. Martin Priestman (Cambridge: Cambridge University Press, 2003), 245–67, pp. 245–6. Compare Tzvetan Todorov, 'The Typology of Detective Fiction', *The Poetics of Prose*, trans. Richard Holmes (Ithaca, NY: Cornell University Press, 1977), 42–52.

20. Spark, 'The Desegregation of Art', 34.

21. Laura Marcus, 'Detection and Literary Fiction', *The Cambridge Companion to Crime Fiction*. See also Andrew Pepper, 'Black Crime Fiction', *Cambridge Companion to Crime Fiction*, 209–26, p. 211; Stephen Soitos, *The Blues Detective: A Study of African American Detective Fiction* (Amherst, MA: University of Massachusetts Press, 1996); Stephen Knight, *Form and Ideology in Crime Fiction* (London: Macmillan, 1980); Dennis Porter, *The Pursuit of Crime: Art and Ideology in Detective Fiction* (New Haven, CT: Yale University Press, 1981); Ernest Mandel, *Delightful Murder: A Social History of the Crime*

Novel (London: Pluto, 1999); Paul Cobley, *The American Thriller: Generic Innovation and Social Change in the 1970s* (Basingstoke: Palgrave Macmillan, 2000); Andrew Pepper, *The Contemporary American Crime Novel: Race, Ethnicity, Gender, Class* (Edinburgh: Edinburgh University Press, 2000).

22. Muriel Spark, 'The Snobs', *The Complete Short Stories* (Harmondsworth: Penguin Books, 2002), 116–23, p. 116.

Further Reading

Primary Texts

Spark, Muriel, 'The Golden Fleece', *Argentor* 3: 1 (1948), 29–32, 70.

Spark, Muriel, 'Poetry and Politics', *Parliamentary Affairs* 1 (1948), 12–23.

Spark, Muriel, 'Poetry and the American Government', *Parliamentary Affairs* 3 (1949), 260–72.

Spark, Muriel, and Stanford, Derek (eds.), *Tribute to Wordsworth: A Miscellany of Opinion for the Centenary of the Poet's Death* (London: Wingate, 1950).

Spark, Muriel, *Child of Light: A Reassessment of Mary Wollstonecraft Shelley* (Hadleigh: Tower Bridge Publications, 1951); revised as *Mary Shelley* (London: Constable, 1988; 1993).

Spark, Muriel, *The Essence of the Brontës: A Compilation with Essays* (London and Chester Spring, PA: Peter Owen, 1952; 1993)

Spark, Muriel (ed.), *A Selection of Poems by Emily Brontë* (London: Grey Walls Press, 1952).

Spark, Muriel and Stanford, Derek (eds.), *Emily Brontë: Her Life and Work* (London: Peter Owen, 1953; London: Arrow, 1985).

Spark, Muriel, *The Brontë Letters* (London: Peter Nevill, 1953).

Spark, Muriel, *John Masefield* (London: Peter Nevill, 1953; revised edition, London: Pimlico, 1992).

Spark, Muriel and Stanford, Derek (eds.), *My Best Mary: Selected Letters of Mary Shelley* (London: Wingate, 1953).

Spark, Muriel, 'The Religion of an Agnostic: A Sacramental View of the World in the Writings of Proust', *The Church of England Newspaper* (27 November 1953), 1.

Spark, Muriel, 'The Mystery of Job's Suffering: Jung's New Interpretation Examined', *The Church of England Newspaper* (15 April 1955), 1.

Spark, Muriel (ed.), *The Brontë Letters* (London: Peter Nevill, 1954).

Spark, Muriel and Stanford, Derek (eds.), *Letters of John Henry Newman: A Selection* (London: Peter Owen, 1957).

Spark, Muriel and Stanford, Derek, *Emily Brontë: Her Life and Work* (London: Peter Owen, 1960).

Spark, Muriel, *The Comforters* (London: Macmillan, 1957; Harmondsworth: Penguin Books, 1963, 1982; New York: New Directions, 1994).

Spark, Muriel, *Robinson* (London: Macmillan, 1958; Harmondsworth: Penguin Books, 1964; London: Macmillan, 1972; New York: New Directions, 2003).

Spark, Muriel, *Memento Mori* (London: Macmillan, 1959; Harmondsworth: Penguin Books, 1961, 1973; New York: New Directions, 2000).

Spark, Muriel, *The Bachelors* (London: Macmillan, 1960; Harmondsworth: Penguin Books, 1963; New York: New Directions, 1999).

Spark, Muriel, *The Ballad of Peckham Rye* (London: Macmillan, 1960; Harmondsworth: Penguin Modern Classics, 1999; New York: New Directions, 1999).

Spark, Muriel, *The Prime of Miss Jean Brodie* (London: Macmillan, 1961; Harmondsworth: Penguin Books, 1965, 1982; New York: Harper Perennial, 1999).

Spark, Muriel, *Voices at Play* (London: Macmillan, 1961; Harmondsworth: Penguin Books, 1961, 1966).

Spark, Muriel, *Doctors of Philosophy: A Play* (London: Macmillan, 1963).

Spark, Muriel, *The Girls of Slender Means* (London: Macmillan, 1963; Harmondsworth: Penguin Books, 1966).

Spark, Muriel, *The Mandelbaum Gate* (London: Macmillan, 1965; Harmondsworth: Penguin Books, 1967).

Spark, Muriel, *The Very Fine Clock*, drawings by Edward Gorey (New York: Alfred A. Knopf, 1968).

Spark, Muriel, *The Public Image* (New York: Alfred A. Knopf, 1968; London, Macmillan, 1969; New York: New Directions, 1993).

Spark, Muriel, *The Driver's Seat* (London: Macmillan, 1970; Harmondsworth: Penguin Books, 1974; New York: New Directions, 1994).

Spark, Muriel, 'The Desegregation of Art', *Proceedings of the American Academy of Arts and Letters*, 2nd series, 21 (1971), 20–7. Reprinted in Joseph Hynes (ed.), *Critical Essays on Muriel Spark* (New York: Maxwell Macmillan International, 1992), 33–7.

Spark, Muriel, *Not to Disturb* (London: Macmillan, 1971; Harmondsworth: Penguin Books, 1974, 1977).

Spark, Muriel, *The Hothouse by the East River* (London: Macmillan, 1973; Harmondsworth: Penguin Books, 1973, 1975).

Spark, Muriel, *The Abbess of Crewe* (London: Macmillan, 1974; Harmondsworth: Penguin Books, 1975; New York: New Directions, 1995).

Spark, Muriel, *The Takeover* (London: Macmillan, 1976; London: Penguin Books, 1978).

Spark, Muriel, *Territorial Rights* (London: Macmillan, 1979; New York: Perigee, 1979; London: Penguin Books, 1991).

Spark, Muriel, *Loitering With Intent* (London: Bodley Head, 1981; London: Virago Modern Classics, 2007).

Spark, Muriel, *The Only Problem* (London: Bodley Head, 1984; London: Granada, 1985; London: Penguin Books, 1995).

Spark, Muriel, *Collected Stories 1* (London: Macmillan, 1985).

Spark, Muriel, *A Far Cry from Kensington* (London: Constable, 1988; London: Penguin Books, 1989, 1991; New York: New Directions, 2000).

Spark, Muriel, *Symposium* (London: Constable, 1990; New York: New Directions, 1990; London: Penguin Books, 1991; London: Virago Modern Classics, 2006).

Spark, Muriel, *Curriculum Vitae: A Volume of Autobiography* (London: Constable, 1992; Harmondsworth: Penguin Books, 1993; Boston, MA: Houghton Mifflin, 1993).

Spark, Muriel, *The Collected Stories* (Harmondsworth: Penguin Books, 1994).

Spark, Muriel, *Reality and Dreams* (London: Constable, 1996; Harmondsworth: Penguin Books, 1997).

Spark, Muriel, *Aiding and Abetting* (London: Viking, 2000; Harmondsworth: Penguin Books, 2001).

Spark, Muriel, *All the Stories of Muriel Spark* (New York: New Directions, 2001).

Spark, Muriel, *The Complete Short Stories* (London: Viking, 2001; Harmondsworth: Penguin Books, 2002).

Spark, Muriel, 'Loser Lucan was too Dull for Goa', *The Guardian* (9 September 2003). http://www.guardian.co.uk//2003/sep/09/biography.murielspark.

Spark, Muriel, *All the Poems* (Manchester: Carcanet, 2004, 2006).

Spark, Muriel, *The Finishing School* (London: Viking, 2004; Harmondsworth: Penguin Books, 2005).

Spark, Muriel, *Walking on Air* (Paris: The American University of Paris; Lewes: Sylph Editions, 2007).

Secondary Texts

Adler, Renata, 'Muriel Spark', in Richard Kostelanetz (ed.), *On Contemporary Literature* (New York: Avon Books, 1964).

Apostolou, Fotini, 'Seduction, Simulacra and the Feminine: Spectacles and Images in Muriel Spark's *The Public Image*', *Journal of Gender Studies* 9: 3 (2000), 281–97.

Apostolou, Fotini, *Seduction and Death in Muriel Spark's Fiction* (Westport, CT and London: Greenwood Press, 2001).

Ashworth, Ann, 'The Betrayal of the Mentor in *The Prime of Miss Jean Brodie*', *Journal of Evolutionary Psychology* 16: 1–2 (March 1995), 37–46.

Bold, Alan (ed.), *Muriel Spark: An Odd Capacity for Vision* (London: Vision Press, 1984).

Bold, Alan, *Muriel Spark*, Contemporary Writers (London: Methuen, 1986).

Bradbury, Malcolm, 'Muriel Spark's Fingernails', *Critical Quarterly* 14: 3 (1972), 241–50.

Brooker, James and Estévez Saá, Margarita, 'Interview with Dame Muriel Spark', *Women's Studies* 33: 8 (2004), 1035–46.

Brown, Peter Robert, '"There's Something about Mary": Narrative and Ethics in *The Prime of Miss Jean Brodie*', *Journal of Narrative Theory* 36: 2 (2006), 228–53.

Carruthers, Gerard, 'The Remarkable Fictions of Muriel Spark', in Douglas Gifford and Dorothy McMillan (eds.), *A History of Scottish Women's Writing* (Edinburgh: Edinburgh University Press, 1997), 514–25.

Carruthers, Gerard, '"Fully to Savour Her Position": Muriel Spark and Scottish Identity', *Modern Fiction Studies* 54: 3 (2008), 487–504.

Cheyette, Bryan, *Muriel Spark* (Tavistock: Northcote House, 2000).

Christensen, Bryce '"The latter end of job": The Gift of Narrative in Muriel Spark's *The Only Problem* and *The Comforters*', *Renascence* 54: 2 (2002), 136–47.

Day, Aidan, 'Parodying Postmodernism: Muriel Spark (*The Driver's Seat*) and Robbe-Grillet (*Jealousy*)', *English* 56: 216 (2007), 321–37.

Dobie, Ann B., 'Muriel Spark's Definition of Reality', *Critique* 12: 1 (1970), 20–7.

Edgecombe, Rodney Stenning, *Vocation and Identity in the Fiction of Muriel Spark* (Columbia, MO and London: University of Missouri Press, 1990).

Elphinstone, Margaret, 'The Human and Textual Condition: Muriel Spark's Narratives', in Ian Brown et al. (eds.), *Edinburgh History of Scottish Literature, Volume 3: Modern Transformations: New Identities (from 1918)* (Edinburgh: Edinburgh University Press, 2007), 207–13.

Frankel, Sara, 'An Interview with Muriel Spark', *Partisan Review* 54 (1987), 443–57.

Gardiner, Michael, *From Trocchi to Trainspotting: Scottish Critical Theory Since 1960* (Edinburgh: Edinburgh University Press, 2006).

Gillham, Ian, 'Keeping it Short: Muriel Spark Talks about Her Books to Ian Gillham', *The Listener* (24 September 1970), 411–13.

Gilliatt, Penelope, 'The Dashing Novellas of Muriel Spark', *Grand Street* 8: 4 (1989), 139–46.

Glavin, John, 'Muriel Spark's Unknowing Fiction', *Women's Studies* 15 (1988), 221–41.

Glavin, John, 'Muriel Spark: Beginning Again', in Abby H. P. Werlock (ed.), *British Women Writing Fiction* (Tuscaloosa, AL and London: The University of Alabama Press, 2000), 293–313.

Greene, George, 'Compulsion to Love: *Collected Stories: I* by Muriel Spark', *The Kenyon Review* 31: 2 (1969), 267–72.

Greene, George, '*Du Côté de Chez Disaster*: The Novels of Muriel Spark', *Papers on Language and Literature* 16 (1981), 295–315.

Gregson, Ian, 'Muriel Spark's Caricatural Effects', *Essays in Criticism* 55: 1 (2005), 1–16.

Harrison, Bernard, 'Muriel Spark and Jane Austen', in Gabriel Josipovici (ed.), *The Modern English Novel: The Reader, the Writer, and the Work* (New York: Barnes & Noble, 1976), 225–51.

Hart, Francis Russell, *The Scottish Novel: From Smollett to Spark* (Cambridge, MA: Harvard University Press, 1978).

Hosmer Jr., Robert E. (ed.), *Contemporary British Women Writers: Texts and Strategies* (Basingstoke: Macmillan, 1993).

Hosmer, Robert, 'An Interview with Dame Muriel Spark', *Salmagundi* 146–7 (2005), 127–58.

Hoyt, Charles Alva, 'Muriel Spark: The Surrealist Jane Austen', in Charles Shapiro (ed.), *Contemporary British Novelists* (Carbondale and Edwardsville, IL: Southern Illinois University Press, 1965; London and Amsterdam: Feffer & Simons, 1971), 125–43.

Hynes, Joseph, *The Art of the Real: Muriel Spark's Novels* (Cranbury, NJ: Associated University Presses, 1988).

Hynes, Joseph (ed.), *Critical Essays on Muriel Spark* (New York, Oxford, Singapore and Sydney: Maxwell Macmillan International, 1992).

Johnson, Abby Arthur, 'The Politics of a Literary Magazine: A Study of *The Poetry Review, 1912–1972*', *Journal of Modern Literature* 3: 4 (1974), 951–64.

Kane, Richard C., *Iris Murdoch, Muriel Spark, and John Fowles: Didactic Demons in Modern Fiction* (Rutherford, NJ: Fairleigh Dickinson University Press, 1988).

Kemp, Peter, *Muriel Spark* (London: Paul Elek, 1974).

Kemp, Jonathan, '"Her lips are slightly parted": The Ineffability of Erotic Sociality in Muriel Spark's *The Driver's Seat*', in *Modern Fiction Studies* 54: 3 (2008), 544–57.

Kermode, Frank. 'Muriel Spark', in *Modern Essays* (Glasgow: Fontana Press, 1990), 267–83.

Labay-Morère, Julie, '"Voices at Play" in Muriel Spark's *The Comforters* and Evelyn Waugh's *The Ordeal of Gilbert Pinfold*', *Études britanniques contemporaines* 30 (2006), 83–93.

Laffin, Garry S., 'Muriel Spark's Portrait of the Artist as a Young Girl', *Renascence* 24: 4 (1972), 213–23.

Lister, Michael, 'Muriel Spark and the Business of Poetry', *Agenda* 40: 4 (2004), 2–4.

Little, Judy, *Comedy and the Woman Writer: Woolf, Spark, and Feminism* (Lincoln, NB: University of Nebraska Press, 1983).

MacKay, Marina, 'Muriel Spark and the Meaning of Treason', *Modern Fiction Studies* 54: 3 (2008), pp. 505–22.

MacLachlan, Christopher, 'Muriel Spark and Gothic', in Susanne Hagemann (ed.), *Studies in Scottish Fiction: 1945 to the Present* (Frankfurt am Main: Peter Lang, 1996), 125–44.

MacLeod, Lewis, 'Matters of Care and Control: Surveillance, Omniscience, and Narrative Power in *The Abbess of Crewe* and *Loitering With Intent*', *Modern Fiction Studies* 54: 3 (2008), 574–94.

McQuillan, Martin (ed.), *Theorizing Muriel Spark: Gender, Race, Deconstruction* (Basingstoke: Palgrave Macmillan, 2001).

Malkoff, Karl, *Muriel Spark* (New York and London: Columbia University Press, 1968).

Massie, Allan, *Muriel Spark* (Edinburgh: Ramsay Head, 1979).

Mengham, Rod, '1973: The End of History: Cultural Change According to Muriel Spark', in Rod Mengham (ed.), *An Introduction to Contemporary Fiction* (Cambridge: Polity Press, 1999), 123–34.

Nixon, Jude V., '"[A] Virginal Tongue Hold": Hopkins's *The Wreck of the Deutschland* and Muriel Spark's *The Girls of Slender Means*', *Renascence* 57: 4 (2005), 299–322.

Page, Norman, *Muriel Spark* (London: Macmillan, 1990).

Parrinder, Patrick, 'Muriel Spark and Her Critics', *Critical Quarterly* 25: 2 (1983), 23–31.

Pero, Allan, '"Look for One Thing and You Find Another": The Voice and Deduction in Muriel Spark's *Memento Mori*', *Modern Fiction Studies* 54: 3 (2008), 558–73.

Potter, Nancy A. J., 'Muriel Spark: Transformer of the Commonplace', *Renascence* 17: 3 (Spring 1965), 115–20.

Randisi, Jennifer Lynn, *On Her Way Rejoicing: The Fiction of Muriel Spark* (Washington, DC: The Catholic University of America Press, 1991).

Rankin, Ian, 'Surface and Structure: Reading Muriel Spark's *The Driver's Seat*', *Journal of Narrative Technique* 15: 2 (1985), 146–55.

Richmond, Velma Bourgeois, *Muriel Spark* (New York: Frederick Ungar, 1984).

Schiff, Stephen, 'Muriel Spark Between the Lines', *The New Yorker* (24 May 1993), 36–43.

Shaw, Valerie, 'Fun and Games with Life-stories', in Alan Bold (ed.), *Muriel Spark: An Odd Capacity for Vision* (London: Vision Press, 1984), 44–70.

Shaw, Valerie, 'Muriel Spark', in Cairns Craig (ed.), *The History of Scottish Literature*, vol. 4 (*Twentieth Century*) (Aberdeen: Aberdeen University Press, 1987), 277–90.

Sheridan, Susan, 'In the Driver's Seat: Muriel Spark's Editorship of the *Poetry Review*', *Journal of Modern Literature* 32: 2 (Winter 2009), 133–42.

Sproxton, Judy, *The Women of Muriel Spark* (London: Constable, 1992).

Stanford, Derek, *Muriel Spark: A Biographical and Critical Study* (Fontwell: Centaur, 1963).

Stanford, Derek, *Inside the Forties: Literary Memoirs 1937–1957* (London: Sidgwick & Jackson, 1977).

Stannard, Martin, *Muriel Spark: The Biography* (London: Weidenfeld & Nicolson, 2009).

Stubbs, Patricia, *Muriel Spark (Writers and Their Work)* (Harlow: Longman, 1973).

Stubbs, Patricia, 'Two Contemporary Views on Fiction: Iris Murdoch and Muriel Spark', *English* 23 (1974), 102–10.

Todd, Richard, 'The Crystalline Novels of Muriel Spark', *Essays on the Contemporary British Novel*, ed. Hedwig Bock and Albert Wertheim (München: M. Hueber, 1986), 175–92.

Tusa, John. 'Interview with Muriel Spark', http://www.bbc.co.uk/radio3/johntusainterview/spark_transcript.shtml.

Updike, John, 'Topnotch Witcheries', in Joseph Hynes (ed.), *Critical Essays on Muriel Spark* (New York, etc.: Maxwell Macmillan International, 1992), 209–12.

Walker, Dorothea, *Muriel Spark* (Boston, MA: Twayne, 1988).

Gavin Wallace and Randall Stevenson (eds.), *The Scottish Novel Since the Seventies: New Visions, Old Dreams* (Edinburgh: Edinburgh University Press, 1993).

Werlock, Abby H. P. (ed.), *British Women Writing Fiction* (Tuscaloosa, AL and London: The University of Alabama Press, 2000).

Whiteley, Patrick J., 'The Social Framework of Knowledge: Muriel Spark's *The Prime of Miss Jean Brodie*', *Mosaic: A Journal for the Interdisciplinary Study of Literature* 29: 4 (1996), 79–100.

Whittaker, Ruth, *The Faith and Fiction of Muriel Spark* (London: Macmillan, 1982).

Whyte, Christopher, 'Queer Readings, Gay Texts: From *Redgauntlet* to *The Prime of Miss Jean Brodie*', in Marco Fazzini (ed.), *Resisting Alterities: Wilson Harris and Other Avatars of Otherness* (Amsterdam: Rodopi, 2004), 159–75.

Notes on Contributors

Gerard Carruthers is Reader in the Department of Scottish Literature, University of Glasgow. He has published extensively on Scottish literature, including *Robert Burns* (2006) and *Scottish Literature: A Critical Guide* (2009). He has edited several volumes, including *The Edinburgh Companion to Robert Burns* (2009), and literary editions of writers, among them Robert Burns, Walter Scott and James Bridie.

Michael Gardiner is Assistant Professor in the Department of English and Comparative Literary Studies at the University of Warwick. As well as creative fiction, comparative cultural history and world literature, his books include *The Cultural Roots of British Devolution* (2004), *Modern Scottish Culture* (2005) and *From Trocchi to Trainspotting; Scottish Literary Theory Since 1960* (2006).

David Goldie is Senior Lecturer in English Studies, University of Strathclyde. He is the author of *A Critical Difference: John Middleton Murray and T. S. Eliot in English Literary Criticism 1919–1928* (1998), and many chapters and articles on twentieth-century Scottish and English literature. He edited, with Gerard Carruthers and Alastair Renfrew, *Beyond Scotland: New Contexts for Twentieth-Century Scottish Literature* (2004).

Vassiliki Kolocotroni is Senior Lecturer in the Department of English Literature and Head of the Graduate School of Arts and Humanities, University of Glasgow. She has written on modern classicism and the international avant-garde, and co-edited collections of travel writings and critical essays on the representation of modern Greece – most recently, with Efterpi Mitsi, *Women Writing Greece* (2008) – and, with Jane Goldman and Olga Taxidou, *Modernism: An Anthology of Sources and Documents* (1998).

Paddy Lyons is Senior Lecturer in the Department of English, University of Glasgow. He has published on Restoration and twentieth-century literature;

147

and writers whose work he has edited include the Earl of Rochester and Mary Shelley. Edited collections include, with G. Bystydzienska and Emma Harris, *Papers in Literature and Culture* (2005), and, with Alison O'Malley-Younger, *No Country For Old Men: Fresh Perspectives on Irish Literature* (2008).

Willy Maley is Professor of Renaissance Studies in the Department of English Literature, University of Glasgow. He writes on both Renaissance and Scottish literature, most recently *Nation, State and Empire in English Renaissance Literature: Shakespeare to Milton* (2002) and *Muriel Spark for Starters* (2009). Edited collections include, with Andrew Murphy, *Shakespeare and Scotland* (2004) and, with Alex Benchimol, *Spheres of Influence: Intellectual and Cultural Politics from Shakespeare to Habermas* (2006).

Drew Milne is Judith E. Wilson Lecturer in Drama and Poetry, Faculty of English, University of Cambridge. He has published extensively on critical theory, modern poetry and poetics, modernist literature, Renaissance drama and Shakespeare, and has edited several books, including *Modern Critical Thought* (2003). His own *The Damage: New and Selected Poems* was published in 2001.

Adam Piette is Professor in the School of English Literature, Language, and Linguistics, University of Sheffield. He has written extensively on modernist literature, and guest-edited a 2002 issue of *Translation and Literature* on modernism and translation. Most recently, he has written *The Literary Cold War, 1945 to Vietnam* (2009) and has edited a collection of essays on the poet Peter Robinson.

Marilyn Reizbaum is Professor in the Department of English at Bowdoin College, Maine. She has written on modernist literature and Scottish and Irish literature, and on James Joyce, Djuna Barnes, Eavan Boland, Neil Jordan, Liz Lochhead, Irvine Welsh, Art Spiegelman, Emma Goldman and Otto Weininger. Her publications include *James Joyce's Judaic Other* (1999) and edited, with Kimberley J. Devlin, *Ulysses: Un-gendered Perspectives* (1999).

Randall Stevenson is Professor of Twentieth-Century Literature in the Department of English Literature, University of Edinburgh. He has written widely on twentieth-century literature, modernism and postmodernism. His publications include *Modernist Fiction* (1998) and *The Oxford English Literary History*, vol. 12, *1960–2000: The Last of England?* (2005), and, with Brian

McHale, *The Edinburgh Companion to Twentieth-Century Literatures in English* (2006).

Matthew Wickman is Associate Professor of English at Brigham Young University, Utah and Senior Lecturer in Scottish Literature at the University of Aberdeen. He is author of *The Ruins of Experience: Scotland's 'Romantick' Highlands and the Birth of the Modern Witness* (2007) and is currently investigating the relationship between Scottish crime fiction and the work and legacy of Martin Heidegger.

Index